Integrated Cyber Space Warfare

Integrated Cyber Space Warfare

Major (Retd.) S.K. Sharma

PRASHANT PUBLISHING HOUSE
DELHI- 110094

PRASHANT PUBLISHING HOUSE
C-34, 28 Foota Road, Gali no-3,
West Karawal Nagar, Delhi-110094
Mob:- 9810396373, 8826258746

Email: prashantpublishinghouse@gmail.com
web- www.pphbooks.co.in

Integrated Cyber Space Warfare

First Published 2019
ISBN- 978-93-88526-05-0

INTED IN INDIA
blished by Mr. R. K. Jha M/s Prashant Publishing House and Published at H.S. Offset House es, Delhi.

Contents

Preface

Cyberspace is constantly under assault. Cyber spies, thieves, saboteurs, and thrill seekers break into computer systems, steal personal data and trade secrets, vandalize Web sites, disrupt service, sabotage data and systems, launch computer viruses and worms, conduct fraudulent transactions, and harass individuals and companies. These attacks are facilitated with increasingly powerful and easy-to-use software tools, which are readily available for free from thousands of Web sites on the Internet.

As a social experience, individuals can interact, exchange ideas, share information, provide social support, conduct business, direct actions, create artistic media, play games, engage in political discussion, and so on, using this global network. They are sometimes referred to as cybernauts. The term cyberspace has become a conventional means to describe anything associated with the Internet and the diverse Internet culture. The United States government recognizes the interconnected information technology and the interdependent network of information technology infrastructures operating across this medium as part of the US national critical infrastructure.

Cyberspace is a domain characterized by the use of electronics and the electromagnetic spectrum to store, modify, and exchange data via networked systems and associated physical infrastructures. In effect, cyberspace can be thought of as the interconnection of human beings through computers and telecommunication, without regard to physical geography.

Network-centric warfare, also called network-centric operations or net-centric warfare, is a military doctrine or theory of war pioneered by the United States Department of Defence in the 1990s. It seeks to translate an information advantage, enabled in part by information technology, into acompetitive advantage through the robust Computer networking of well informed geographically dispersed forces.

Cyberwarfare has been defined as "actions by a nation-state to penetrate another nation's computers or networks for the purposes of causing damage or disruption," but other definitions also include non-state actors, such as terrorist groups, companies, political or ideological extremist groups, hacktivists, and transnational criminal organizations.

Understanding the effectiveness of the strategic culture and utilization of cyber warfare capability by the challenging/rising hegemon against the hegemon will have consequences on U.S. national security doctrine. United States as one of the most "wired" states in the world shows a potential vulnerability against cyber-attacks. Globalization -fueled by technological advancement and spread of cyber space in physical space- is a manifestation of new means through which power is exercised and distributed. On the same token such power comes with a vulnerability that states such as North Korea and China are trying to separate themselves from by keeping their critical infrastructure isolated from internet reach.

This book provides deep insight into various dimensions of issues relating to the subject.

—*Editor*

1

Countering Threats through Cyber Space

In the United States, surveillance has been at the heart of changes in traditional defence, as well as attempts to counter so-called "asymmetric" security threats. Guided by the principle that "what can be seen can be hit," battlefield surveillance was at the heart of the U.S., "revolution in military affairs" during the 1970s, 1980s, and 1990s. Two asymmetric threats in particular have caught the imaginations of those within the United States who have worked consistently to increase government surveillance capabilities: the threats of terrorism and cyber attack.

The idea that information-age conflict in general, and the fight against terrorism in particular, constitute a global "battle for hearts and minds" has been popular among U.S., defence and security professionals for at least a decade. Various observers have worried about terrorist use of the Internet as a tool for fundraising, organising, recruiting, and propaganda. It is in this spirit that Arquilla has urged the U.S., government to remove terrorist web sites from the Internet. Likewise, it is in this spirit that groups of self-organised, online volunteers engage in various types of online activities in support of the U.S., "war on terrorism," including intelligence gathering and counter-propaganda activities.

The work of Shannen Rossmiller and her group Phoenix Global Information Systems is the most notable example of intelligence-focused, volunteer cyber-counterterrorism. In response to the terrorist attacks of September 11, 2001, Rossmiller, a municipal judge from a small town in Montana, began trolling jihadist web sites to learn more about those who had attacked the United States and what they might be planning next. In January 2003, Rossmiller joined forces with at least six other individuals whom she met in the online discussion forum. They created a web site and began calling themselves 7-Seas Global Intelligence.

Members of 7-Seas live in the United States, Canada, Australia, and Singapore and include an economist, a physicist, a computer systems engineer, a corporate security consultant, and a private investigator. Rossmiller and members of 7-Seas have used a number of techniques to gather intelligence about terrorists online. These have included creating multiple false personas complete with pictures and detailed life histories. To appear as convincing as possible to her targets, Rossmiller has learned Arabic, studied the Quran, and read Arabic literature. They also employ translation software, tools to map the IP addresses of the online jihadists with whom they interact, software to mask their own IP addresses and make it appear that they are located in the Middle East or South Asia, and even spyware that is remotely installed on the computers of some of those that they investigate.

While their initial goal was to predict future terrorist attacks, they soon shifted to gathering and analysing information from terrorist web sites, forums, and chat rooms, and then turning that information over to authorities. Rossmiller's efforts in particular have contributed to two high-profile arrests of would-be terrorists, including the 2004 case of Specialist Ryan Anderson, a Washington state National Guardsman who attempted to sell classified information about vulnerabilities of U.S., weapons systems to an al-Qa'ida member that he met online.

That al-Qa'ida member was actually Rossmiller. Anderson is now in prison serving five consecutive life sentences, the harshest penalty yet dealt to an American in the war on terrorism. In another case, and again posing online as a member of al- Qa'ida, Rossmiller uncovered a plot by Pennsylvania resident and al-Qa'ida sympathiser, Michael Reynolds, to blow up several gas pipelines and oil refineries in the United States. Reynolds was convicted and is now serving fifty seven years in prison. Rossmiller is reported to have provided information to U.S., law enforcement or intelligence in as many as 240 other cases, leading to the detention of dozens of suspects worldwide and even some arrests and deportations of terrorism suspects from the United States.

For all the success that Rossmiller and 7-Seas has had, there remains a great deal of ambivalence, ambiguity, and tension in their relationship with authorities. On the one hand, the volunteers are motivated in part by calls by authorities to be vigilant. They believe authorities' claims about the seriousness of the threat of terrorism and want to help. One the other hand, they are also motivated by feelings that the government is either unable or unwilling to counter extremists' use of the Internet. Similarly, while Rossmiller has received a great deal of praise and assistance from authorities—the FBI has compensated her for her expenses, provided her with Arabic translation services, and provided her with security, a former Secretary of Commerce has said that she deserves a medal, she has been consulted by the Defence Intelligence Agency, and she has been an invited speaker at an FBI cyber security conference—these agencies have also sometimes expressed concern or doubt about her work and the work of others like her.

For her part, Rossmiller has at times complained that her work is being undervalued by authorities and has been clear to assert her independence from the state. But for all the tensions between authorities and volunteers, and for all that Rossmiller and 7-Seas have tried to distance themselves from the authorities, they nonetheless seek both approval and profit from the authorities. Both 7-Seas and later Phoenix Global Intelligence Systems have sought government contracts and intelligence and security consulting work for government clients.

In 2009, Rossmiller announced at an FBI-sponsored cyber security conference that she had formed a company and was seeking a partnership with a defence contractor to offer cyber-intelligence training and services to the government. She has been encouraged to do so by former CIA Director, James Woolsey. In the end, there are real reasons for tension and for concern. Both sides are right. The authorities likely cannot monitor and analyse that much Web content, making the work of the volunteers indispensable.

However, the volunteers do not have the ability to physically arrest suspects or materially disrupt terrorist planning or operations in any significant way, making the capabilities of the state indispensable in achieving their goals. Additionally, there are clear difficulties in making the relationship work. Sometimes authorities and volunteers can work at cross purposes. If authorities rely too much on volunteers, or if the role of volunteers becomes formally institutionalised, then their main value can be compromised. Finally, Michael Reynolds' defence strategy—i.e., claiming that he too was just trying to catch terrorists online like Rossmiller—also points to some of the potential difficulties in this new relationship between producers and consumers of security online.

THE MEANING OF SPACE

If you go far away from the lights of the city on a clear and moonless night and you gaze into the sky, you will behold the awe-inspiring vastness of space; millions of stars and galaxies will twinkle at you across incomprehensible distances, beckoning you to come, to explore, to discover! What is this universe, you may ask yourself. And what is our place in it? How was it made? Who else lives here? These are timeless questions that even our most distant ancestors asked, for the very nature of space calls to us in ways that we cannot escape. It confronts us with some of the most basic and fundamental questions about our existence, our past, and our destiny; and the depths of space, its vastness and incomprehensibility, embody for us a set of meanings that are unlike any other.

For example, space, the concept of outer space and its sheer enormity, makes us wonder how rare life might be in the universe; it makes us think about the possibility of voyages across the unlimited black emptiness from our world to others. It manifests the apparent outcome of billions of years of history emanating from a single explosion of incomprehensible power, and all of this combines to make space one of the most provocative and compelling concepts among all the enduring icons that burn within human consciousness. Among the approximately 6.5 billion people who are alive today, only a tiny handful are likely to ever venture into space during the course of their lifetimes. Fifty, one hundred, perhaps five hundred, or maybe even 5000 will have the opportunity to escape Earth's gravity and then gaze back upon our small planet.

What will this experience mean to them? For these few, the idea of "outer space" will surely have a unique and transcendent meaning, for it might well be the unique and defining experience of a lifetime, an experience without parallel, an epiphany.

For the rest of us, however, the meaning of space doesn't have to be any less profound even though it will necessarily lack the vital dimension of experience. This is so because space carries meanings that are unique and unmatched by any other aspect of the human experience, either on Earth or off of it we can all partake of these meanings regardless of whether our status is astronaut or armchair astronaut.

Still the very words I've used to convey the nature of space - "vast," "inconceivable," "incomprehensible," "emptiness" - these words and any others that we might choose are still inadequate to express the scale and scope of space, and we find in the end that our language is simply insufficient for the task. The meaning of space is beyond the capacity of our expression, as it is also in many very real ways far beyond our comprehension.

And yet we must try to understand what it does mean, and we must try to express that meaning, for space is the context and container of life on Earth, of our life. It is our local neighborhood in this tiny part of the galaxy we call home.

Space is also, perhaps our destiny, for although a mass exodus to space may yet be centuries in the future, we who are living today cannot escape the idea that a human diaspora will eventually bring human civilization to numerous bodies throughout the solar system. We must also consider the possibility that an active human presence in space is not only our challenge, but also our responsibility. And finally, it is certainly true that whatever we see in space, or imagine that we see, is merely a reflection of ourselves, and the incomprehensible scale of space makes it simply a mirror of the incomprehensible depth within ourselves. These are four meanings of space - the local neighborhood; human destiny; responsibility; and the psychology of space - that we will explore in this chapter.

Welcome to the Neighborhood

Five decades ago space travel was a dream, but then with billions of dollars and the capabilities of thousands of brilliant and dedicated scientists and engineers, humans launched the space age. And so it is in our own lifetimes that the meaning of space has changed from the domain of science fiction, to that of science. Space is no longer just the realm of imagination or possibility, but of actuality, and in this process our neighborhood has grown.

While forty years is a mere instant on the Earth's vast scale of billions of years, in the context of human history and human civilization forty decades is a significant span of time, and during this period as we have witnessed the transformation of space from a fantasy to a reality, we have also seen a transformation in the reality of human life back on Earth. We see ourselves differently now, for we have looked back from the moon to see the tiny blue ball, and this perspective has nurtured a much greater appreciation for our extraordinary planet. We know and do things differently now, for space science has transformed meteorology (with weather satellites), agriculture (with mapping and analysis from space), transportation (with GPS), communication (with radio, television, and cell satellites), medicine (with telemetry) as well as astronomy, physics, all of the materials sciences, rocketry, and also, sadly, warfare.

Spacecraft have charted all the major bodies in our solar system, and human footprints still dot the face of the Moon (along with the debris we've left there, and on other neighbors as well). Within a few years Voyager will cross the conceptual boundary between the solar system and what lies beyond, and continue on its journey into the unknown.

Forty years along, the space movement has also affected our attitudes and expectations, for it has given us some perspective on how small the Earth is, and how unique life might be. A little more knowledge about our neighborhood has indeed been transformational for the human race.

PATROLLING NATIONAL BORDERS IN CYBER SPACE

Online, volunteer cyber-surveillance efforts have also been used to aid in the production of more traditional forms of security, such as defending territorial integrity by patrolling national borders. Since, 9/11, the debate over immigration from the global South has been increasingly linked to the "War on Terror." Part of this linkage can be found in the actions and discourse of what are collectively called "Minutemen" groups. Minutemen groups are most known for their use of physical presence on the U.S.-Mexico border, especially in 2005, a presence spurred by organisers who wanted to draw attention to what they perceived to be the government's lack of intervention in illegal immigration.

Although the Minutemen are not a government agency, their border-watching efforts were meant to supplement—and not replace —the physical intervention of the U.S., Border Patrol; thus the Minutemen appropriated part of the state's power of surveillance without impinging on the state's monopoly on the use of force. In addition, Minutemen groups have also deployed "Cyber Minutemen," extending surveillance onto the Web. Using a mix of fibre-optic fencing, Web cameras, motion detectors, infrared sensors, and even aircraft, various Minutemen groups have posted images and live streams to a variety of Web sites.

This use of relatively inexpensive surveillance and Web technology is touted by Cyber Minutemen as a viable, high-tech, modern way for citizens to succeed where the state has ostensibly failed in stemming the flow of immigrants across the Mexican border. Jim Wood, founder of the nowdefunct Border Fence Project, argues that citizen groups are more efficient and cost-effective than state efforts to secure the border. "The bottom line is this," he argues in a letter to supporters, "Despite bureaucratic refusals, delays and boondoggles, we civilians on the border can build a national Border Fence without them, repairing the old and erecting the new... Therefore, we as American citizens and patriots must stand up and do this ourselves." Part of the efficiency arises from the use of distributed volunteers across the Web; volunteers from as far away as Australia have reportedly spotted illegal border crossings.

In this case, the convergence of state aims and privately deployed technologies echoes previous, new media "crowdsourcing" efforts such as Wikipedia and the NASA Clickworkers project. As in the other convergence security cases, Cyber Minutemen have enjoyed some support from the state, as well as from Internet entrepreneurs. Texas governor Rick Perry, the Texas Border Sheriff's Coalition, and private landowners joined Internet company BlueServo in a "publicprivate partnership" to distribute live feeds of the border to Web volunteers.

This public-private partnership is a for-profit endeavor. BlueServo claims, "Because www.BlueServo.net is an internet social network, in the future, BlueServo anticipates that high volume of traffic to its web site will generate advertising revenue to defray the operations cost of the Virtual Community Watch to the Texas Border Sheriff's Coalition." Thus, in keeping with convergence media business practices, BlueServo intends to meld the Cyber Minutemen desire to secure the border with the political economy of attention found in other Web 2.0 sites such as Facebook and YouTube. This entrepreneurial form of convergence border security has also been proposed by the Heritage Foundation.

However, as with other convergence security groups, the Minutemen have had ambivalent, ambiguous, and tense relationships with the state. Although Texas Governor Perry and California Governor Arnold Schwarzenegger publicly endorsed the movement, George W. Bush referred to them as "vigilantes". The Department of Homeland Security rejected a proposal to formally integrate volunteer citizen patrols into the Border Patrol.

For their part, the Minutemen groups have not sought integration with the state. Rather, they have largely called for an increased police or military presence at the border; they tend to frame their activity as drawing attention to the perceived problem of illegal immigration, drug trafficking, and terrorism. In the main, the Minuteman movement has been strict with members about the use of violence; thus the Minutemen have been careful not to infringe on the state's monopoly on violence for fear of political and legal repercussions.

A large Minuteman group, the Minutemen Civil Defence Corps (MCDC), disbanded in 2010 not long after a leader in that organisation called for a "locked and loaded"—i.e., publicly armed—patrol of the border. The "locked and loaded" muster was intended as a show of arms rather than an explicit call to violence. However, the proposed muster led to an enthusiastic response among members that the MCDC leadership interpreted as potentially violent, stoking fears within the organisation that the MCDC would not be able to prevent members from using weapons on alleged illegal border crossers, thus echoing Bush's earlier fears of vigilantism. The leaders of the MCDC did not want to cross the border between civil society groups and state-sponsored military groups.

Ultimately, in the case of the Minutemen, their proposed virtual surveillance of the border was accepted by the state far easier than their proposed, *embodied* patrol of the border. While the MCDC disbanded in light of the potential use of force by members, BlueServo and its Web camera network remains active to this day. State officials who decry potential vigilantism at the border tend to ignore or tolerate the use of Web-based surveillance. Most state officials who want increased border security eschew Minutemen-style groups and opt instead for state-sanctioned groups such as the U.S., Border Patrol, the National Guard, or new bureaucratic formations such as the Department of Homeland Security.

Conclusion

We draw two key conclusions from these case studies. First, we see the value in applying media studies theories to security studies. Media studies is currently grappling with many of the transitions, ruptures, and continuities that digitisation has wrought; likewise, scholars and policymakers alike have grappled with the implications of digitisation for security. Synthesising the two fields will produce new insights for those working in security studies. Second, at the level of politics, convergence security points to a fruitful critique of Hardt and Negri: the boundary between biopower and biopolitical production is not so neat as their work makes it seem.

Further work in convergence security analysis will likely continue to blur that boundary; however, we also see convergence security as a means to continue Hardt and Negri's call for true democracy. These case studies indicate that Jenkins's claim that convergence will apply in other areas beyond entertainment and media is borne out. General Clapper's statement indicates that the idea has made its way into the minds of influential professionals of security. Thus, applying convergence to understand changes in security affairs is necessary; moreover, the value of convergence points to other possible media studies theories that could be used in future security studies.

Specifically, we should also consider applying the work of other media scholars like Mark Deuze's work on digital culture, Axel Bruns on "produsage," and Hector Postigo's and Tiziana Terranova's exploration of online volunteers and free labour. Media studies could further help us to understand the changes occurring within traditional security organisations, as well as between traditional producers and consumers of security. Convergence security also undermines Hardt and Negri's perhaps too neat separation between biopower and biopolitical production; there is more continuity between the production of security and the production of other "immaterial goods" than once thought. In fact, it is possible to describe security itself as one of those immaterial goods created via biopolitical production.

This has implications for the political project that Hardt and Negri map in *Multitude* and *Commonwealth*. While these findings do not entirely contradict or invalidate Hardt and Negri's belief that biopolitical production is "the social basis on which it is possible today to begin a project of the multitude"—i.e., the project of creating real democracy—they do call our attention to the fact that the multitude can be appropriated to do the work of the state, and often quite happily so.

Further empirical and theoretical work is required to problematise the border between biopower and biopolitical production. For example, Deibert and Rohozinski point to the privatisation and outsourcing of knowledge production about and response to threats to and through cyber space, particularly among "patriotic hackers" in Russia, China, and Iran. We agree with their call for more research on this phenomenon, but we also note that it is not just adversaries of the U.S., that have such groups.

The U.S., has "patriotic hackers" as well, and there are powerful policymakers calling for the U.S., government to do more to recruit and support these groups. Clearly, the courting and integration of biopolitical "patriotic hackers" into the auspices of the state is another, emerging form of convergence security.

All this said, Hardt and Negri's basic premise that the creative, affective, and immaterial labour of the multitude can lead to real democracy is not necessarily invalidated by convergence security; it is simply nuanced. For proponents of real democracy, the question becomes: how do we integrate the passions, desires, and skills of these groups into a more democratic polis?

CYBERSPACE AT A GLANCE

For the most part, the Internet is built upon national and international telecommunications infrastructures, including the landlines of most public phone systems and wireless, and satellite communications. Beyond the Internet, these telecommunications infrastructures tend to be highly dependent on computing technology. Thus, by our definition, they are part of cyberspace. There are currently about 1.3 billion Internet users worldwide. The Internet now comes to ground in over 200 "countries" (Top-Level Domains, i.e. the letters which follow the dot after the domain name).

This enormous growth has been achieved since the early 90s. The only thing growing faster than the Internet is cellular telephony, with about three billion phones in use, to which 1.6 million users are added every day. The fact that soon cellular telephones will be a platform for the Internet means that at least a billion new users will have access to this resource, and this expansion will mostly be in developing countries.

(In)Security (Internet Security) at a Glance

The architecture, design, and practice of the Internet emphasize *access* (ease of use, low cost, universality). It has almost never considered security as a primary or important factor. It is an unfortunate result of the history of the way the Internet was developed that the protocols used by the Internet today are derived from those that were established in the early days of the ARPANet, where there were only a few wellrespected researchers using the infrastructure, and they were trusted to do no harm. Consequently, security considerations were not built in to the Internet. All cybersecurity measures taken today to protect the Internet are add-on measures that do not remedy the underlying security deficiencies.

The situation we have as a result is that current technology asymmetrically favors the attackers; it provides them great "nonlinear leverage", and attackers get their innovations into practice more quickly and effectively than defenders. If we make a comparison between cyber attacks and modern warfare, we would say that it is an asymmetrical conflict.

While the state, because of its capacity, has a huge technological advantage over terrorists, the problem is that the kinds of nonlinearities associated with what terrorists do in cyberspace give leverage to those with relatively little technical capability. What has always been thought of as one of the great advantages of the networks can also threaten them: They give a small number of relatively weak people extensive access to a lot of information, each other, potential recruits and sympathizers, and prospective targets. There is also a negative aspect of tightening access against terrorists or other malicious users more generally because it would compromise access and privacy for many, many more "good" users.

The functionality of the Internet ranges greatly. Of particular concern for those aware of the threat of terrorism is the fact that SCADA (Supervisory Control and Data Acquisition) systems now more commonly use the Internet to transmit data and control instructions, rather than the dedicated networks that had been used before. Additionally, very few of the "cyber" parts of the critical infrastructures were designed or implemented with security as much of a consideration, if it was considered at all. Most are riddled with vulnerabilities, which are defined as weaknesses that can be exploited through either hostile attacks or accidents. It would be almost impossible to create "patches" to protect programs from malicious people who seek to find and exploit these vulnerabilities.

Another problem to recognize is that Internet defense pushes the burden outward to the end user organizations; most of these find it difficult, and often increasingly difficult, to defend themselves.

In particular, most of the over two hundred connected countries have little or no national cybersecurity capabilities.

International Threats Arising from Globalization

One area of concern that extends broadly across all of the stages of defense is that globalization creates new populations of "insiders"—people who have authorized access with the potential for abuse that can cause great harm. Insiders still probably account for a majority of successful penetrations for criminal purposes. The problem is complicated by changes in organizational relations and technical architectures that make "inside" and "outside" more difficult even to define. The possibility that a terrorist or a terrorist sympathizer might gain employment that would enable him or her to conduct a devastating attack or to provide critical information or access to others cannot be discounted or ignored.

The two most general ways of dealing with infiltration are through deep preemployment investigations, something that most non-government entities are neither capable of doing nor permitted to do in many countries, and through stronger forms of containment and compartmentalization of access within an organization. Globalization has meant that the Internet is now less secure, with vulnerabilities resulting from new systems "intimacies". Transfer of information now takes place in unprecedented transnational contexts.

A particular problem for those who want to control or police the Internet is the spread and ownership of, and access to, transnational transportation infrastructures. Much of the day to day running is outsourced, and offshoring (outsourcing to foreign entities) means that any attempts to control the Internet require international cooperation.

Terrorists in Cyberspace

What do we know or anticipate that terrorists want to do in cyberspace? I believe the answers to this question fall into three categories:

1. Terrorists want to support their activities and infrastructure, but not directly through an attack, using the Internet.
2. They may want explicitly to attack parts of the cyber infrastructure.
3. They may use cyberspace as a means of attacking other targets. These might include compromising transportation or other supervisory control systems to cause disasters resulting in extensive consternation and costing many lives.

It is certain that terrorists and their supporters have been engaging in extensive activities under category 1, and that they will continue to do so.

This would cover communications, including encrypted communications with each other; recruiting and "advertising" (for example, via Web sites); and financial transactions such as money transfers and laundering. Training manuals for terrorists, including information about bomb-making and avoiding detection, are freely available. Terrorists are also likely to be scouring cyberspace for information on potential targets and on weapons of mass destruction.

As far as we can tell, terrorists have not been responsible for any of the major attacks or accidents that have occurred in recent years under categories 2 or 3.

So much has been written about such possibilities—and they have had some prominence in the media—that it is inconceivable that terrorists are not aware of them. So far, for reasons we can only speculate about, they do not seem to have chosen to pursue these possibilities with vigor and effect, or perhaps they have tried and failed.

Systems and Networks at Risk

Should an attack be launched against systems and networks, the following would be at risk:

1. The Internet.
2. Embedded/real-time computing (e.g. avionics systems for air traffic control, SCADA systems used by the amenities, routing for shipping containers, and process control for toxic chemical production, switching of telecommunications, bank teller machines, floodgates).
3. Dedicated computing devices (e.g. desktop computers).

Each has a different role, and may be the subject of different kinds of attack. Terrorists might attack the Internet physically or "through the wires", the latter being potentially more destructive. One type of attack that we see is directed against Internet operations. Such attacks are often based on self-replicating programs (worms and viruses) that are transmitted from system to system, consuming prodigious amounts of router processing time and network channel bandwidth. In recent years, some of these worms and viruses have been transmitted without explicitly destructive payloads and yet have been able to disrupt key Internet backbone subnetworks for several days. Another kind of attack on Internet operations seeks to corrupt the routing tables that determine how a packet should travel through the Internet.

In both cases, the intent of the attack is to reduce the normally expected functionality of the Internet for some significant portion of its users—that is, a denial-of-service attack in intent, although not one necessarily based on flooding traffic. An attacker might also target the Internet's Domain Name System (DNS), which translates domain names (e.g. "example.com") to specific Internet Protocol (IP) addresses (e.g. 123.231.0.67) denoting specific Internet nodes.

A relatively small number of "root name servers" underpins the DNS. Although the DNS is designed to provide redundancy in case of accidental failure, it has some vulnerability to an attack that might target all name servers simultaneously. Although Internet operations would not halt instantly, an increasing number of sites would, over a period of time measured in hours to days, become inaccessible without root name servers to provide authoritative translation information. Physical replacement of damaged servers would be achievable in a matter of days, but changing the IP addresses of the root name servers would be more complicated.

Recommendations: Focus on Terrorists

It is only a matter of time before cyber terror attacks, at present largely a threat, become a reality. Both government and private sector need to focus on preparations. There are a number of measures that must be taken. Build Much Stronger Defenses, More Integrated Emergency Preparedness and Response Systems, and Improve the Processes for Their Use. The first order of business is to provide indications and warnings that an attack is taking place. This is a difficult area, and intrusion detection has become a particularly active area in research and development. Not surprisingly, detection and notification are more difficult and prone to false positives during the early stages of an attack, before significant damage has been done.

To prevent penetration of the system at risk from the outside, we try to erect barriers and otherwise harden it. Both cyber and physical approaches are necessary. Passwords are the oldest, and still most widely used, cybertechnique. More recent and somewhat widely used techniques are firewalls and proxy servers. Like all forms of cyberdefense, these can be defeated, although it is possible to make them real barriers against many attempted attacks. Physical protection needs to consider several forms of penetration or attempts to isolate the system. These include attacks on electronics using electromagnetic pulses, and attempts to cut cable endings. A wide variety of forms of physical protection are possible, ranging from fences to biometrics.

In the event of an attack there needs to be a system for incident management, mitigating an attack, and damage limitation. A next line of defense is internal compartmentalization and containment. In this instance, the goals are to limit penetration and damage, protect surviving assets, and protect and gather information to help with recovery and response after the attack. Approaches include creating internal physical barriers and cyberbarriers through compartmentalization and need-to-know access controls, intrusion tolerance schemes, setting up decoys, maintaining protected redundancies, and hiding assets. All have both static (pre-positioned and unchanging during the attack) and dynamic variants.

Another approach is automatic or partial shutdown and reallocation. A system that senses it is under attack would start erecting internal barriers that would not be tolerable during normal operations, in an attempt to isolate those parts of the system that had been compromised.

It would also involve load-shedding strategies to reallocate surviving capabilities to the most important functions required by the organization. All of this amounts to various forms of real-time reassignment and reconfiguration under rapid degradation. Particular attention needs to be given to preserving and collecting information during an attack.

This is done most easily if the attack has a clear and precise starting time and backups are made regularly, or if the organization maintains a redundant "shadow" system. More insidious attacks that build up slowly present a much more difficult problem in identifying a state where the system is free from inserted malicious code. It is also important to have strong audit functions to identify when an attack starts and to collect information that might assist in the identification and apprehension of the attacker and help the organization better defend itself against similar attacks in the future.

Organizations should establish security policies and plans for defending against attacks. Special attention should be given to preventing and dealing with insider attacks. Staff should know who to call for help. It might be a good idea to test the plan through the use of exercises. However, most organizations avoid live "fire drills" because they can be expensive, disruptive, and risky in their own right. Many information systems are delicate and their owners are afraid something will go wrong, resulting in the selfinflicted equivalent of a serious attack.

Improve the security of systems that control physical processes (e.g., SCADA).

From the standpoint of counter terrorism, we would imagine that attacking physical targets via control and management systems would result in the kind of mass casualties, damage, fear, and loss of confidence that terrorists favor. Many of these systems are vulnerable to tampering with control signals, especially by insiders.

Increasing the security for DC/SCADA systems poses particularly difficult problems. These systems are often small and self-contained, and have constrained power needs (including backup). Security may not readily fit with the space, real-time, or power requirements. Security measures could also reduce performance or be problematic in the synchronization of other more extensive processes. Additionally, most of these systems are in the private or mixed sectors (for example, airports). Their owners and operators may not have sufficient resources to secure them more effectively. National governments that are in positions to do so should give priority to protecting the small percentage of cyberspace users who are private owners and operators of digital control and management systems. This would include providing them with various forms of assistance and technology. Particular attention should be given to transportation systems because for decades they have been highly favored by terrorists both as targets and as the means of delivering an attack.

This kind of defensive work is essentially "target hardening". This can be defined as the use of various technologies and products and procedures (for example, those governing outside dial-in or reconstitution and recovery) to protect the information technology (IT) assets owned or operated by an individual or organization.

It is important to notice that many of these recommendations would have more general value than just vs. terrorists (e.g., they would help against accidents, natural disasters, serious crime, and non-terrorist forms of conflict). However, as defense does not involve serious risk or impose a penalty on the attacker, there is also the need to develop deterrents. For this we need laws:

Design and Implement a Stronger "System of Justice", Especially Its International Dimensions

International cooperation should concentrate on effective intelligence operations. This is an area where a considerable amount of success could be expected, which would create the atmosphere for a long-term international legal framework.

The problems of jurisdiction are greatly compounded by the easy transnational access provided by many components of cyberspace, most notably the Internet. What may be perceived as serious in one country whose cyberinfrastructure may be used as part of a terrorist action may not even make the legal radar screen of others that are part of an attack that crosses multiple sovereign physical jurisdictions. Most countries have given little or no thought to making serious crimes of the various forms of cyberattack, and "without law there is no sin". Seeking widely adopted national laws at least criminalizing attacks against or using the networks is an important objective. Legislating against the support functions to which terrorists put the Internet would be a more distant prospect. The enforcement and prosecution of these laws are also critical elements of cybersecurity.

Given the many technical and evidentiary problems of identifying cybercriminals and prosecuting them, nobody has any delusion that such laws would end criminal or terrorist activities in cyberspace. Nonetheless, they might reduce the enormous amount of malicious "noise" in cyberspace, and this would help make it easier to more readily identify more serious activities. They would also provide a necessary basis for encouraging people to report malicious cyberactivities, and for international cooperation in dealing with several kinds of problem.

CIIP at Every Stage

Security must become a criterion for any system used for CII from the design stage onwards. The priorities in design have been access and throughput. Added security is not just costly; it may also result in reduced efficiency and functionality. Furthermore, so far there does not seem to be much incentive for people to design or redesign systems to be much more secure. There has been much speculation that the design or redesign of systems will occur only in the aftermath of a "digital Pearl Harbor" or in response to the forces of legal liability or insurance necessities and standards. Even better, security should be a factor to be considered over the entire life cycle of such systems. Organizations should build cadres of capable defenders, and contingency plans (including internationally) for crisis and emergency conditions need to be in place. There could be national-level CERTs or CSIRTs (Cybersecurity Incident Response Teams).

A postdesign and implementation variant is to try to prevent attacks by finding and fixing vulnerabilities before an attacker can try to exploit them. Red teams, test beds, or simulations may be used to do this. Another approach, at least to the often-serious threat of possible insider attacks, is to more thoroughly screen employees with potentially sensitive access. It is clear that for a number of these measures operational contingencies among owners and operators and their governments need to be established.

2

Terrorists in Cyberspace

Terrorists have moved into cyberspace to facilitate traditional forms of terrorism such as bombings. They use the Internet to communicate, coordinate events, and advance their agenda. While such activity does not constitute cyberterrorism in the strict sense, it does show that terrorists have some competency using the new information technologies.

By 1996, the headquarters of terrorist financier Osama bin Laden in Afghanistan was equipped with computers and communications equipment. Egyptian "Afghan" computer experts were said to have helped devise a communication network that used the Web, e-mail, and electronic bulletin boards. Hamas activists have been said to use chat rooms and e-mail to plan operations and coordinate activities, making it difficult for Israeli security officials to trace their messages and decode their contents. The Revolutionary Armed Forces of Columbia (FARC) uses e-mail to field inquiries from the press.

The Web is especially popular as a medium for reaching a global audience. For example, after the Peruvian terrorist group Tupac Amaru stormed the Japanese Ambassador's residence in Lima on December 17, 1996 and took 400 diplomatic, political, and military officials as hostage, sympathizers in the United States and Canada put up solidarity Web sites. One site included detailed drawings of the residence and planned assault.

In February 1998, Hizbullah was operating three Web sites: one for the central press office (www.hizbollah.org), another to describe its attacks on Israeli targets, and the third for news and information. That month, Clark Staten, executive director of the Emergency Response & Research Institute (ERRI) in Chicago, testified before a U.S. Senate subcommittee that "even small terrorist groups are now using the Internet to broadcast their message and misdirect/misinform the general population in multiple nations simultaneously." He gave the subcommittee copies of both domestic and international messages containing anti-American and anti-Israeli propaganda and threats, including a widely distributed extremist call for "jihad" (holy war) against America and Great Britain.

In June 1998, *U.S. News & World Report* noted that 12 of the 30 groups on the U.S. State Department=s list of terrorist organizations are on the Web. Now, it appears that virtually every terrorist group is on the Web. Forcing them off the Web is impossible, because they can set up their sites in countries with free-speech laws. The government of Sri Lanka, for example, banned the separatist Liberation Tigers of Tamil Eelam, but they have not even attempted to take down their London-based Web site. Even in democracies, however, there are limits to what terrorists can post on the Net. After a group of anti-abortionists put up a Web site terrorizing doctors who performed abortions, a federal jury ordered the pages be taken down and damages of more than $100 million paid. The Nuremberg Files site had listed the names of about 200 abortion providers under the heading of "baby butchers." Readers were invited to send in such personal details as the doctors' home addresses, license plate numbers, and the names of their children. Three doctors whose names appeared on the list were killed, and after each, the doctor's name was promptly crossed out. Doctors named on the site testified that they lived in constant fear and used disguises, bodyguards, and bulletproof vests. In ordering the site down, the federal jury said the site and "wanted" posters amounted to death threats against the doctors.

Many terrorists are using encryption to conceal their communications and stored files, compounding the difficulties of providing effective counter-terrorism. Hamas, for example, reportedly has used encrypted Internet communications to transmit maps, pictures, and other details pertaining to terrorist attacks.

Ramsey Yousef, a member of the international terrorist group responsible for bombing the World Trade Centre in 1994 and a Manila Air airliner in late 1995, encrypted files on his laptop computer. The files, which U.S. government officials decrypted, contained information pertaining to further plans to blow up eleven U.S.-owned commercial airliners in the Far East. The Aum Shinrikyo cult, which gassed the Tokyo subway in March 1995, killing 12 people and injuring 6,000 more, also used encryption to protect their computerized records, which included plans and intentions to deploy weapons of mass destruction in Japan and the United States.

CAPABILITY OF CYBERTERROR

The following three levels of cyberterror capability is defined by Monterey group:

- Simple-Unstructured: The capability to conduct basic hacks against individual systems using tools created by someone else. The organization possesses little target analysis, command and control, or learning capability.
- Advanced-Structured: The capability to conduct more sophisticated attacks against multiple systems or networks and possibly, to modify or create basic hacking tools. The organization possesses an elementary target analysis, command and control, and learning capability.
- Complex-Coordinated: The capability for a coordinated attack capable of causing mass-disruption against integrated, heterogeneous defenses (including cryptography). Ability to create sophisticated hacking tools. Highly capable target analysis, command and control, and organization learning capability.

Concerns

As the Internet becomes more pervasive in all areas of human endeavor, individuals or groups can use the anonymity afforded by cyberspace to threaten citizens, specific groups (i.e. with membership based on ethnicity or belief), communities and entire countries, without the inherent threat of capture, injury, or death to the attacker that being physically present would bring. Many groups such as Anonymous, use tools such as Denial-of-service attack to attack and censor groups who oppose them, creating many concerns for freedom and respect for differences of thought.

Many believe that cyberterrorism is an extreme threat to our economy, and fear an attack could potentially lead to another Great Depression. Several leaders agree that cyberterrorism has the highest percentage of threat over other possible attacks on U.S. territory. Although natural disasters are considered a top threat and have proven to be devastating to people and land, there is ultimately little that can be done to prevent such events from happening. Thus, the expectation is to focus more on preventative measures that will make Internet attacks impossible for execution.

As the Internet continues to expand, and computer systems continue to be assigned increased responsibility while becoming more complex and interdependent, sabotage or terrorism via the Internet may become a more serious threat and is possibly one of the top 10 events to "end the human race."

Dependence on the internet is rapidly increasing on a worldwide scale, creating a platform for international cyber terror plots to be formulated and executed as a direct threat to national security. For terrorists, cyber-based attacks have distinct advantages over physical attacks. They can be conducted remotely, anonymously, and relatively cheaply, and they do not require significant investment in weapons, explosive and personnel. The effects can be widespread and profound. Incidents of cyberterrorism are likely to increase. They will be conducted through denial of service attacks, malware, and other methods that are difficult to envision today.

In an article about cyber attacks by Iran and North Korea, the New York Times observes, "The appeal of digital weapons is similar to that of nuclear capability: it is a way for an outgunned, outfinanced nation to even the playing field. 'These countries are pursuing cyberweapons the same way they are pursuing nuclear weapons,' said James A. Lewis, a computer security expert at the Center for Strategic and International Studies in Washington. 'It's primitive; it's not top of the line, but it's good enough and they are committed to getting it.'"

History

Public interest in cyberterrorism began in the late 1980s. As 2000 approached, the fear and uncertainty about the millennium bug heightened, as did the potential for attacks by cyber terrorists.

Although the millennium bug was by no means a terrorist attack or plot against the world or the United States, it did act as a catalyst in sparking the fears of a possibly large-scale devastating cyber-attack. Commentators noted that many of the facts of such incidents seemed to change, often with exaggerated media reports.

The high profile terrorist attacks in the United States on September 11, 2001 and the ensuing War on Terror by the US led to further media coverage of the potential threats of cyberterrorism in the years following. Mainstream media coverage often discusses the possibility of a large attack making use of computer networks to sabotage critical infrastructures with the aim of putting human lives in jeopardy or causing disruption on a national scale either directly or by disruption of the national economy.

Authors such as Winn Schwartau and John Arquilla are reported to have had considerable financial success selling books which described what were purported to be plausible scenarios of mayhem caused by cyberterrorism. Many critics claim that these books were unrealistic in their assessments of whether the attacks described (such as nuclear meltdowns and chemical plant explosions) were possible. A common thread throughout what critics perceive as cyberterror-hype is that of non-falsifiability; that is, when the predicted disasters fail to occur, it only goes to show how lucky we've been so far, rather than impugning the theory.

U.S. military

The US Department of Defense (DoD) charged the United States Strategic Command with the duty of combating cyberterrorism. This is accomplished through the Joint Task Force-Global Network Operations, which is the operational component supporting USSTRATCOM in defense of the DoD's Global Information Grid. This is done by integratingGNO capabilities into the operations of all DoD computers, networks, and systems used by DoD combatant commands, services and agencies. On November 2, 2006, the Secretary of the Air Force announced the creation of the Air Force's newest MAJCOM, the Air Force Cyber Command, which would be tasked to monitor and defend American interest in cyberspace. The plan was however replaced by the creation of Twenty-Fourth Air Force which became active in August 2009 and would be a component of the planned United States Cyber Command.

On December 22, 2009, the White House named its head of Computer security as Howard Schmidt to coordinate U.S Government, military and intelligence efforts to repel hackers. He left the position in May, 2012. Michael Daniel was appointed to the position of White House Coordinator of Cyber Security the same week and continues in the position during the second term of the Obama administration.

Estonia and NATO

The Baltic state of Estonia was target to a massive denial-of-service attack that ultimately rendered the country offline and shut out from services dependent on Internet connectivity for three weeks in the spring of 2007. The infrastructure of Estonia including everything from online banking and mobile phone networks to government services and access to health care information was disabled for a time.

The tech-dependent state was in severe problem and there was a great deal of concern over the nature and intent of the attack. The cyber attack corresponded to an Estonian-Russian dispute over the removal of a bronze statue depicting a World War II-era Soviet soldier from the center of the capital, Tallinn. In the midst of the armed conflict with Russia, Georgia likewise was subject to sustanined and coordinated attacks on its electronic infrastructure in August 2008. In both of these cases, circumstantial evidence point to coordinated Russian attacks, but attribution of the attacks is difficult; though both the countries point the finger at Moscow, proof establishing legal culpability is lacking.

Estonia joined NATO in 2004, therefore NATO carefully monitored its member state's response to the attack and worried both about escalation and the possibility of cascading effects beyond Estonia's border to other NATO members. In 2008, directly as a result of the attacks, NATO opened a new center of excellence on cyberdefense to conduct research and training on cyber warfare in Tallinn.

China

The Chinese Defense Ministry confirmed the existence of an online defense unit in May 2011. Composed of about thirty elite internet specialists, the so-called "Cyber Blue Team," or "Blue Army," is officially claimed to be engaged in cyber-defense operations, though there are fears the unit has been used to penetrate secure online systems of foreign governments.

Israel

May 2011 Israeli Prime Minister Benjamin Netanyahu announced the establishment of the National Internet Defense Taskforce, charged with developing tools to secure vital Israeli online infrastructure. "The main responsibility of the taskforce will be to expand the state's ability to defend vital infrastructure networks against cybernetic terrorist attacks perpetrated by foreign countries and terrorist elements."

Examples

An operation can be done by anyone anywhere in the world, for it can be performed thousands of miles away from a target. An attack can cause serious damage to a critical infrastructure which may result in casualties. Attacking an infrastructure can be power grids, monetary systems, dams, media, and personal information. Some attacks are conducted in furtherance of political and social objectives, as the following examples illustrate:

- In 1996, a computer hacker allegedly associated with the White Supremacist movement temporarily disabled a Massachusetts ISP and damaged part of the ISP's record keeping system. The ISP had attempted to stop the hacker from sending out worldwide racist messages under the ISP's name. The hacker signed off with the threat, "you have yet to see true electronic terrorism. This is a promise."

- In 1998, Spanish protesters bombarded the Institute for Global Communications (IGC) with thousands of bogus e-mail messages. E-mail was tied up and undeliverable to the ISP's users, and support lines were tied up with people who couldn't get their mail. The protestors also spammed IGC staff and member accounts, clogged their Web page with bogus credit card orders, and threatened to employ the same tactics against organizations using IGC services. They demanded that IGC stop hosting the Web site for the Euskal Herria Journal, a New York-based publication supporting Basque independence. Protestors said IGC supported terrorism because a section on the Web pages contained materials on the terrorist group ETA, which claimed responsibility for assassinations of Spanish political and security officials, and attacks on military installations. IGC finally relented and pulled the site because of the "mail bombings."
- In 1998, ethnic Tamil guerrillas attempted to disrupt Sri Lankan embassies by sending large volumes of e-mail. The embassies received 800 e-mails a day over a two-week period. The messages read "We are the Internet Black Tigers and we're doing this to disrupt your communications." Intelligence authorities characterized it as the first known attack by terrorists against a country's computer systems.
- During the Kosovo conflict in 1999, NATO computers were blasted with e-mail bombs and hit with denial-of-service attacks by hacktivists protesting the NATO bombings. In addition, businesses, public organizations, and academic institutes received highly politicized virus-laden e-mails from a range of Eastern European countries, according to reports. Web defacements were also common. After the Chinese Embassy was accidentally bombed in Belgrade, Chinese hacktivists posted messages such as "We won't stop attacking until the war stops!" on U.S. government Web sites.
- Since December 1997, the Electronic Disturbance Theater (EDT) has been conducting Web sit-ins against various

sites in support of the Mexican Zapatistas. At a designated time, thousands of protestors point their browsers to a target site using software that floods the target with rapid and repeated download requests. EDT's software has also been used by animal rights groups against organizations said to abuse animals. Electrohippies, another group of hacktivists, conducted Web sit-ins against the WTO when they met in Seattle in late 1999. These sit-ins all require mass participation to have much effect, and thus are more suited to use by activists than by terrorists.

- In 2000, a Japanese Investigation revealed that the government was using software developed by computer companies affiliated with Aum Shirinkyo, the doomsday sect responsible for the sarin gas attack on the Tokyo subway system in 1995. "The government found 100 types of software programs used by at least 10 Japanese government agencies, including the Defense Ministry, and more than 80 major Japanese companies, including Nippon Telegraph and Telephone." Following the discovery, the Japanese government suspended use of Aum-developed programs out of concern that Aum-related companies may have compromised security by breaching firewalls. gaining access to sensitive systems or information, allowing invasion by outsiders, planting viruses that could be set off later, or planting malicious code that could cripple computer systems and key data system.
- In March 2013, the New York Times reported on a pattern of cyber attacks against U.S. financial institutions believed to be instigated by Iran as well as incidents affecting South Korean financial institutions that originate with the North Korean government.
- In August 2013, media companies including the New York Times, Twitter and the Huffington Post lost control of some of their websites Tuesday after hackers supporting the Syrian government breached the Australian Internet company that manages many major site addresses. The Syrian Electronic Army, a hacker group that has previously

attacked media organisations that it considers hostile to the regime of Syrian president Bashar al-Assad, claimed credit for the Twitter and Huffington Post hacks in a series of Twitter messages. Electronic records showed that NYTimes.com, the only site with an hours-long outage, redirected visitors to a server controlled by the Syrian group before it went dark.

Sabotage

Non-political acts of sabotage have caused financial and other damage, as in a case where a disgruntled employee, Vitek Boden (aka Peter Markan) caused the release of 800,000 litres of untreated sewage into waterways in Maroochy Shire, Australia.

More recently, in May 2007 Estonia was subjected to a mass cyber-attack in the wake of the removal of a Russian World War II war memorial from downtown Tallinn. The attack was a distributed denial-of-service attack in which selected sites were bombarded with traffic to force them offline; nearly all Estonian government ministry networks as well as two major Estonian bank networks were knocked offline; in addition, the political party website of Estonia's current Prime Minister Andrus Ansip featured a counterfeit letter of apology from Ansip for removing the memorial statue.

Despite speculation that the attack had been coordinated by the Russian government, Estonia's defense minister admitted he had no conclusive evidence linking cyber attacks to Russian authorities. Russia called accusations of its involvement "unfounded," and neither NATO nor European Commission experts were able to find any conclusive proof of official Russian government participation. In January 2008 a man from Estonia was convicted for launching the attacks against the Estonian Reform Party website and fined.

During the Russia-Georgia War, on 5 August 2008, three days before Georgia launched its invasion of South Ossetia, the websites for OSInform News Agency and OSRadiowere hacked. The OSinform website at osinform.ru kept its header and logo, but its content was replaced by a feed to the Alania TV website content.

Alania TV, a Georgian government supported television station aimed at audiences in South Ossetia, denied any involvement in the hacking of the websites. Dmitry Medoyev, at the time the South Ossetian envoy to Moscow, claimed that Georgia was attempting to cover up information on events which occurred in the lead up to the war.

One such cyber attack caused the Parliament of Georgia and Georgian Ministry of Foreign Affairs websites to be replaced by images comparing Georgian president Mikheil Saakashvili to Adolf Hitler. Other attacks involved denials of service to numerous Georgian and Azerbaijani websites, such as when Russian hackers allegedly disabled the servers of the Azerbaijani Day.Az news agency.

Website Defacement and Denial of Service

Even more recently, in October 2007, the website of Ukrainian president Viktor Yushchenko was attacked by hackers. A radical Russian nationalist youth group, the Eurasian Youth Movement, claimed responsibility. In 1999 hackers attacked NATO computers. The computers flooded them with email and hit them with a denial of service (DoS). The hackers were protesting against the NATO bombings of the Chinese embassy in Belgrade. Businesses, public organizations and academic institutions were bombarded with highly politicized emails containing viruses from other European countries.

In fiction

- The Japanese cyberpunk manga, *Ghost in the Shell* (as well as its popular movie and TV adaptations) centers around an anti-cyberterrorism and cybercrime unit. In its mid-21st century Japan setting such attacks are made all the more threatening by an even more widespread use of technology including cybernetic enhancements to the human body allowing people themselves to be direct targets of cyberterrorist attacks.
- Dan Brown's *Digital Fortress*.
- Amy Eastlake's *Private Lies*.

- In the movie *Live Free or Die Hard,* John McClane (Bruce Willis) takes on a group of cyberterrorists intent on shutting down the entire computer network of the United States.
- The movie *Eagle Eye* involves a super computer controlling everything electrical and networked to accomplish the goal.
- The plots of *24* Day 4 and Day 7 include plans to breach the nation's nuclear plant grid and then to seize control of the entire critical infrastructure protocol.
- The Tom Clancy created series Netforce was about a FBI/ Military team dedicated to combating cyberterrorists.
- Much of the plot of *Mega Man Battle Network* is centered around cyberterrorism.
- In the 2009 Japanese animated film *Summer Wars,* an artificial intelligence cyber-terrorist attempts to take control over the world's missiles in order to "win" against the main characters that attempted to keep it from manipulating the world's electronic devices.
- In the 2012 film Skyfall, part of the James Bond franchise, main villain Raoul Silva (Javier Bardem) is an expert cyberterrorist who is responsible for various cyberterrorist incidents in the past.
- Cyberterrorism plays a role in the 2012 video game Call of Duty: Black Ops II, first when main antagonist Raul Menendez cripples the Chinese economy with a cyberattack and frames the United States for it, starting a new Cold War between the two powers. Later, another cyberattack with a computer worm leads to Menendez seizing control of the entire U.S drone fleet. Finally, one of the game's endings leads to another attack similar to the latter, this time crippling the U.S' electrical and water distribution grids. An alternate ending depicts the cyberattack failing after it is stopped by one of the game's characters pivotal to the storyline.
- The plot of the 2013 video game Watch Dogs is heavily influenced by cyber-terrorism. In which players take control

of the game's protagonist, Aiden Pierce, an accused murder suspect, who hacks into a ctOS (Central Operating System), giving him complete control of Chicago's mainframe in order to hunt down his accusers.

- The video game *Metal Slug 4* focuses on Marco and Fio, joined by newcomers Nadia and Trevor, to battle a terrorist organization known as Amadeus that is threatening the world with a computer virus.
- The visual novel *Baldr Force* has the main character Tooru Souma joining a military organization to fight cyberterrorism to avenge the death of his friend.
- The Japanese Manga and Live Action *Bloody Monday* is Highly influenced with Hacking and Cracking, the main character Takagi Fujimaru is a Super Elite hacker which use his hacking knowledge to fight against his enemies.

CYBER-TERRORISM: THE EMERGING THREAT

A number of economies were thrown into disarray with the recent financial turmoil. Opinions remain divided on which way the road ahead leads to. But even when household names and industry heavyweights were being brought down to their knees, technology remained steadfast. In fact, technology today has so inconspicuously become a business enabler that it's almost easy to overlook.

The United Nations telecommunications agency warns that the next world war could well be in cyberspace. This should come as no surprise. Wars have often included attacks on installations or facilities that are critical to the enemy, delivering a crippling blow to gain the higher ground. Considering the sheer magnitude of dependence that the modern world places on technology, it would logically make a fine target if a war were to ensue.

Cyber-Terrorism

A new page in the information warfare book comes in a sinister form. Cyber-terrorism involves highly targeted efforts made with the intention of terrorism. It is an emerging threat that has the potential to cause serious damage. While we'd often associate terrorism with loss of life, we cannot overlook important results like intimidation or coercion that can be brought about by cyber-terrorism.

A prolonged and targeted terrorism campaign against a country has the potential to render it weak in the long-run. Given the varied economic, financial, and even psychological effects such a campaign could have, cyber-terrorism poses a significant hurdle in times to come. Technology is the backbone of most countries in the world today. A hard hit on such a critical backbone would be an ideal strategy for attackers.

Non-Tech? Think Again!

The long-held belief that terrorists are unorganized and non-technical has been clearly shattered in modern times. The most recent example of this could be seen in the 2008 terror attacks in Mumbai (India), where satellite phones using VoIP technology, complex GPS systems, and, allegedly, even Google Earth were all used to aid the acts of terror. As far back as 1998, the, now-exterminated, terrorist organization in Sri Lanka, known as the Tamil Tigers, overloaded Sri Lankan embassies with more than 800 e-mails per day for two weeks. In more recent times, cyber attacks directed at India from terrorist organizations and others with similar malicious intentions is commonplace. Israel has significant threats from organizations such as Hamas and Hezbollah. Today, terrorists share information by embedding it in image files and sharing these images over e-mail. The image with embedded information is strikingly similar to the original and does not appear to be different by just looking or comparing visually. This technique is commonly classified under what is known in the security world as "steganography". There are free tools available on the Internet to do this.

While the bleak prospect of having an image embedded with information being intercepted even exists, another method allows terrorists to plot without even sending e-mail. By saving e-mails as drafts and never sending them, terrorists effectively communicate with each other without even really sending an e-mail. The communicating parties simply share the password to the e-mail account. No e-mail sent means no e-mail intercepted.

Why should you care? As a direct or indirect victim of a cyber-terror attack, you could be left groping around in the dark if you aren't reasonably well-prepared. The impacts are pretty much the same as any other hacker attack on an organization, except that you'll be a pawn in a broader terrorist agenda.

Another significant reason lies in the fact that we don't live in a vacuum. Cyber threats can have the same impacts as real world threats. The economic and political impacts alone are enough causes to worry, and cyber-terror attacks are not limited to geographic borders or reach. The world is much smaller due to technology. When the very technology that enables this is attacked, it may not matter which part of the world you're in when an attack takes place if the objective and magnitude of the attack is large enough.

Countering Cyber-Terrorism

Preparing against the threat of cyber-terrorism requires the same level of planning and preparation to survive an economic or financial crisis. One of the biggest concerns that organizations have when protecting against an emerging threat is the cost associated with it. In fact, the costs associated with countering cyber-terrorism are not new costs at all. Your existing information security strategy need only be tweaked and adapted to be well-prepared.

Responsible Attitude

To be able to counteract the threat posed by cyber-terrorism, the first need would be to take it seriously. Even if you were to believe that the threat will never materialize, being prepared for it is the responsible thing to do. You do not want to be caught unaware.

Program, Policies, and Procedures

Your existing information security program should already provide a guideline on how to deal with information security threats. You need only add guidelines on how to specifically approach the threat of cyber-terrorism. Ensure that policies and procedures guide the organization to know when to activate the incident response mode. Switching to this mode could be expensive, so ensure that the guidelines are accurate, clear, and well-documented.

Incident Response

An organization's incident response capability will be severely tested in the event of a cyber-terror attack. A good incident response plan is critical to address the threat adequately. Ensure that the plan includes steps on monitoring, prevention, communication, and escalation. Testing should be performed on a periodic basis with documented test results and future improvement steps. It is also important to interface and interact with advisories such as the CERT to keep abreast with current events and happenings.

Technical Security Assessments

Technical assessments such as external and internal penetration tests, audits, vulnerability assessments, social engineering engagements, and application hacking engagements are generally performed by many organizations. While these could arise from regulatory requirements, they greatly benefit the organization's information security posture as a whole.

Technical security assessments, if performed thoroughly and accurately, can transform an organization into an impenetrable fortress.

While the regulatory compliance will be a pleasant by-product, your secure organizational information is of utmost importance to protecting your assets.

Business Continuity Planning

Business continuity is another vital ingredient in preparations to counter the threat of cyber-terrorism.

The business continuity plan ensures that your organizational operations will continue to run profitably even in the event of a cyber-terror attack. Although real-world terrorist attacks are often included in business continuity plans, it is a good idea to include virtual-world terrorist attacks as well. Ensure on regular data backups and full-recovery testing.

Awareness Training

Generating awareness of emerging threats is critically important. The information security industry is one that is ever changing and evolving. Hence, training and awareness efforts need to keep pace. The employees of an organization are the ultimate implementers of information security and so training them correctly should be considered vital to a secure and profitable business operation. The best awareness training efforts utilize a variety of approaches in order to avoid monotony. Such methods include seminars, newsletters, intranet forums, awareness posters, and many others. The key is to keep it interesting.

Moving Forward Sensibly

Borders between countries have been greatly diminished in modern times, in large part due to technology. Real-world terrorism is arguably the biggest challenge faced by the world today, and perhaps the best opportunity for committed terrorists. When this translates into the virtual-world, the impacts could be disastrous and debilitating. Recent trends suggest that this migration to cyber-terrorism has already begun.

Being mindful of the emerging threat of cyber-terrorism when protecting your organization's information will enable a wholesome approach to information security. As the world strides into the future, sensible organizations will be wary of the threat looming large at the horizon and take precautions to ward against potential threats.

TERRORISM TO CYBERTERRORISM

The definition of "terrorism" has been well studied, defined, and documented. There is also a degree of understanding of the meanings of *CyberTerrorism*, either from the popular media, other secondary sources, or personal experience. This paper examines the future of CyberTerrorism - a term the author coined a decade ago, as the indicia of technological dependence and frailty were forming in our New World disOrder. Indeed, that future has come to fruition, today.

The face of terrorism is changing. While the motivations remain the same, we are now facing new and unfamiliar weapons. The intelligence systems, tactics, security procedures and equipment that were once expected to protect people, systems, and nations, are powerless against this new, and very devastating weapon. Moreover, the methods of counter-terrorism that our world's specialists have honed over the years are ineffectual against this enemy. Because, this enemy does not attack us with truckloads of explosives, nor with briefcases of Sarin gas, nor with dynamite strapped to the bodies of fanatics. This enemy attacks us with one's and zero's, at a place we are most vulnerable: the point at which the *physical* and *virtual* worlds converge. Let us first define theses two domains.

The Physical World

The physical world is matter and energy - light, dark, hot and cold, all physical matter - that place in which we live and function.

The Virtual World

The virtual world is symbolic - true, false, binary, metaphoric representations of information - that place in which computer programs function and data moves.

The physical and virtual worlds are inherently disparate worlds. It is now the intersection, the convergence, of these two worlds that forms the vehicle of CyberTerrorism, the new weapon that we face.

Reliance and Dependence

This convergence of the physical and virtual worlds, this lattice, is growing larger and more complex as we venture further into technological dependence. Each day, we move ahead with blinding speed into the computerization of every task and process that we face. We are becoming ever more inextricably reliant and dependent on the convergence of these two worlds.

Points of Convergence

What are some of the more obvious points of convergence?

- A garage door opener.

- A heart pacemaker.
- The computer chip in a late model car.
- A microwave oven.

These are all things taken for granted. Yet, as we progress into a far more technological world, what other points of convergence are taken for granted?

- Food processing plants
- Pharmaceutical processing plants
- Electric and natural gas utilities
- Train crossings and traffic control systems
- Next generation air traffic control systems
- Virtually all modern military equipment
- Military and public safety communications
- Civilian communications

Convergence Drivers

What is driving the convergence of these two worlds? There are three goals:

1. Access: the goal of universal, ubiquitous interface;
2. Control: the goal of remote administration; and
3. Mining: the goal of knowledge acquisition.

Convergence Vehicles

To achieve these goals, there are four vehicles:

- Transmission: longer lines across land and through space;
- Connections: more links to more points;
- Aggregation: more information centralized, and disconnected information linked; and
- Retrieval: more ways of retrieving information, and more importantly, knowledge.

Achieving CyberTerrorist Goals

So how does a CyberTerrorist achieve his mission? Like any terrorist, a CyberTerrorist actively exploits the goals of the target population in areas in which they take for granted. There are three potential acts in CyberTerrorism at the point of convergence:

1.Destruction;

2.Alteration; and

3.Acquisition and retransmission (these are a unit).

As we will see, these three types of acts are most heinous at the point where the physical and virtual worlds converge.

To achieve a true terrorist goal, as we know, we must have *scale* and *publicity*. So how does the CyberTerrorist approach a new age - an age of convergence of the physical and virtual worlds? An age where, thanks to our goals, he can perform his CyberTerrorist acts from his living room, undetected, from 8,000 kilometers away?

Cracker or CyberTerrorist?

A great deal of "cracks" are committed for the purposes of anarchy, humor, or as often stated by the perpetrators, "to be annoying." However, is this the mindset of a CyberTerrorist? Does the CyberTerrorist make a garage door go up and down? Does he change an Internet web site to say a country's government is evil? Does he hack into a major corporation's voice mail system to make long distance calls? No - that is not the domain of the CyberTerrorist - that is the domain of the amateur cracker community that exists worldwide.

A CyberTerrorist's mindset is quite different. A CyberTerrorist would not alter a voice mail, or even abuse credit cards.

Potential CyberTerrorist Acts

Let us examine some example CyberTerrorist acts. Based on the definitions of terrorism, a determination can be made if they in fact constitute terrorism:

- A CyberTerrorist will remotely access the processing control systems of a cereal manufacturer, change the levels of iron supplement, and sicken and kill the children of a nation enjoying their food. That CyberTerrorist will then perform similar remote alterations at a processor of infant formula. The key: the CyberTerrorist does not have to be at the factory to execute these acts.
- A CyberTerrorist will place a number of computerized bombs around a city, all simultaneously transmitting unique

numeric patterns, each bomb receiving each other's pattern. If bomb one stops transmitting, all the bombs detonate simultaneously. The keys: 1) the CyberTerrorist does not have to be strapped to any of these bombs; 2) no large truck is required; 3) the number of bombs and urban dispersion are extensive; 4) the encrypted patterns cannot be predicted and matched through alternate transmission; and 5) the number of bombs prevents disarming them all simultaneously. The bombs *will* detonate.

- A CyberTerrorist will disrupt the banks, the international financial transactions, the stock exchanges. The key: the people of a country will lose all confidence in the economic system. Would a CyberTerrorist attempt to gain entry to the Federal Reserve building or equivalent? Unlikely, since arrest would be immediate. Furthermore, a large truck pulling along side the building would be noticed. However, in the case of the CyberTerrorist, the perpetrator is sitting on another continent while a nation's economic systems grind to a halt. Destabilization *will* be achieved.
- A CyberTerrorist will attack the next generation of air traffic control systems, and collide two large civilian aircraft. This is a realistic scenario, since the CyberTerrorist will also crack the aircraft's in-cockpit sensors. Much of the same can be done to the rail lines.
- A CyberTerrorist will remotely alter the formulas of medication at pharmaceutical manufacturers. The potential loss of life is unfathomable.
- The CyberTerrorist may then decide to remotely change the pressure in the gas lines, causing a valve failure, and a block of a sleepy suburb detonates and burns. Likewise, the electrical grid is becoming steadily more vulnerable.

In effect, the CyberTerrorist will make certain that the population of a nation will not be able to eat, to drink, to move, or to live. In addition, the people charged with the protection of their nation will not have warning, and will not be able to shut down the terrorist, since that CyberTerrorist is most likely on the other side of the world.

Sadly, these examples are not science fiction. All of these scenarios can be executed today. As you may know, some of these incidents already have occurred in various nations. More of such acts will take place tomorrow. Are you prepared?

CyberTerrorists: Who, Where, and Why?

The purpose of this paper is to help you understand the threats that exist, and hopefully, to help you prevent these types of atrocities. But know this - there are people out there with very different goals, who are our real threats, and who are, or will be, attacking us. Make no mistake, *the threats are real, today.* Who are the CyberTerrorists? There a great many poor movies and too many works of fiction about the hacker and cracker communities. In the popular media, there recently was the Kevin Mitnick incident, where one cracker broke into another cracker's systems. This spawned endless press and at least two best selling books. While this incident received much attention, the events amounted to meaningless children's games.

By and large, the cracker community, based primarily in the United States, Europe, the Middle East, Asia, and in the nations of the former Soviet Union, is composed of individuals who see the cracking process merely as a challenge, a brain teaser, a puzzle. They view themselves as not only being innocent of any crime, but perhaps even doing something righteous, something to counter the dark monoliths of the corporate and government worlds. They believe they are being persecuted. These individuals believe that what they are doing is not doing any true damage. At its least harmful, these crackers just look at information. However, privacy issues and military secrecy can render such infiltrations acts of terror.

Sometimes crackers make minor changes, just for fun, to be annoying, or to make a statement. The potential for damage here is enormous.

Crackers as Facilitators

Individuals with a background in intelligence are aware that a frequent element of case execution is enlisting the indigenous, sometimes called "facilitators," to assist in a campaign. At the convergence of the physical and virtual worlds, the indigenous are the crackers. There is the incorrect assumption in the cracking community that they, the crackers, are so sophisticated or so knowledgeable as to know when they are being approached for a truly illicit reason (e.g., to be enlisted as a facilitator to commit an act of terrorism). However, despite cracker arrogance, these individuals are easy targets for enlistment.

What about those crackers who actively *wish* to cross the line, or more basically, need money? To a teenager, a $1,000 U.S. can purchase a good many compact disks, a new modem, and a great deal of libation. Beyond youths, there are professionals in this arena as well.

Historically, individuals engaged in the practice of terror tended not to be people working upon a computer 20 hours per day. Terrorists have not been in the business of tracking the latest holes found in UNIX or an obscure government telnet opportunity. There *are* people, however, who are in that business - for illicit as well as good cause. As stated, just as indigenous people may be turned into soldiers, so can crackers be turned into CyberTerrorists. Sometimes such a transition may be motivated by money or prestige. Usually, this transition will occur without the cracker's cognizance. The potential threat from such transitions is mind boggling, considering the damage even one mis-directed cracker can cause.

Further, as young, educated people are brought into the folds of terrorist groups, this new generation will have the talent to execute the acts of CyberTerrorism of which we have spoken.

We are going to see increasing levels of in-house expertise, and concomitant exponential increases CyberTerrorism. Unlike other methods of terrorism, CyberTerrorism is safe and profitable, and difficult to counter without the right expertise and understanding of the CyberTerrorist's mind. Combine our increasing vulnerability, with the explosive increases in the level of violence, and increasing expertise available inside terrorist organizations through new blood and outside through facilitators, and we can see that at the point where the physical and virtual worlds converge, the old models of managing terrorism are obsolete.

Methods of Protection: No Easy Answers

We must consider the following elements when building a counter-CyberTerrorist program:

- We must accept that while the theories of terrorism stand true, the way in which we approach counter-terrorism, in this case, counter-CyberTerrorism, must change.
- We must cooperate and share intelligence in ways we have never have before.
- We must enlist the assistance of those individuals who understand the weapons we are facing and have experienced fighting these wars.
- We must learn the new rules, the new technologies, and the new players.

Unfortunately, one cannot learn how to fight this very unconventional warfare from someone who hasn't been there, nor from someone whose experience is in the old ways and old technologies. The old data processing, auditing, and computer security models in use today are obsolete. On this battlefield, against this weapon, the terrorist is already far ahead. The building of a counter-CyberTerrorist team *must* be real-time and dynamic, as the weapons will continually change, to morph, in an attempt to beat you, your systems, and your people. There is no re-machining, and unlike other terrorists, if the CyberTerrorist loses today, he does not die - he learns what did not work, and will use that information against you tomorrow.

TERRORISM USING INTERNET

The presence of terrorist groups on the internet is a relatively new phenomenon, the growth of which has exploded in the past decade. Accurate estimates on the number of active terrorist group's websites vary due to difficulties measuring but, there is a general consensus that in 1996 there was just under 100 websites and to well over 5000 websites today.

It is also widely accepted that all Foreign Terrorist Organisation's listed by the U.S. Department of State website have established an online presence of some form.

Only after 9/11 has governmental and public interest really been focussed on terrorists and the internet shown by the large number of articles examining the issue in the media which primarily occurred due to evidence recovered from Al Qaeda computers in Afghanistan, that indicate the Internet was being used to collect intelligence and send encrypted messages. The definition of terrorism used in this document is that of the new academic consensus definition: that terrorism is "a politically motivated tactic involving the threat or use of force or violence in which the pursuit of publicity plays a significant role".

Terrorist Groups use of the Internet

Growth in the use of the internet by terrorist groups is due to the key characteristics of the internet: ease of access which facilitates the possible massive worldwide audiences, few laws when compared to the physical world, little censorship, rapid and 'always on' flow of information, the low cost, anonymity of communication and a multimedia environment. The following is a breakdown of the main purposes that terrorist groups utilise the Internet for:

Cyberterrorism

Directly after 9/11, much was made of the possibilities of a large-scale cyber-terrorism attack by the media. However, several academics in the pending years published papers focusing on the terrorist groups utilize the Internet as it was designed to be; a means to communicate and collaborate, therefore the terrorists have stronger reasons to keep it up and online. Hence the apparently impending large scale cyber-terrorist attack that would cripple the internet has not materialised although Al Qaeda has taken full advantage of this fear.

Publicity and Propaganda

As stated by Dr Maura Conway, terrorism researcher: "Every machine connected to the internet is potentially a printing press, a broadcasting station or place of assembly." The internet is an un-paralleled media suite. Terrorists no longer have to have their messages diluted and edited by the media. Instead they can disseminate information of their choice to aid their causes. In most cases, this is achieved by the terrorists focusing on their grievances in order to justify why they are resorting to terrorist activities. This is usually achieved by the publication of various articles combined with pictures galleries, although this may be supplemented by video and audio files in which the terrorists themselves orally defend their actions. An example of this would be a gallery of atrocities against innocent civilians in Iraq supposedly carried out by foreign forces in order to generate local as well as international support for the terrorists.

In some cases, the terrorists choose to distribute information displaying their acts of violence or relating actions although this is not common. Again, these can be through written articles describing the violence, but are more often videos and pictures. Examples of these would be the pre-mission pictures published on the Tamil Tigers website of the Air Tiger squadron that a few days earlier had carried out its successful inaugural air attack on Sri Lankan governmental forces. A rather more extreme example was the distribution of the beheading of the journalist Daniel Pearl by the terrorist organisation 'The National Movement for the Restoration of Pakistani Sovereignty'.

Data Mining

The Internet is a vast resource of information which anyone can tap into and terrorists are well aware of this. According to Secretary of Defence Donald Rumsfeld, speaking on January 15, 2003, an al Qaeda training manual recovered in Afghanistan tells its readers that: "Using public sources openly and without resorting to illegal means, it is possible to gather at least 80 percent of all information required about the enemy."

The Internet allows access to highly detailed maps, schematics and various other sources of data that would allow terrorists gather information for potential targets. More importantly, once this data has been collated, it is compiled into volumes or "How to" manuals that are distributed between terrorist organisations.

Fund Raising

Terrorist groups have made full use of the Internet's ability to create funds; whether legitimately or otherwise. The main methods that the terrorists achieve this is by: Goods selling: merchandise that is directly related to the terrorist organisation, for example, CDs, DVDs and books from the LTTE.

Website and email based appeals: sending emails to sympathizers who registered interest on a group's website, posting messages on newsgroups/forums and their own websites that give directions as to how and where donations can be made.

Deception: using seemingly legitimate charities or businesses that unknown to the donator, directs the funds to terrorist organisations. Criminal activity: Illegitimate means of gaining funds that terrorist groups are known to use include credit card fraud, online brokering and gambling.

Recruitment

This chapter is inherently tied-in with Propaganda. Terrorist organisations are able to monitor users who browse their websites, capture their profile and information about them and if deemed possibly useful to their cause, are contacted. This grooming process starts from when the user begins to absorb the propaganda on the website, for example the often discussed "charismatic" style of delivery that Osama Bin Laden employs on his video messages. Perhaps motivated by this video, the user seeks answers to questions and goes to internet chat-rooms and discussion boards. Possible recruits are spotted by lurking recruiters who through gradual encouragement of discussion of religious issues to gradually including more political discussions. This grooming leads the recruits to become more and more entangled in terrorist related discussions and are led through a maze of private chat-room's until personal indoctrination occurs which is often through the use of the secure software Paltalk.

Communication & Networking

Terrorist groups have changed recently from having a clearly defined hierarchy in the organisations with designated leaders, to having multiple, semi-independent cells with no clear distinct leader in order to allow them to remain hidden. The Internet facilitates communication between cells which allows exchange of information and manuals. The Internet also assists with internal communication within a cell particularly in relation to the planning of attacks. To avoid being detected and targeted by security forces, Messages are often sent by conspirators through emails which are often sent using public email systems such as Hotmail and Yahoo and may also be sent from public libraries and internet cafes. Chat rooms may also be used for this purpose.

In addition, steganography may be used to hide information embedded within graphic files on websites. Graphic files may also used to send very subtle messages, such as reversing the orientation of a gun graphic may indicate that the next stage of a plan is to proceed. Other methods of concealing instructions and messages may be through the use of coded language, such as that used by Mohamed Atta's final email to the other terrorists who carried out the attacks of 9/11 is reported to have read: The semester begins in three more weeks. We've obtained 19 confirmations for studies in the faculty of law, the faculty of urban planning, the faculty of fine arts, and the faculty of engineering.

This is believed to be in reference to the four targets that the planes were planned to strike; 'architecture' being the World Trade Centre, 'arts': the Pentagon, 'law': the Capitol and 'politics': the White House. An even more secure method of communication is that which involves using one-time anonymous public email accounts; two terrorists who wish to communicate to open 30 anonymous email accounts whose usernames and passwords are known by each side. To communicate, one terrorist creates a web-based email and instead of sending it, saves it as a draft online. The "recipient" then logs onto this account, reads this message and deletes. The next day, a new account is used; this increases the difficulty of traceability of the users.

The Audiences of the Terrorist Websites

The first group of people that will frequent these websites are current supporters and future supporters. The websites typically include information relative to their activities, their allies, and their competitors. In addition, many websites offer items for sale. The second group of people that will enter these websites will be members of the outside community. In hopes of appealing to people all over the world, many terrorist organizations offer their websites in multiple languages. The websites typically include historical background information and general information about the organization itself. Only some of the websites address the enemy or citizens of a country currently under attack by terrorists. The terrorists hope weaken public support within countries and in some cases will threaten attacks if the government fails to do as they ask.

CYBERTERRORISM TODAY AND TOMORROW

It seems fair to say that the current threat posed by cyberterrorism has been exaggerated. No single instance of cyberterrorism has yet been recorded; U.S. defence and intelligence computer systems are air-gapped and thus isolated from the Internet; the systems run by private companies are more vulnerable to attack but also more resilient than is often supposed; the vast majority of cyberattacks are launched by hackers with few, if any, political goals and no desire to cause the mayhem and carnage of which terrorists dream. So, then, why has so much concern been expressed over a relatively minor threat?

The reasons are many. First, as Denning has observed, "cyberterrorism and cyberattacks are sexy right now.... [Cyberterrorism is] novel, original, it captures people's imagination." Second, the mass media frequently fail to distinguish between hacking and cyberterrorism and exaggerate the threat of the latter by reasoning from false analogies such as the following: "If a sixteen-year-old could do this, then what could a well-funded terrorist group do?" Ignorance is a third factor. Green argues that cyberterrorism merges two spheres—terrorism and technology—that many people, including most lawmakers and senior administration officials, do not fully understand and therefore tend to fear. Moreover, some groups are eager to exploit this ignorance. Numerous technology companies, still reeling from the collapse of the high-tech bubble, have sought to attract federal research grants by recasting themselves as innovators in computer security and thus vital contributors to national security. Law enforcement and security consultants are likewise highly motivated to have us believe that the threat to our nation's security is severe. A fourth reason is that some politicians, whether out of genuine conviction or out of a desire to stoke public anxiety about terrorism in order to advance their own agendas, have played the role of prophets of doom. And a fifth factor is ambiguity about the very meaning of "cyberterrorism," which has confused the public and given rise to countless myths.

Verton argues that "al Qaeda [has] shown itself to have an incessant appetite for modern technology" and provides numerous citations from bin Laden and other al Qaeda leaders to show their recognition of this new cyberweapon. In the wake of the 9/11 attacks, bin Laden reportedly gave a statement to an editor of an Arab newspaper claiming that "hundreds of Muslim scientists were with him who would use their knowledge... ranging from computers to electronics against the infidels." Sheikh Omar Bakri Muhammad, a supporter of bin Laden and often the conduit for his messages to the Western world, declared in an interview with Verton, "I would advise those who doubt al Qaeda's interest in cyber-weapons to take Osama bin Laden very seriously. The third letter from Osama bin Laden... was clearly addressing using the technology in order to destroy the economy of the capitalist states."

"While bin Laden may have his finger on the trigger, his grandchildren may have their fingers on the computer mouse," remarked Frank Cilluffo of the Office of Homeland Security in a statement that has been widely cited. Future terrorists may indeed see greater potential for cyberterrorism than do the terrorists of today. Furthermore, as Denning argues, the next generation of terrorists is now growing up in a digital world, one in which hacking tools are sure to become more powerful, simpler to use, and easier to access. Cyberterrorism may also become more attractive as the real and virtual worlds become more closely coupled. For instance, a terrorist group might simultaneously explode a bomb at a train station and launch a cyberattack on the communications infrastructure, thus magnifying the impact of the event. Unless these systems are carefully secured, conducting an online operation that physically harms someone may be as easy tomorrow as penetrating a website is today.

Paradoxically, success in the "war on terror" is likely to make terrorists turn increasingly to unconventional weapons such as cyberterrorism. The challenge before us is to assess what needs to be done to address this ambiguous but potential threat of cyberterrorism—but to do so without inflating its real significance and manipulating the fear it inspires. Denning and other terrorism experts conclude that, at least for now, hijacked vehicles, truck bombs, and biological weapons seem to pose a greater threat than does cyberterrorism. However, just as the events of 9/11 caught the world by surprise, so could a major cyberassault. The threat of cyberterrorism may be exaggerated and manipulated, but we can neither deny it nor dare to ignore it.

CYBERTERROR THREAT EXAGGERATED

Amid all the dire warnings and alarming statistics that the subject of cyberterrorism generates, it is important to remember one simple statistic: so far, there has been no recorded instance of a terrorist cyberattack on U.S. public facilities, transportation systems, nuclear power plants, power grids, or other key components of the national infrastructure. Cyberattacks are common, but they have not been conducted by terrorists and they have not sought to inflict the kind of damage that would qualify them as cyberterrorism.

When U.S. troops recovered al Qaeda laptops in Afghanistan, officials were surprised to find its members more technologically adept than previously believed. They discovered structural and engineering software, electronic models of a dam, and information on computerized water systems, nuclear power plants, and U.S. and European stadiums. But the evidence did *not* suggest that al Qaeda operatives were planning cyberattacks, only that they were using the Internet to communicate and coordinate physical attacks. Neither al Qaeda nor any other terrorist organization appears to have tried to stage a serious cyberattack. For now, the most damaging attacks and intrusions, experts say, are typically carried out either by disgruntled corporate insiders intent on embezzlement or sabotage or by individual hackers—typically young and male—seeking thrills and notoriety. According to a report issued in 2002 by IBM Global Security Analysis Lab, 90 percent of hackers are amateurs with limited technical proficiency, 9 percent are more skilled at gaining unauthorized access but do not damage the files they read, and only 1 percent are highly skilled and intent on copying files or damaging programs and systems. Most hackers, it should be noted, concentrate on writing programs that expose security flaws in computer software, mainly in the operating systems produced by Microsoft. Their efforts in this direction have sometimes embarrassed corporations but have also been responsible for alerting the public and security professionals to major security flaws in software.

Moreover, although there are hackers with the ability to damage systems, disrupt e-commerce, and force websites offline, the vast majority of hackers do not have the necessary skills and knowledge. The ones who do, generally do not seek to wreak havoc. Douglas Thomas, a professor at the University of Southern California, spent seven years studying computer hackers in an effort to understand better who they are and what motivates them. Thomas interviewed hundreds of hackers and explored their "literature." In testimony on July 24, 2002, before the House Subcommittee on Government Efficiency, Financial Management and Intergovernmental Relations, Thomas argued that "with the vast majority of hackers, I would say 99 percent of them, the risk [of cyberterrorism] is negligible for the simple reason that those hackers do not have the skill or ability to organize or execute an attack that would be anything more than a minor inconvenience."

His judgment was echoed in *Assessing the Risks of Cyberterrorism, Cyber War, and Other Cyber Threats*, a 2002 report for the Centre for Strategic and International Studies, written by Jim Lewis, a sixteen-year veteran of the State and Commerce Departments. "The idea that hackers are going to bring the nation to its knees is too far-fetched a scenario to be taken seriously," Lewis argued. "Nations are more robust than the early analysts of cyberterrorism and cyberwarfare give them credit for. Infastructure systems [are] more flexible and responsive in restoring service than the early analysts realized, in part because they have to deal with failure on a routine basis." Many computer security specialists believe it is virtually impossible to use the Internet to inflict death on a large scale and scoff at the notion that terrorists would bother trying. The resilience of computer systems to attack, they point out, is no accident but rather the result of significant investments of time, money, and expertise. Nuclear weapons and other sensitive military systems enjoy the most basic form of Internet security. They are "air-gapped," meaning that they are not physically connected to the Internet and are therefore inaccessible to outside hackers. The Defence Department has been particularly vigilant in protecting key systems by isolating them from the Internet and even from the Pentagon's internal computer network. All new software must be submitted to the National Security Agency for security testing.

The 9/11 hijackings understandably led to an outcry that airliners are particularly susceptible to cyberterrorist attacks. In 2002, for instance, Senator Charles Schumer (D-N.Y.) described "the absolute havoc and devastation that would result if cyberterrorists suddenly shut down our air traffic control system, with thousands of planes in mid-flight." In fact, cybersecurity experts give some of their highest marks to the Federal Aviation Authority, which separates its administrative and air traffic control systems. And there is a reason the 9/11 hijackers used box-cutters instead of keyboards: it is impossible to hijack a plane remotely, which eliminates the possibility of a high-tech 9/11 scenario in which planes are used as weapons. Another source of concern is terrorist infiltration of the intelligence agencies. But here, too, the risk is described by Internet experts as slim. The CIA's classified computers are also air-gapped, as is the FBI's entire computer system.

That leaves less-well-protected secondary targets such as power grids, oil pipelines, and dams that do not present opportunities as nightmarish as do nuclear weapons systems but that nonetheless might be used to inflict other forms of mass destruction. Because most of these systems are in the private sector, they tend to be less secure than government systems. In addition, as noted above, companies increasingly use the Internet to manage SCADA systems that control such processes as regulating the flow of oil in pipelines and the level of water in dams. To illustrate the supposed ease with which terrorists could seize control of a dam, a story in the *Washington Post* in June 2003 on al Qaeda cyberterrorism related an anecdote about a twelve-year-old who hacked into the SCADA system at Arizona's Theodore Roosevelt Dam in 1998 and was, according to the article, within mere keystrokes of unleashing millions of gallons of water upon helpless downstream communities. However, a subsequent investigation by the tech-news site CNet.com revealed the tale to be largely apocryphal; investigators concluded that the hacker could not have gained control of the dam and that no lives or property were ever at risk.

To assess the potential threat of cyberterrorism, experts such as Denning suggest that two questions be asked: Are there targets that are vulnerable to cyberattacks? And are there actors with the capability and motivation to carry out such attacks? The answer to the first question is yes: critical infrastructure systems are complex and therefore bound to contain weaknesses that might be exploited, and even systems that seem "hardened" to outside manipulation might be accessed by insiders, acting alone or in concert with terrorists, to cause considerable harm. But what of the second question?

Few people besides a company's own employees possess the specific technical know-how required to run a specialized SCADA system. The most commonly cited example of SCADA exploitation bears this out. In April 2002, an Australian man used an Internet connection to release a million gallons of raw sewage along Queensland's Sunshine Coast after being turned down for a government job. When police arrested him, they discovered that he had worked for the company that designed the sewage treatment plant's control software.

It is possible, of course, that such disgruntled employees might be recruited by terrorist groups, but even if the terrorists did enlist inside help, the degree of damage they could cause would still be limited. As Joshua Green argues in "The Myth of Cyberterrorism" (which appeared in the *Washington Monthly* in November 2002), the employees of companies that handle power grids, oil and gas utilities, and communications are well rehearsed in dealing with the fallout from hurricanes, floods, tornadoes, and other natural disasters. They are also equally adept at containing and remedying problems that stem from human action.

In August 1999, the Centre for the Study of Terrorism and Irregular Warfare at the Naval Postgraduate School (NPS) in Monterey, California, issued a report titled *Cyber-terror: Prospects and Implications*.

The report concluded that terrorists generally lack the wherewithal and human capital needed to mount attacks that involve more than annoying but relatively harmless hacks. The study examined five types of terrorist groups: religious, New Age, ethnonationalist separatist, revolutionary, and far-right extremists. Of these, only the religious groups were adjudged likely to seek the capacity to inflict massive damage. Hacker groups, the study determined, are psychologically and organizationally ill suited to cyberterrorism, and any massive disruption of the information infrastructure would run counter to their self-interest.

In October 2000, the NPS group issued a second report, this one examining the decision-making process by which substate groups engaged in armed resistance develop new operational methods, including cyberterrorism. The report concluded that while substate groups may find cyberterror attractive as a nonlethal weapon, terrorists have not yet integrated information technology into their strategy and tactics and that significant barriers between hackers and terrorists may prevent their integration into one group.

Another illustration of the limited likelihood of terrorists launching a highly damaging cyberattack comes from a simulation sponsored by the U.S. Naval War College. The college contracted with a research group to simulate a massive cyberattack on the nation's information infrastructure.

Government hackers and security analysts gathered in July 2002 in Newport, R.I., for a war game dubbed "Digital Pearl Harbor." The results were far from devastating: the hackers failed to crash the Internet, although they did cause serious sporadic damage. According to a CNet.com report on the exercise published in August 2002, officials concluded that terrorists hoping to stage such an attack "would require a syndicate with significant resources, including $200 million, country-level intelligence and five years of preparation time."

3

Information Warfare: The Unethical Use of Cyberspace

Over 35 years ago, computer scientists of the United States Department of Defense, and four western-state universities were constructing the precursor to the Internet. Named ARPANET, for Advanced Research Projects Agency Network, one of the projects goals was to study how communications could be maintained in the event of an all-out nuclear attack, as this was the middle of the Cold War.

After realizing that ARPANET would not be immune to a nuclear assault, the computer scientists using it recognized that assisting human communication was the most fundamental advance that the ARPANET made possible. Today, the Internet provides incredible opportunities for the hundreds of millions of users around the world. Globalization is due, in part, to the connections nations and corporations have been able to establish on behalf of the Internet. Previously, most computerized information was stored on disks or hard drives, but the Internet has allowed for easier access of data by storing information on networks so that it may be accessed from, and sent to any connected location.

Expanding at a phenomenal rate, 200 million Americans used the Internet in 2000, and the number of websites doubles every 37 days, according to the Federal Bureau of Investigation. The convenience and ease of transmitting information around the globe in seconds makes the Internet priceless for business, government agencies and anyone else who can go on-line. The Internet is now one of several regions that create the ever-growing entity known as Cyberspace. Governments, corporations, and educational institutions the world over became conscious of the potential of cyberspace, in which they could communicate, conduct business, and share information in ways previously unavailable.

The benefits of this new medium were appealing not only to those using computers for productive means, but for those who sought to unlawfully use information in order to cause damage in a variety of ways. And thus, the unethical use of computers helped create Information Warfare.

According to the Institute for The Advanced Study of Information Warfare, "Information warfare is the offensive and defensive use of information and information systems to deny, exploit, corrupt, or destroy, an adversary's information, information-based processes, information systems, and computer-based networks while protecting one's own. Such actions are designed to achieve advantages over military or business adversaries."

Although a global menace, a focus on the causes and effects of Information Warfare threatening Canada, and mainly the United States will demonstrate the extent to which this phenomenon may reach. Granted, militaries and governments rely on computers for day-to-day operations, this essay will focus more on the aspect of computers that are used and depended on by the general public.

Although virtually every nation in the world could be the victim or purveyor of an Information attack, the most likely target is the United States. The US military is arguably the most powerful in the world and most enemies cannot match their arsenal and power. Rather than try to build an equivalent military, a more efficient alternative of attack would be through computers, with Information Warfare, i.e. cyber terrorism and cyber warfare.

The most severely threatening and destructive forma of Information Warfare are indeed the most difficult to defend against, says the Canadian Security Intelligence Service (CSIS). Terrorist groups and criminal hackers are often far more educated in the area of computers than law enforcement agents, and they have the knowledge and equipment to stay ahead of advances in protective security. Targets could include governments of all levels, military and police forces, political groups and prominent individuals; basically anyone with a computer hooked up to a modem. Using the Internet for terrorist activity reduces the chances of detection or capture. Terrorists can cause disruptions and economic damage to their target by attacking computer systems, rather than using weapons that inflict physical damage. Industrialized nations that are heavily reliant on computer systems are vulnerable to Information Warfare attacks.

A 1999 report by the Center for Strategic and International Studies, "Cybercrime…Cyberterrorism…Cyberwarfare" warned of the severe risk to the critical infrastructures in the United States. Current defenses are inadequate to protect against an attack as the Pentagon estimates that a coordinated attack by fewer than 20 strategically placed computer experts, with a budget of $10 million, could cripple the United States. Within a matter of seconds, a cyber attack could cripple a nation's government and economy, not to mention its society. It is interesting to note that the Internet was created by the US military and now they must protect themselves and their country from others who want to attack the US by means of computers and the Internet.

All industrialized nations, especially those of the Group of Eight Industrialized Nations, G8, are becoming increasingly dependent on their critical infrastructures, which virtually keep nations running. Critical infrastructures, of the government and private sector, are essential to the routine operations of the economy and government, and are both physical and cyber based. Technological advances have linked many infrastructures, such as telecommunications, energy, banking and finance, transportation, water, sewage and emergency systems, and these systems are becoming progressively automated. The reliance and importance of infrastructures have created potential targets for physical and cyber attacks.

The vulnerability of critical infrastructures, and the unique risks associated with networked computing have been recognized by the U.S. for some time, but not until 1998 was this issue applied the urgent status it deserves. The Presidential Decision Directive 63 was approved by Bill Clinton, and a national infrastructure protection policy was developed. The National Infrastructure Protection Center (NIPC), run by the FBI, and the Critical Infrastructure Assurance Office (CIAO), run by the Department of Commerce were created in order to protect and examine infrastructure vulnerabilities. Both the NIPC and CIAO are an administrative types of protection, whereas major cyber-terrorist attacks or network sabotages are handled by the Federal Computer Emergency Response Team (Fed Cert), which is likened to a SWAT team. By creating these agencies, and addressing the threats they face, the US government has made cyberspace security and Information Warfare a top priority. None of these agencies mention the moral and ethical implications of Information Warfare, as this aspect is not evident to be a military or law enforcement concern.

The Canadian Security Intelligence Service is concerned with foreign governments, terrorist groups and politically motivated extremists who may now use Information Warfare instead of traditional method of attack. Terrorism and industrial espionage, among many other malicious acts, are unethical regardless if committed with the aid of computers or not. However, using a computer, the Internet or other forms of IT to facilitate Information Warfare can be considered even more unethical than traditional methods of terrorism and related offences. Compared to the U.S., Canada is less economically and politically influential on the rest of the world, and is fortunately not an enemy to as many foreign states. However, this does not give Canada immunity from transnational Information Warfare. Director of the FBI, Louis J. Freeh, characterized Canada as a "hacker haven" as a result of our "sophisticated information technology system and our open society."

John Deutch, Director of Central Intelligence, testified before an American congressional committee and warned that, "an electronic Pearl Harbour was now a real threat" because, "criminal hackers were offering their services to so-called rogue states with various schemes to undo vital US interests through computer intrusions."Previously, terrorist groups used to take credit for their actions so their objectives would be well known, but a new trend is to avoid responsibility, which is quite easy with cyber attacks, so tracking such organizations is becoming increasingly difficult.

Information Warfare has international implications and virtually any one with access to a particular district of cyberspace is at risk. Several of the many features that make the Internet so unique, such as the speed at which information can be transferred, the ability to remain anonymous, and the ease of accessibility, attract many people, including the criminally minded. The broad range of crimes committed on the Internet, or with the aid of computers, poses new challenges for governments and law enforcement agencies around the world.

Transnational computer crimes, such as cyber terrorism and cyber warfare, are pertinent global matters that must be prevented if cyberspace is to prosper in the future. The future of cyberspace depends on the prevention of the most destructive types of crimes. Therefore, governments, aided by law enforcement agencies and private corporations must address and prevent the most severe threats to cyberspace. Again, ethical implications are not considered.

Not only must industry continue to develop security policies and safeguards for their networks and systems, but it should also continue its efforts to identify security flaws that threaten the Internet. These massive companies, such as Microsoft, Cisco, and Oracle have the knowledge, resources and personnel to create effective solutions. The technology to monitor vast areas of cyberspace, in real time, are available, as well as methods to detect network intrusions. These companies have the ability to inform governments of potential attacks, if and where there is a gap in an infrastructures security system, and they can block against many types of attacks and intrusions.

These abilities could be extremely beneficial for cyberspace as a whole by protecting governments, infrastructures and economies. As well these types of technologies could be incorporated into combating smaller scale crimes. The reason these measures are not commonplace is the initial costs incurred. As well, many companies do not want their vulnerabilities to be known for fear of further violations and loss of consumer confidence. Countless businesses, e-business and real space as well, rely on IT corporations for their products and innovations. Perhaps even more importantly, these corporations provide the global market with the hardware and software needed to access and effectively use cyberspace, and subsequently make the economy even more computer dependent.

These companies made and continue to manufacture the products now in use by terrorists and others who engage in Information Warfare.

Although their products intended use is not for such malevolent activities, American and Canadian made products can be used by terrorists to carry out their attacks on the American economy and government networks. These major corporations have a moral obligation to research and fund protective measures that can prevent and shield infrastructures, themselves, governments, not to mention cyberspace as a whole.

The private sector cannot depend on law enforcement agencies for protection. Raymond Kendall, Secretary General of Interpol, (International Criminal Police Organization, consisting of 178 nations) told senior executives of large and growing companies, "The private sector must shoulder the responsibility for its own defense because government agencies do not have the technology necessary to do the job."

DEFINITION OF INFORMATION WARFARE

Information Warfare (IW) was formally launched in December 1992 with the dissemination of DOD Directive 3600.1. (Note 1) From the outset, widespread discussion and understanding of IW were hampered by its Top Secret classification. (Note 2) In September 1995 the Assistant Secretary of Defense for Command, Control, Communications and Intelligence (ASD(C3I)) published the formal DOD unclassified definition of IW:

Actions taken to achieve information superiority by affecting adversary information, information-based processes, and information systems, while defending one' s own information, information-based processes, and information systems.

This description clearly underscores both the defensive, as well as offensive aspects of IW. In the summer of 1994, the Defense Science Board(Note 3) (DSB), drawing heavily from expertise within DOD, published the most comprehensive and authoritative discussion of IW to date. The report highlighted the distinction between information in warfare and information warfare. Information in warfare pertains to "getting [information] it where it is needed in a timely and reliable manner. (Note 4) " It encompasses the collection, processing, and dissemination of information and is synonymous with the "C4I for the Warrior" vision released by the Joint Staff in 1992.

C4I for the Warrior addresses the concept of a global Command, Control, Communications, Computer, and Intelligence system directly linking military units around the globe in an interoperable, fully integrated fashion spanning the range of military operations from peace to war. (Note 5) Information in warfare capitalizes on the national information infrastructure (NII). Characterized as an "information highway,6 the NII is the growing worldwide information infrastructure which transcends industry, media, and the military and includes government and non-government entities. Most activities now rely on the information infrastructure including the banking' transportation, manufacturing, and electrical power industries. The Defense Information Infrastructure (DII) is an integral part of the NII with over 95 percent of DOD' s worldwide telecommunications needs satisfied by commercial telecommunications carriers. (Note 7) Military activities relying on the DII include transportation, logistics, financial, manpower, and personnel and training.

While C4I for the Warrior focuses on harnessing ever-increasing computer storage and exchange capabilities, IW targets these information systems. The distinction between C4I for the Warrior and IW is extremely important. IW employs offensive techniques such as deception, electronic jammers, munitions and advanced technologies to deceive, deny, exploit, damage, or destroy adversary information systems, while at the same time protecting friendly information systems from disruption, exploitation and damage by an adversary. (Note 8) The target of IW may range from influencing national level decisionmakers to corrupting the automated control of transportation systems. (Note 9) defensive IW protects friendly information systems from disruption, exploitation and damage by an adversary. (Note 10) or example, the Army's ongoing digitization of the battlefield is an application of information in warfare at the operational and tactical levels. Defensive IW, on the other hand, focuses on identifying and protecting vulnerabilities which arise from this increased reliance on technology.

The emergence of Command and Control Warfare (C2W) has been fundamental in understanding IW. (Note 12) In article in Signal magazine LTGen James Clapper, then Director Defense Intelligence Agency (DIA), wrote "the closest description of information warfare might be found in the definition of command and control warfare." (Note 12) IW and C2W, however, are not interchangeable terms. C2W is a subset of IW. The Chairman of the Joint Chiefs of Staff (CJCS) Memorandum of Policy (MOP) 3O, states "C2W is the military strategy which implements IW on the battlefield." (Note 13) C2W is designed as an essential part of an overall theater campaign plan. It is implemented during "joint military operations when U.S. military forces unilaterally or as part of an allied/coalition force are opposed or threatened by an organized military or paramilitary force." (Note 14) C2W focuses on an adversary's military command and control when military force is applied. On the other hand, the use of the word "warfare" in the term IW does not limit IW to a military conflict, declared or otherwise. is IW targets the entire information infrastructure of an adversary - political, economic, and military throughout the continuum of operations from peace to war.

Organizational Imperative

IW, as this definitional discussion highlights, is a complex issue. Organizations are essential in actually implementing this new concept and achieving a viable IW architecture. IW will only become institutionalized if activities actually take responsibility for planning and executing IW. Today IW offices have been stood up throughout DOD focusing on offensive and defensive IW capabilities, but for the most part the budgets and staffs of these elements are very limited. They represent an important start in what will likely be a long and slow process.

IWExecutive Board: The Deputy Secretary of Defense chairs an IW Executive Board established in May 1995 which comprises senior officials within the department including the Vice Chairman Joint Chief of Staff (VCJCS) (Note 16). Supporting the IW Executive Board is an IW Council chaired by the Assistant Secretary of Defense for Command, Control, Communications and Intelligence (ASD(C3I)).

The Executive Board is chartered to address IW roles and responsibilities and serve as the DOD focal point for IW discussion at the national level. The Board is a welcome addition as it demonstrates an awareness by senior DOD officials of the need to coordinate IW, not only within the department, but in the interagency arena. However, senior officials are too busy to spend a great deal of time on any one issue, particularly one that has not reached crisis proportions. This is the point Robert McNamara makes in his book In Retrospect when discussing the evolution of U.S. policy in Vietnam during the Kennedy and Johnson administrations and the same is true today. (Note 17) You need to have the pull from the top, but it is important that lower levels are fully energized.

ASD C31: The ASD(C3I), as the senior IW advisor to the Secretary of Defense, has organized a small IW Directorate comprising less than ten personnel to help him execute his responsibilities. It was the forerunner to this office which drafted the original IW directive in 1992. The IW Directorate conducts centralized planning, coordination, and oversight for IW and conducts program reviews of selected Service and defense agency IW efforts. In May 1995 the IW Directorate sponsored an IW wargame for senior government officials designed to raise the profile of the threat to the U.S. information infrastructure. (Note 18)

The IW Directorate has also focused on initiating a DOD "Red Team" effort. This was one of the IW recommendations from the 1994 Defense Science Board report to "jump start Defensive IW." (Note 19) Under this concept personnel knowledgeable in adversaries' offensive IW form a team to "attack" the DOD information infrastructure. Given the magnitude of the vulnerabilities, the objective would be to have this capability distributed throughout DOD and carried out at various levels and locations. This concept dovetails with the Computer Emergency Response Team (CERT) which reacts to real world intrusions into computer systems. The Defense Information Systems Agency (DISA) has stood up small offices which accomplish both these tasks, but a more comprehensive program is necessary. In the twelve months prior to July 1994 DISA detected roughly 3,600 attacks on military networks, but officials estimate they detected only two percent of all the attacks, raising the estimated number to 182,000. (Note 20)

The "Red Team" program is designed to increase awareness throughout DOD of the vulnerabilities of automated systems and improve the overall security posture. A comprehensive "Red Team" effort can significantly reduce vulnerabilities in the near term as many existing problems are attributed to inadequate training of operators and system administrators. As the head of a CERT team stated, "the problem...is a lack of understanding and awareness and a lack of training and technical competence on the part of the user community." (Note 21) The "Red Team" is a laudable objective, but ASD(C3I) presently only coordinates and does not direct action. The Joint Staff has designated the Joint Command and Control Warfare Center (JC2WC) at San Antonio, Texas as executive agent to support the OSD IW Red Team effort. However, implementation of the "Red Team" concept is evolving slowly given budget constraints and manpower reductions in the Services and defense agencies.

USD(P): In 1995 the Under Secretary of Defense (Policy) (USD(P)) created an Infrastructure Policy Directorate. This office focuses on emergency preparedness and shaping the role of DOD in the protection of infrastructures, including coordination between DOD and nonDOD government, and civilian/corporate owned infrastructures. (Note 22) These are important responsibilities which clearly fall under the heading of defensive IW. As this office matures, it will be incumbent upon the IW Council and Executive Board to insure IW activities within ASD(C3I) and USD(P) are delineated and deconflicted, if necessary.

Joint Staff: In the Joint arena, IW organizations have also emerged. On the Joint Staff, proponency for IW is now shared between the Directorate for Operations, J3, and the J6, Directorate for Command, Control, Communications, Computers, and Intelligence (C4I) under a Memorandum of Understanding signed in October 1994. While conceptually this may have merits with each directorate bringing a unique dimension of IW, in reality as Lt Gen Clapper, former Director, DIA, has recommended, the Operations Officer should be the overall staff coordinator as he is for all other operations issues. (Note 23)

The current arrangement on the Joint Staff presents some unique challenges as no one is actually in charge. The J3 and J6 principals are too busy to dedicate the constant attention this area requires and day-to-day responsibility for IW on the Joint Staff is delegated. A need exists for direct flag officer sponsorship to orchestrate joint IW policy and doctrine development, conduct operational planning, and establish requirements. A dedicated flag officer sponsor would greatly facilitate coordination with Services, OSD, the Intelligence Community and as IW matures, the interagency and civilian sectors. It would also send a strong message that IW is an important joint warfighting issue requiring immediate highlevel attention. Within the Joint Staff J3, responsibility for offensive IW now resides within the Information Warfare /Special Technical Operations Division (IW/STOD). This division is responsible for coordinating compartmented planning between the Services, Combatant Commands, and DOD agencies. Bob Woodward writes in The Commanders, the Special Technical Operations Center (STOC) is "a command and communications center for operations involving the sensitive "black" programs known only to those cleared to the special-access compartments." (Note 24) The IW/STOD also has responsibility for coordinating all facets of C2W for the Joint Staff including policy, doctrine, and operational issues. It is this office which authored MOP 30, led the preparation of Joint Pub 3-13 and will draft IW doctrine. This arrangement underscores the important linkage between C2W and IW. As the military proceeds to operationalize IW, the IW/STOD represents the linchpin for ensuring the integration of all dimensions of joint IW.

It has been suggested that, just as we continue to use a Single Integrated Operational Plan (SIOP) for strategic nuclear warfare, DOD might consider the use of an "IW SIOP" which addresses offensive and defensive deconfliction and intelligence equity issues. (Note 25) If this were implemented, the task would be assigned to the IW/STOD to coordinate the task. Today the IW/STOD focuses principally on support to the Combatant Commands, but as IW matures with both its non- lethal and deterrence potentials, greater interagency participation and coordination will undoubtedly occur.

JC2WC: The activation of the Joint Command and Control Warfare Center (JC2WC) at San Antonio, Texas in October 1994 provided a valuable resource for the Commanders of the Combatant Commands (CINCs). (Note 26 As a field-operating agency of the Joint Chiefs of Staff and headed by a flag officer, (Note 27) the JC2WC is fully engaged in the warfighting application of IW. With 163 assigned personnel, the JC2WC dispatches tailored teams to augment CINC and Joint Task Force staffs and provide C2W expertise in all joint exercises and contingency operations. Personnel from the JC2WC have participated in U.S. efforts in Bosnia and contingency operations in both Kuwait and Haiti. Given the high turnover of personnel on CINC staffs, the JC2WC is very much in demand for its C2W expertise. (Note 28) The JC2WC is in the unique position of being able to cross fertilize and share C2W lessons learned between the Combatant Commands. Accordingly, the organization has played a major role in developing joint C2W doctrine and will contribute significantly to the preparation of a follow-on C2W Joint Tactics, Techniques, and Procedures (JTTP) publication. At the present time, the JC2WC is fully engaged accomplishing its assigned tasks with respect to C2W. It is only now beginning to analyze its newly assigned responsibilities as executive agent in support of the OSD IW Red Team effort. As IW evolves and DOD' s role in the larger IW arena is clarified, a natural progression will be for this organization to serve as the nucleus for a Joint IW center.

Joint COMSEC Monitoring Activity. The JCMA is another field operating agency of the Joint Chiefs of Staff having IW applications. It was created in 1993 by a Memorandum of Agreement between the Service Operations Deputies and Directors of the Joint Staff and NSA. The JCMA is charged with conducting "COMSEC monitoring (collection, analysis, and reporting) of DOD telecommunications and automated information systems (AIS) and monitoring of related noncommunications signals." (Note 29) Its purpose is to identify vulnerabilities exploitable by potential adversaries and recommend countermeasures and corrective actions. The JCMA focuses on unencrypted DOD systems and "does not perform traditional telephone monitoring," as this function remains a Service responsibility. (Note 30) The Joint Staff Director for Operations has been assigned primary responsibility for JCMA affairs. This facilitates coordination between the JC2WC and the JCMA. The JCMA supports both real-world operations, as well as joint exercises and DOD systems monitoring. The JCMA, more so than the JC2WC, already has the expertise to perform the Red Team mission. Rather than further diluting the already stretched resources and expertise of the JC2WC, it would make better sense to designate the JCMA as executive agent to support the OSD Red Team IW initiative.

Joint Spectrum Center. The DOD Joint Spectrum Center (JSC) was activated in September 1994 under the direction of the Joint Staff J6. The JSC assumed all the mission and responsibilities previously performed by the Electromagnetic Compatibility Center, as well as additional functions. The JSC deploys teams in support of the CINCs and serves as the DOD focal point for supporting spectrum supremacy aspects of IW. Notably the JSC assists warfighters in developing and managing the Joint Restricted Frequency List (JRFL) and assisting in the resolution of operational interference and jamming incidents. While informal coordination occurs on IW related issues between the Joint Spectrum Center, the Joint COMSEC Monitoring Activity, and the Joint C2W Center, each organization interfaces separately with the CINC staffs. No formal mechanism is yet in place to ensure the warfighters obtain a coordinated IW support package.

Combatant Commands: The focus of warfighters at the Combatant Commands remains planning and executing C2W. All of the geographic CINCs now have C2W staff officers assigned in their Operations Directorates, but organizing the diverse elements which comprise C2W is a challenge for CINC staffs. U.S.

Central Command (CENTCOM) has actually physically consolidated the staff officers responsible for orchestrating electronic warfare, operational security, military deception and psychological operations into a single branch.

This organization can serve as the nucleus as new IW capabilities emerge and are apportioned to the CINCs. Defensive IW poses a more significant challenge. While the CINCs can take incremental measures to unilaterally reduce vulnerabilities of their information systems, given their ultimate dependence on the national information infrastructure, defensive IW must be undertaken as part of a larger DOD sponsored initiative.

Services: Each of the Services have created or are participating in Information Warfare Centers or Activities. The Air Force leads the Services and in September 1995, the Chief of Staff and Secretary of the Air Force published the 17 page, Cornerstones of Information Warfare which describes how "Air Force doctrine should evolve to accommodate information warfare." (Note 31) The Air Force was also the first to establish their Information Warfare Center (AFIWC) at San Antonio, Texas in October 1993. This was accomplished by consolidating the Air Force cryptologic support center and the electronic warfare center. The AFIWC serves as the Air Force command and control warfare executive agent with approximately 1000 military and civilian personnel assigned. The Center is subordinate to the Air Intelligence Agency closely aligning it with the Intelligence Community. The Center applies the teaming concept integrating the intelligence component with operators, engineers, communications and computer specialists, both offensive and defensive. (Note 32) The AFIWC also has an ongoing "Red Team" and CERT effort designed to improve network security in the Air Force. The Center is collocated with the JC2WC and both organizations work closely together. Personnel from the AFIWC regularly team with the JC2WC on major deployments.

On 1 October 1995, the Air Force created its first Information Warfare Squadron at Shaw Air Force Base, South Carolina. The squadron's primary purpose will be to protect Air Force computers and communications, as well as assisting in "infiltrating an enemy's computer and communications systems." (Note 33) The squadron will support the 9th Air Force commander who is assigned the

Central Command area of operations. Eventually, the Air Force will set up more squadrons to assist air commanders responsible for other geographic areas. While the IW Squadron at Shaw AFB presently only has two officers assigned, there will be as many as 40 by August 1996, when the squadron is slated to be operational. Eventually, the squadron might grow to 85 people. (Note 34) The Air Force recognizes it is pushing the envelope, but as General Joseph Ralston, chief of Air Combat Command, stated:

You can sit around for another 10 years and debate about what some of the problems might be [with setting up an information warfare squadron]...but you will never know until you actually get into them and try to make it work operationally. (Note 35)

The Navy established the Navy Information Warfare Activity (NIWA) in August 1994 to serve as their focal point for IW activities. (Note 36) Directly subordinate to the Naval Security Group, the NIWA is located at Fort Meade, Maryland and is closely linked to the National Security Agency.

Given the rapid pace of advancing technology the Navy has given the NIWA special authority to generate requirements and procure systems. Traditionally there has been a sharp separation in the Navy between organizations responsible for setting requirements and those charged with overseeing their acquisition. However, with new generations of computers and information systems unveiled on average about every 18 months, the Navy has adopted a more streamlined approach. As John Davis, technology adviser to the Navy's Space and Electronic Warfare Directorate, indicated, "If we fall more than one cycle behind. we could find industry putting information warfare systems into potentially hostile nations at the same time that US force receive the same equipment." (Note 37)

The Navy also has established the Fleet Information Warfare Center (FIWC) at Little Creek, Virginia from existing Fleet Deception/C2W Group assets. (Note 38) The FIWC serves as the link between the NIWA and the Atlantic and Pacific Fleets. With personnel deployed on carrier battle groups throughout the world, the FIWC fulfills a similar mission for the Navy that the JC2WC does for the joint warfighter. The IW organizational structure created by the Navy enables the FIWC to focus on near term operational requirements, while the NIWA assumes a more long-term perspective keeping abreast of IW advances and developing and acquiring systems.

Rather than create a separate IW organization, the Marines intend to assign liaison officers to the respective Service IW centers to benefit from their efforts. The Navy and Marines have also teamed up to develop policy guidance for Navy and Marine IW/C2W operations. In February 1995, the Marine Corps Commandant and Chief of Naval Operations approved a plan which states, "Navy and Marine Corps must have a fully integrated IW/C2W capability...team must organize, train, and equip its forward deployed forces to conduct IW/C2W." (Note 39)

The Army is the latest Service to establish an IW activity. Officially activated in May 1995, the Land Information Warfare Center (LIWA) is subordinate to the Army Intelligence and Security Command (INSCOM) but is under the operational control of the Headquarters Department of the Army, Deputy Chief of Staff for Operations (DCSOPS). As with the Air Force and Navy, the Army has closely aligned its IW effort with the Intelligence Community. The LIWA is a totally new organization in contrast to the Air Force and Navy efforts which reorganized existing activities. It is also the smallest of the three Service IW activities with a projected end strength of 50-75 personnel. The primary focus of the LIWA is to provide operational support at the Army Corps and higher levels. The Army is also coordinating closely with the Marines to assign personnel to the LIWA. Given its small size, the LIWA draws upon existing capabilities in the Army including psychological operations, electronic warfare, and operational security. The Army is in the process of institutionalizing a "Red Team" effort from existing INSCOM assets, and there is close coordination and collaboration with NSA on mutual IW efforts.

The Services' efforts during a period of serious budget constraints underscore a recognition of the importance of IW. Except for the general responsibilities delineated in the original DOD IW directive, Services have received no additional policy guidance on how to implement IW. In reviewing Service responses to IW, they have established organizations which best suit their near term needs. Manpower and funding for Service IW initiatives have been reallocated internally with the Air Force taking the most aggressive approach.

Over time Service organizations can be expected to evolve as IW matures. Today much of their focus is on implementing C2W, the military application of IW. Services have also implemented "Red Teams" to train personnel and improve security awareness of the vulnerabilities associated with information systems. Additionally, while the linkages of Service IW organizations with the Intelligence Community is valuable, it is important IW does not become an intelligence activity. IW needs to be controlled and fully managed by the warfighters as an integral part of an overall strategy. In that regard, the recent activation of the IW Squadron by the Air Force, separate and distinct from the AFIWC, is a positive step.

Intelligence Community: Within the Intelligence Community there exists an acute appreciation of the enormous impact IW has on their efforts. Each organization, DIA, CIA and NSA has established an office to orchestrate IW related activities and satisfy the needs of their consumers. NSA, in addition to it its intelligence mission, has a unique responsibility for developing "standards, techniques, systems, and equipment" for classified information. (Note 40) NSA has demonstrated success at protecting classified systems, but has achieved less success in the increasingly vulnerable area of unclassified computer networks where it plays a supporting role.

Under the 1987 Computer Security Act, the National Institute for Standards and Technology (NIST) was assigned responsibility for developing government wide standards and guidelines for "unclassified, sensitive information." (Note 41) The law also directed NIST to draw upon technical computer security guidelines developed by NSA. (Note 42) To clarify the relationship between NIST and NSA, a Memorandum of Agreement (MOW) was formalized in 1989 establishing mechanisms for implementing the Computer Security Act of 1987. The MOU has been controversial because of concerns in Congress and elsewhere that it cedes NSA much more authority than was intended under the act. (Note 43) The act envisioned NIST requesting NSA expertise as needed, but instead the MOU has involved NSA in all NIST activities related to information security.

Protecting unclassified, sensitive information is essential in developing an effective IW architecture. Given the growing threat to our information system, NSA officials are lobbying for increased efforts to protect unclassified networks. (Note 44) While NSA certainly has tremendous expertise and is the national authority on cryptographic protection, there are reservations about having it assume a greater role. Some perceive a conflict of interest between NSA's information protection role and its principal intelligence mission. Additionally, leadership in cryptography does not imply leadership in other areas of defensive IW. DOD has assigned the responsibility of protecting its own information infrastructure to the Defense Information Systems Agency. (Note 45) As national defensive IW policy is formulated, the security of unclassified, sensitive information must be addressed.

Non DOD Organizations: Although defensive IW has not been officially embraced outside of DOD, several standing organizations focus on this issue. The National Communication System (NCS) was established in 1963 to coordinate the planning of national security and emergency preparedness communications for the federal government under all circumstances, including crisis or emergency, attack, recovery, and reconstitution. The NCS receives policy direction directly from the National Security Council (NSC) but is managed through the Department of Defense. (Note 45) The NCS's National Coordinating Center for Telecommunications is staffed full time by both government and telecommunications industry representatives whose mission is to respond to both military and civil emergencies: ea., Desert Storm, Hurricane Andrew and, more recently, the bombing of the Federal building in Oklahoma city. (Note 47)

The National Security Telecommunications Advisory Council (NSTAC) was established during the Reagan Administration to advise the President on national security and emergency preparedness issues. This senior body is composed of presidents and CEOs of major telecommunications and defense information systems companies. NSTAC works closely with NCS.

The Federal Communications Commission (FCC) also plays a strong role in reliability and privacy issues regarding the public switched telephone network. The Network Reliability Council (NRC) was created in 1992 by the FCC to investigate the reliability of the public switched network following a series of service outages in 1991. The efforts culminated in a one-thousand page document, "Network Reliability." The FCC expanded the membership of the NRC in July 1994 and gave it a new charter. Today the NRC is composed of CEOs from telephone companies, equipment suppliers, state agencies, and federal, corporate, and consumer users.

Each of these organizations, as well as NIST, are involved in aspects of defensive IW. What is lacking, however, is an overarching framework linking these disparate efforts into a coordinated effort. Within the government someone needs to be in charge. The NCS may serve as a blueprint for this effort. Not only does it have in place representatives and links to all major government agencies, including the Intelligence Community, but it is a model for governmentindustry cooperation. To be successful, defensive IW must have the support of private industry. Not only must awareness of vulnerabilities be increased, but coordinated steps taken to reduce the risk. That is the exactly the success which NCS has achieved in the telecommunications sector. As national policy is developed for IW, strong consideration should be given to creating an organization like the NCS to serve as the focal point for this effort and having it possibly work directly for the Vice President. DOD should play a role in the organization but as an active participant, not the leader.

FUNDAMENTALS OF INFORMATION WARFARE

The information technology explosion that's out there sweeping the world is an important matter, not just for the military services, but also for industry, the government, and our whole way of life. I have been looking forward to this opportunity to share with you what the Air Force is doing to capture the potential of new information realities. I see information warfare as having both an ascending and a transcending role in military operations. To understand why I say this, I will draw a little bit upon my academic background.

The history of the Second World War offers great examples of the military and civilian leadership manipulating information, even in a very crude fashion, to achieve rather spectacular results. In those days, as we thought about dominating the information spectrum, we turned to the cryptographers who were on the leading edge of these efforts, the so-called "code breakers." These specialized folks focused intently upon breaking the Japanese and German codes. In Europe, the ULTRA project -- "ULTRA" for the "ULTRA secret" -- produced spectacular results. Our code breakers literally worked miracles.

After the Normandy invasion, the German 7th Army attempted a counterattack to drive the Allied forces from the rather tenuous beachhead that they held. But with the help of ULTRA's ability to read the German mail and message traffic, we knew precisely what they were doing as they began to gather their forces to make this attack. We were able to put the British Second Tactical Air Force and the United States Ninth Tactical Air Force immediately upon these armor formations just as they massed. ULTRA gave us the critical information that allowed us to defeat the German forces before they ever came in contact with our ground forces.

By comparison, if you think to December of 1944 and the Battle of the Bulge, we see an example of where the Germans were able to catch us by surprise. They used an alternative communications network, and the Allies did not realize that the Germans had made this switch. It was our lack of information that really fueled the initial German success in the Battle of the Bulge. We had come to rely on ULTRA and had developed a little bit of self-delusion -- and the Germans took advantage of it very effectively.

Our ability to monitor the enemy's communications and use that information as an integral part of our operations is really nothing new. There is another example we should not forget. That's how we control the information that we allow the enemy to receive. Again, I am going back to the Second World War and talking about disinformation, particularly the disinformation campaign that centered on General Patton before and during the D-Day landings.

At that time, the Allies understood the other guy's ability to intercept our open signals, so we devised a rather elaborate plan that played to this emerging capability on the part of the Germans. The Allies set up a fake Army headquarters and generated false communications transmissions in England. As a result, the Nazis ended up with a significant number of troops placed in the wrong positions.

Even as they started to pick up indications that there was this great Allied armada that was going to invade Normandy, the Germans refused to believe that there could actually be an Allied invasion of Europe led by anyone but Patton. We played on that expectation in a way that kept Patton associated with his fake headquarters. Even as the Germans began to get higher and higher fidelity intelligence that indicated a real attack at Normandy, their leaders were frozen in indecision and, as a result, tied down considerable forces in France across from the shortest invasion route from England.

For instance, the aircraft we will fly over this time frame are fundamentally the same kinds of aircraft we are flying today. Some will have more advanced avionics, more advanced stealth characteristics or other features; but in the main, aircraft will remain fundamentally aircraft as we know them today. Ships will remain fundamentally ships as we know them today. The same holds true for tanks and armored personnel carriers.

Information warfare is not the exclusive domain of the Air Force, or any other service. I think information warfare has different meanings to a soldier, sailor, Marine, or airman. For instance, the soldier's focus may be on what happens at the corps level and below. The sailor's and Marine's focus is on the maritime and littoral regions. At the same time, an airman's focus is theater-wide, from the front lines to the adversary's capital. You begin to see how IW covers the entire battlefield. But, because of these divergent views and unique needs, I think it's critical that all services come to grips with and develop capabilities for their respective mediums of operations -- that is land, sea, and air. Then, it falls to the joint force commander, or the regional commander-in-chief, to integrate these capabilities to accomplish the mission.

The Air Force has put considerable effort into developing our concepts. In fact, over the past four months, we have had a team travel to every commander-in-chief (CINC) of a U.S. unified command and brief them on our efforts to incorporate IW into our doctrine and to integrate these concepts into our force employment. Most importantly, we want to be sure that what we are doing and how we approach the subject as an institution will be consistent with the way the CINCs intend to fight. And we want to make sure that what we are doing will meet their needs.

As a practitioner of the profession of arms, I view information technology advances with a single-minded interest. I am motivated by the fact that throughout history, soldiers, sailors, Marines, and airmen have learned one extremely valuable lesson relative to engagement with an opposing force. That is, if you can analyze, act, and assess faster than your opponent, you will win.

The information explosion discussed here today is going to make dramatic changes in how this nation fights wars in the future. Such technology will allow a commander's vision and view of the battlefield to be shared at the lowest level -- to the flight for the airman, to the company on the ground, and to the ship's bridge. Simultaneously, soldiers, Marines, sailors, and airmen on the front lines will be able to see and exploit opportunities as they occur.

What this means is our joint forces may enjoy what some are calling "dominant battlefield awareness." We have some of this kind of capability today. We've made significant enhancements to our ability to leverage our forces with faster command and control and intelligence networks. Among other capabilities, these networks are dramatically reducing the time required to detect and destroy a target.

This process starts with how we gather data. Our intelligence, surveillance, and reconnaissance efforts have been significantly and dramatically improved since Desert Storm. If you are familiar with our TALON programs, you will appreciate what we are doing to reduce the sensor-to-shooter loop -- that is injecting what is detected by our space-based assets directly into the cockpit or a flight deck. We are making similar advances with the systems that operate within the earth's atmosphere. For example, our AWACS early warning aircraft have been greatly improved. Their current radar upgrade allows us to detect cruise missiles at twice the range that we could previously. The AWACS is being fitted with the Joint Tactical Information Distribution Systems, or JTIDS. We will start the initial JTIDS operational test this August. I expect that we will reach full operational capability before the end of the decade. JTIDS alone will give us some pretty significant capabilities. It is not restricted just to AWACS. It also gives our warfighters a secure and jam-resistant data link between Air Force, Navy, Army, and Marine units and future coalition partners -- on land, at sea, and in the air. What that really means is all the players will have a real-time picture and awareness of both what is happening on the ground and what is going on in the air above those forces. JTIDS will give us a tremendous capability to know, at a much higher fidelity, the location of both the enemy and our own forces.

We are also making similar improvements in how we plan and control air operations. Today, we are fielding CTAPS -- the Contingency Theater Automated Planning System. CTAPS will connect our command and control from the joint forces air component commander (JFACC) to the air wings and the base-level planning cells. It will allow us to generate, disseminate, and monitor the progress of the daily air tasking order much faster than we ever have been able to do before. CTAPS also will tie in with the Combat Intelligence System which will provide us the enemy's order of battle through imagery and integrated threat data.

What does this really mean to us? During Desert Storm, it took us about 48 hours to plan and disseminate the ATO. That doesn't mean that it took 48 hours to execute a request from the field. But, it means that the deliberative process that planners went through to service targets was a 36- to 48-hour process. And you had to have someone manually intervene with an immediate air request to get inside those planning cycles. What the CTAPS system will do for us is take this 48-hour cycle and compress it to 12 hours. This really isn't some pie-in-the-sky system that we're dreaming about or visualizing. This is something that is in full use in exercises today and will be operational across the force next year. We have a similar planning tool that has been operational with our global air mobility forces for about three years.

These are a couple of examples of the kinds of tools we are putting in place. They are going to do more than replace the grease pencil and butcher block paper that (retired Air Force General) Chuck Horner and his staff had to use to run the air war during Desert Storm. These systems are going to help us dominate the information spectrum. I am convinced that this capability will be critical the next time our forces are employed in combat.

If you recall, I described information warfare in terms of how we deny, corrupt, or destroy our adversary's information base while we protect our own. Much of this activity has a very offensive element to it. I think we have been doing this for some time, but perhaps we didn't use that term. For example, during Desert Storm, we targeted many of the Iraqi communications nodes and physically destroyed Saddam Hussein's ability to talk to his troops through normal channels. We forced him into sub-optimum modes of communicating.

In the future, we will approach this objective by viewing our adversary's information activities as a system, and we will engage that system in a variety of ways. In fact, rather than put a precision guided munition into the central telephone exchange in Baghdad and destroy it next time, we may elect to leave it standing so we can better exploit it through our advances in information warfare. So, there will be trade-offs between lethal and non-lethal dimensions in the IW arena.

In the same manner, we have been doing some things along the way that we could properly classify as offensive information operations. There are ways that we corrupt information available to the enemy to deceive him. They include using psychological operations and our electronic warfare assets, like the Compass Call aircraft. I think that these kinds of measures that are designed to corrupt information the enemy has are really critical tools that we provide to the CINCs today. They open the envelope for the potential of further operations tomorrow. Again, if you think back to what we did on D-Day with disinformation, and you consider the tremendous advances in technology since 1944, you begin to appreciate the tremendous potential that exists in this area.

If we recognize an adversary's information network as a lucrative target, an adversary will view our data banks and weapon systems the same way. Information security -- the classic OPSEC, COMSEC, and the more recently stressed computer security -- takes on a whole new level of urgency. As a result, the Air Force is taking some rather significant measures to safeguard our assets. This year, we are spending more than $80 million on defensive measures alone, including establishing a base network control center to protect access to computers and communications. This same center will permit us to see if someone has tried to gain access to our system and, hopefully, will allow us to track down who tried to intrude on the system. These initiatives are important because we run a tremendous risk if we look at information warfare as something that is unique to America. It is not, and by the same token, the U.S. military is not alone in this vulnerability.

Our commercial sector, other elements of the government, and our industrial sectors rely on information systems just as much, if not more, than the military. If you've read Tom Clancy's recent thriller, Debt of Honor, you're familiar with what may be plausible. In this fictional tale, Clancy describes the problems caused when someone infects the stock exchange's computers with a virus, literally bringing the stock market to a standstill. To me, Clancy's work reinforces how the information threat is more than just a unique military concern.

As I look at information warfare and how it relates to the services, I'm reminded of a story about a football team. It seems that during one of the games, the local team had to put in a back-up quarterback late in the fourth quarter. They were ahead, and they were just trying to hang on. So, they put this relatively untested young man into the game, and all he had to do was avoid making a mistake and the team would win. So, the coach grabbed the guy as he was about to go on the field and said, "OK, here's what I want you to do. Run the ball three times, and then punt." So, the kid understood that and goes out onto the field.

His first run gains 20 yards -- great. On the second play, he gains 30 yards. Now, this is going a lot better than he ever expected. On the third play, he gains 30 more yards. Now they are down on the 10-yard line, the fans are going crazy, and it appears they're going to wrap this thing up. All he has to do is score, and he'll seal the victory for sure. So, the center snaps the ball to him and he punts. Everyone is stunned by this. His coach pulls him over to the sidelines and asks him what he was thinking. And the quarterback replied, "I was thinking that since you didn't change that play, I must have the dumbest coach around."

It is not enough to make a game plan and go with it. You must act and react to what is happening around you. What we're doing today with information warfare is a little bit like that football game -- IW gives us the ability to plan faster with better information so that we can call the optimum play. It may allow us to know what defensive stunt the other team is going to use. It may allow us to give our opponent false information on what play we're about to use. And, most importantly, it may allow us to call an audible and adjust to a fluid situation.

But unlike the game that I just described, when America sends her military forces into action, we don't want a close, exciting game, and we don't want an inexperienced quarterback. This nation has come to expect in our military operations nothing but blow-outs -- 100 to nothing is a good score. And, I believe that exploiting this new and emerging information technology is going to be the key to making this happen. As we approach tomorrow, we need to do more as a service and with the other services. Let me touch just briefly on what we are doing in terms of changing the way we organize, train, and equip our forces.

First, in terms of organizing, in September 1993, the United States Air Force stood up the Air Force Information Warfare Center in San Antonio. This center has more than 1,000 men and women chartered to support IW planning, intelligence gathering, weapon system analysis, and related activities. This group will be a source of IW support teams to go out and assist the CINCs and JFACCs during crises or exercises. They will help build information warfare into the air campaign planning and execution. The Air Force is not alone in this. The Army has an Information Warfare Center at Fort Belvoir, Virginia, and the Navy has created a center at Fort Meade, Maryland.

Additionally, the Air Force is adjusting our training and education programs to include IW concepts. We have had a course for our major air command and numbered air force staffs to give them basic understanding of the issues. We are incorporating IW into our doctrine, so that airmen everywhere will share a common foundation and a common terminology. We're adjusting our mid- and senior-level professional military education schools at Maxwell Air Force Base, Alabama. You see part of this effort here today. We have four Air Force officers attending the inaugural class of the National Defense University's School for Information Warfare.

Finally, and most significantly, we are beginning to procure weapon systems with a mindset that places high priority on maximizing their performance as an information warfare platform. One example of that is the United States' new air superiority fighter, the F-22. This aircraft is the first platform to be built around information technologies. This was an established objective when we started the program, not something added after the fact. A lot of people have heard about the F-22's stealth. You've heard about its supercruise capability -- that is the ability to cruise faster than the speed of sound in military power. And possibly you've heard about the fact that it has tremendous agility in the air-to-air arena. But, you cannot begin to appreciate its potential until you sit in the concept demonstrator and see how the F-22's integrated avionics work. The quality of the composite picture that's compiled from a variety of sources will literally water your eyes, particularly if you're an old-time fighter pilot. For the first time, you'll be able to sit with those flat glass displays and have tremendous situational awareness readily available to you. That is something we've needed for years, and we're finally in the process of getting it. It will allow our pilots to act and assess faster even when outnumbered. And I tell you it isn't just a concept -

- it's being put into production today! The F-22 is just one of many Air Force programs that we're continuing to push forward. You see the same thought processes in the space-based infrared system, in our Joint STARS, and in our precision munitions program. As we move forward, we are establishing an additional requirement for our weapon systems -- that is security against the information threat -- that's being written into the requirements documents.

This new mindset is found throughout our acquisition strategy. We are changing how we view our modernization needs. We're taking another look at IW capabilities, like those associated with command and control, and we're treating them more like force structure than support structure. It's part of how we must change the way we do business to incorporate the fundamentals of information warfare.

This broad approach means that we must get the lawyers involved. When I first heard about bringing in the lawyers, I thought we had really slipped off the deep end one more time. I apologize if I offend any lawyers out there -- I always have held lawyers in fairly high esteem. The more I thought about bringing the lawyers into the equation, the more I realized we need their expertise. Because exploiting the information spectrum will readily cross international borders, we must be cognizant of what the law allows and will not allow.

When do you begin information warfare in the spin up to a conflict? When do you begin to go out there and intrude in somebody's banking system? When do you begin to get into somebody's telecommunications system? These are all very difficult questions. Clearly, information warfare is not something that is focused solely on the confines of a constrained battle area. While we will fight in a theater, information warfare will force us to be engaged worldwide. Thus, we must have some good advice as we pursue this capability.

I appreciate this opportunity to share with you what the Air Force is doing to try and keep up with the information technology explosion. The American way of war has very strong roots in understanding the value of exploiting information to deny information to our adversary, to corrupt what data he has, and to exploit what we know. World War II was filled with many examples of information warfare. Perhaps Winston Churchill offered the best summary of its importance. At the Tehran conference, when discussing the Allied plans to manipulate information before D-Day, many of these same ethical questions came up. When do we do it? How do we do it? Who are the innocent victims of this thing? And Churchill, addressing the other Allied leaders said, "In wartime, truth is so precious that she should always be attended by a bodyguard of lies" (Anthony Cave Brown, Bodyguard of Lies (New York: Harper and Row, 1975), p. 10). Something to think about. Later, there was a book written with that title by Anthony Brown. If you read his thick volume, it is rather chilling to see what was possible in that era, and then think about how much more is possible today with the technology that's available.

Today and in the future, information warfare is, in fact, going to be this nation's bodyguard. It is essential for the success of our joint forces. To succeed, we are going to need help from a lot of people, including all the very interested people in this room. You understand the far-reaching implications of systems like LANDSAT or SATCOM which are readily available and widely employed at relatively low cost. You appreciate the potential for information technology to allow an adversary to build small, capable, autonomous, operating systems that can threaten U.S. forces on land, sea, or in the air. Such devices might operate relatively unseen and unobserved until they unleash their destructive power.

INFORMATION WARFARE AND INFORMATION STRATEGY

Information warfare is often thought of as being defined by a particular target setudecision makers, information, information processes, and information systems. The "battlespace" associated with IW has been a constantly expanding one, moving far beyond traditional military situations. In some quarters, IW has even been associated with the leveraging of information technologies to achieve greater effectiveness and efficiency. This has stretched the meaning of IW to the breaking point and has sowed more confusion than enlightenment. For this reason, this treatment of the subject uses the term "information strategies" to refer to the recognition and utilization of information and information technologies as an instrument of national power that can be independent of, or complementary to, military presence and operations.

The scope, or battlespace, of information warfare and strategy (IWS) can be defined by the players and three dimensionsùthe nature of their interactions, the level of their interactions, and the arena of their interactions. Nation states or combinations of nation states are not the only players. Non-state actors (including political, ethnic, and religious groups; organized crime; international and transnational organizations; and even individuals empowered by information technology) are able to engage in information attacks and to develop information strategies to achieve their desired ends.

The term "war" has been used so loosely in recent times (e.g., War on Poverty, War on Drugs, War on Crime) that is should be no surprise that IW has evolved over the past several years to become a "catch-all" term that encompasses many disparate activities, some of which have long been associated with competition, conflict, and warfare, and others that are of more recent origin. These include activities that range from propaganda campaigns (including Media War), to attacks (both physical and non-physical) against commanders, their information sources, and the means of communicating with their forces. Under this rather large umbrella that has become known as IW, one can find activities long associated with military concepts and operations, including deception, command and control warfare (C2W), and psychological operations (Psyops). Technological advances have added new forms such as electronic warfare (EW) and "hacker warfare."

The term "defensive information warfare" (IW-D) is used here to refer to all actions taken to defend against information attacks, that is, attacks on decision makers, the information and information-based processes they rely on, and their means of communicating their decisions. Strictly speaking, since these attacks can be launched during peace time at nonmilitary targets by nonmilitary groups, both foreign and domestic, the term IW-D should be IWS-D. However, IW-D is currently in wide use.

This overview of IW-D does not attempt to deal with the problems of defending against all of the different kinds of information attacks, but rather focuses its attention on the subset of IW that involves attacks against our information infrastructure, including what has become known as "hacker warfare" and in its more serious form, "digital warfare."

Analogies and Realities

Defending against information attacks has a number of characteristics in common with societal efforts to combat disease, drugs, and crime. Noting these similarities helps to put this problem into perspective, provides some potential useful lessons learned, and serves as a benchmark.

Before reviewing the specific similarities between combating IWS and these long-standing problems, it should be noted that, while eradicating information attacks may not be a realistic expectation, significant progress can be made in defending against all forms of information attacks, enough so that the risks can be kept at acceptable levels. Defending, as it is used here, includes preventing attacks, blunting attacks, and controlling the damage caused by attacks.

The problem of IW-D is similar to the problems encountered in the "wars" on disease, drugs, and crime in a number of dimensions. First, the solution to any of these problems requires the efforts of a number of organizations, both public and private. Second, it is unlikely, given the competition for resources, that any of these efforts will be fully funded. Therefore, we can expect that there will never be what those who have IW-D responsibilities think are a sufficient level of funding for IW-D programs. Third, these are not static problems. Drug cartels and criminals certainly learn from their mistakes. Even viruses "learn." Thus, defense forces will be continuously locked in a battle to keep up with attackers. Fourth, public awareness and concern will reach peaks, often accompanied by frenzied efforts to solve the problem. These relatively short periods of interest will be followed by longer periods when the urgency to solve the problem will give way to apathy. Maintaining funding and progress during these periods of waning public interest will be one of the key challenges of leadership in this area. Fifth, organizations and individuals will learn to make adjustments in their behavior to deal with IW attacks and their often unintended consequences. These adjustments will be made so that those organizations and individuals can accommodate some level of painùa dynamic equilibrium of sortsùas the cost of doing business in the Information Age. Finally, solutions will, of necessity, involve compromises. This is due to the natural tensions that exist among the various stakeholders. Tensions between the law enforcement and the protection of civil liberties are classic examples that have already arisen in the information domain.

Current Situation

Attacks on information systems are already a fact of life in the Information Age. Although a small portion of these attacks result in significant loss or damage, the vast majority of them result in little or no damageù the crime equivalents of trespassing, public nuisance, minor vandalism, and petty theft. It has been estimated that more than 90 percent of these attacks are perpetrated using available tools and techniques (based upon incidents reported to CERT), that only 1 attack in 20 is noticed by the victim, and that only 1 in 20 gets reported (these last two statistics were a result of a Defense Information Systems Agency (DISA) study and similar rates have been reported by others). However, it appears that reporting rates may be on the increase.

Of more concern is the presence of a technically feasible "strategic" threat. That is, the means exist to cause significant damage and disruption to U.S. public and private information assets, processes, and systems, and to compromise the integrity of vital information. Analysts also have no difficulty identifying groups with the motivations and opportunities to launch such attacks. Given our present vulnerabilities as a nation, a well-planned, coordinated IW attack could have strategic consequences. Such an attack, or the threat of such an attack, could thwart our foreign policy objectives, degrade military performance, result in significant economic loss, and perhaps even undermine the confidence of our citizens in the Government's ability to protect its citizens and interests. While no "smoking keyboard" has been found to validate such a threat, the very existence of the means to carry out such an attack, when coupled with the myriad of motives and opportunities that exist, results in our present state of vulnerability. These circumstances have created a situation that calls for prudent defensive actions to be taken in the public interest. We need to be proactive rather than be forced to react after an Information Age "Pearl Harbor." Moreover, a successful strategic attack would point the way and encourage others to plan similar attacks. Hence, we need to go on the offensive with a vigorous defense.

Digital War

Each age has seen war transformed by modern technologies and concepts. The Information Age promises to be no different. Some have called the Gulf War the first "Information War" - others have called it the last "Industrial Age" war. The power of information was clearly demonstrated in the context of traditional conflict. Information was leveraged to significantly improve the effectiveness of all aspects of warfare from logistics to command, control, communications, and computers, intelligence, surveillance, and reconnaissance (C4ISR).

The effectiveness of the U.S. and its allies in the Gulf War has surely deterred potential adversaries from taking on our forces in the rather symmetrical manner that Iraq attempted and has stimulated thinking about other strategies for countering conventional forces. Digital war, enabled by advances in technology and its widespread adoption as well as the globalization of economics and commerce, is surely a strategy that potential adversaries are thinking about to achieve some of the objectives that have previously been sought by means of traditional warfare.

Digital war, a subset of what we call information war, involves non-physical attacks on information, information processes, and information infrastructure that compromise, alter, damage, disrupt, or destroy information and/or delay, confuse, deceive, and disrupt information processing and decision making.

Digital war intrinsically possesses in ultimate form some of the same characteristics that traditional military planners are striving for, including low-cost precision, standoff, and stealth.

Digital war threatens the ability of a nation state's military to interpose itself between its population and "enemies of the state," thereby causing a loss of sanctuary. The importance of sanctuary can be inferred by our willingness to spend significant resources on air, sea, and missile defenses to provide our citizens with a workable sanctuary with respect to territorial intrusions.

Another characteristic of information attacks stems from the loss of sanctuary. Attacks of this sort, particularly when they consist of more than an isolated incident, create a perception of vulnerability, loss of control, and loss of confidence in the ability of the state to provide protection. Thus, the impact can far exceed the actual damage that has occurred. This non-linear relationship between actual damage and societal damage makes the problem of digital war a particularly challenging one because it creates a mismatch between rational defense responses and their effectiveness.

How does one respond to a serious set of information attacks? Responding with traditional military forces may be politically unacceptable or in fact, may be ineffectual. Currently there is no consensus, even among those in the defense establishment who think about these issues, regarding how to deal with such an attack.

Given the potential effectiveness of digital war, particularly as an instrument of power for niche competitors and non-state actors, we need, as a society, to take this Information Age form of war very seriously. If we do not, and if we rely solely on traditional weapons and concepts of war, we may be building our own 21st Century Maginot line that can be flanked with the speed of light.

Inadvertent Robustness

There are some who have suggested that we are not as vulnerable to information attacks as has been claimed because the collection of our legacy systems provides a certain amount of inherent robustness and resiliency. They point to the overlaps and duplications in these systems and argue that it would be very hard for anyone to completely disrupt a given set of services.

They point to the lack of interoperability among legacy systems and the firewalls that are thereby created and argue that it would be impossible for attackers to get very far by penetrating the weakest systems and using them as launching pads for attacks on other systems. They argue that our current legacy systems and their interrelationships are difficult (even for us) to understand, so it must follow that potential adversaries will also be confused.

Clearly there is some truth in each of these arguments. But this unruly collection of legacy systems also carries with it significant disadvantages.

As far as security considerations are concerned, five points need to be made. First, this issue is not whether or not an attack could totally destroy or disrupt a particular system or type of service, but whether or not there could be sufficient damage to trigger the perception of a failure and result in panic behavior that could in turn create a significant national problem.

Second, the redundancies in the systems are only partial and unplanned. Hence, they are neither complete nor reliable. Third, our legacy systems, many having been designed and built with little or no attention to security, are difficult to protect and secure. Fourth, as the need for interconnectivity and interoperability increases, more and more systems are being lashed together with "work-arounds."

These patches, in many cases, compromise security. Lastly, the lack of security that these systems provide is dampening the demand for services that could make operations more effective and efficient in many areas. Our current collection of legacy systems has other disadvantages as well. For example, the lack of interoperability wastes resources and impairs operations. Thus, it should be clear that the disadvantages of our current collection of legacy systems are not a blessing in disguise but rather the source of problems that need to be addressed so that we can take full advantage of the opportunities that information technologies can provide.

Formulating the Problem

The first step in tackling any problem involves developing an understanding of the possible environments that may be faced (or the "states of nature"), one's options, and the objective that is being sought. This requires an identification of the variables that are relevant, that is, those that can significantly influence the outcome as well as the subset of these relevant variables that are controllable, which form the basis for designing options. In a problem as complex as IW-D, working to formulate the problem accomplishes three things. First, it provides a useful framework for discussion. Second, it serves to keep the focus on those specific areas that are either unknown or in dispute. Third, it serves as a benchmark for measuring progress.

In this case, the states of nature correspond to the nature of the threat that will be faced vis-a-vis the vulnerabilities of our information infrastructure while our options correspond to the strategies we adopt and the actions we take to defend ourselves. The objective being sought corresponds to a level of infrastructure performance, its definition and measure being a major challenge in and of itself.

A good place to start is to try to develop an understanding of the nature of the threat, or more accurately the spectrum of relevant threats. This involves the identification of potential threats and the estimation of their likelihoods. Normally one would construct a set of states of natures that are mutually exclusive and collectively exhaustive so that a probability density function could be used. For the purposes of this discussion, the states of nature referred to correspond to potential threats grouped in some logical fashion to facilitate analysis of how well each defensive strategy deals with each of these threats.

Having an initial concept of the nature and range of potential threats, one can develop alternative defensive strategies and corresponding sets of action to counter one or more of these threats. A great deal depends upon what variables we believe we can and should control. Each defensive strategy, with its corresponding set of actions, then needs to be analyzed with respect to each of the threats. The results of these analyses will be a characterization of the results or outcomes from pursuing each of the defensive strategies with respect to each of the threats. These outcomes, which are basically descriptions of results (e.g., number of penetrations and their consequences), then need to be translated into value measures that represent their impact. These costs and benefits provide a rational basis for determining an appropriate defensive strategy. Much will depend upon how we measure success. Given the central role that the threat topology plays in problem formulation, we will now turn our attention to examining this topology.

Threat Topology

The irregular nature of the space is meant to indicate that its boundaries are not well defined. Nevertheless, one can group threats in order of the seriousness of their consequences (from left to right). The consequences associated with a failure to counter a specific attack range, on the one hand, from isolated and limited consequences to, on the other hand, consequences of catastrophic proportions.

There are a relatively small number of threats that most everyone would agree have strategic implications and must be defended against with considerable vigor. Attacks against our systems that control and safeguard weapons of mass destruction (WMD) and our minimum essential emergency communication network (MEECN) clearly fall into this category. Others that fall into this category would include the information and communication systems associated with the National Command Authority (NCA), some of our command, control, communications and intelligence (C3I) systems, and some of our intelligence systems, particularly information regarding sources and methods. A review of other Government information and information systems would result in additional information and systems that should be added to this list. Beyond those sets of threats that clearly fall into either the Everyday or Strategic categories, there are classes of threats that span the threat spectrum.

Attacks on our national, or for that matter international, infrastructure do not fall neatly into one area of the threat topology but in fact populate all three classes of threat. These attacks on our public safety, energy, financial, and communications systems and services have different implications and consequences depending on the specific nature of the attacks and the circumstances surrounding the attack.

The vast majority of attacks on infrastructure are by hackers whose motives run the full gamut from financial motives, to having some fun, or to more serious forms of antisocial behavior. While some of these attacks may have serious consequences in the form of significant losses of data, interrupted services, or stolen assets or services, only a small number of these lone perpetrator attacks are likely to have potential strategic consequences. This is not to say that it is impossible that some set of circumstances would result in the snowballing of one of these hacker attacks into a national security concern, but rather that this outcome is unlikely.

However, infrastructure attacks can be quite serious if they are well planned and coordinated. Arguably this would require an adversary with seriousness of purpose and with some sophistication and organization. This kind of attack would be better named digital warfare rather than be included as part of the group referred to as hacker attacks. Depending on the level of sophistication of a digital warfare operation, its consequences could range from a "high-end" hacker attack to an attack with strategic consequences.

A key point to be made involves the chaotic nature of the transition between topological boundaries for infrastructure attacks. Chaotic behavior involves a non-linear relationship between input and output where prediction becomes extremely difficult if not impossible. Two distinct scenarios serve to illustrate the chaotic nature of infrastructure attacks. In the first case, a particular infrastructure attack may trigger a series of proximate consequences that are difficult to predict and that greatly magnify the effects of the attack. In the second case, a series of attacks will exhibit chaotic behavior when the sum of their consequences can not be determined by adding up their individual consequences, or when their cumulative effect far exceeds the sum of the individual effects of a series of independent events. These are not uncommon patterns. Valid scientific disciplines of complexity, catastrophe, and complexity theory have been developed because these patterns occur throughout nature.

It is much the same story for attacks on commercial targets. In the Everyday category are attacks that amount to Information Age versions of fraud and theftùa continuation of white collar crime and a transformation of some more violent crime into a non-physical form. As Dr. Horton (PDASD (C3I)) has pointed out, one of the more notorious bank robbers of the 20th century, when asked why he robbed banks (given that they were often so well defended), was purported to remark, "that's where the money is." Well, digital money (assets and services) is where the money is in the Information Age. As with attacks on infrastructure, attacks on commercial targets can range from Everyday threats to Strategic ones depending on the circumstances. Attacks on commercial targets by competing organizations usually do not target money directly, but rather target vital information (e.g., trade secrets) and have the potential for more serious consequences than isolated thefts or embezzlements. These attacks, in the form of commercial espionage, have Potentially Strategic consequences, particularly when key industries are targeted by foreign companies.

Commercial espionage turns into economic war which could have Strategic consequences when it involves concerted efforts by state actors, international organizations, or other foreign-controlled groups.

Threat Characteristics

As can been seen from the series of graphical depictions of the threat topology presented above, the threat we face is multidimensional, somewhat messy and, with respect to the consequences of information attacks, can behave in a chaotic manner. The dynamic and interactive nature of the threat makes defending against attacks all the more challenging.

Unfortunately, the attackers possess some inherent advantages. For example, the attacker can pick the time, place, medium, and method of the attack. The technology edge also goes to the attacker, for it is very difficult to develop perfect defenses at an affordable cost. Therefore, there will always be "holes." Which ones will be exploited are unknown until attacks occur, thus the offense usually is one step ahead of the defense. Those who choose to orchestrate coordinated attacks on infrastructure also have the advantage that comes from being able to control their attack more easily than can a number of loosely coupled defenders.

In any event this is a learning environment for both attackers and defendersùa dynamic one at that. In this organic environment, attackers learn from undetected attacks, whether successful or not, while both sides learn from detected attacks, whether successful or not. Both attackers and defenders make adjustments and the "game" continues.

This aspect of the threat means that defense is not a one time thing. It must be a continuous activity. It also means that collection and analysis of information about attacks is vital to maintaining parity with attackers. Finally, it means that defenders must be proactive and undertake efforts designed to anticipate methods of attack so that timely defenses can be developed.

IW-D Considerations

The problem of how best to defend against a variety of potential digital information attacks is exacerbated by the following three characteristics of the problem: our inability to develop a simple relationship between a type of attack or threat and an organization, the essentially non-linear relationship between outcome and value, and the fact that key variables are not within our control.

Being able to decompose a problem often helps us to make progress, at least on some fronts, by facilitating the delegation of either functional or jurisdictional responsibility along organizational lines. As we have seen, the problem of IW-D resists decomposition along organizational lines. This is because there is a weak mapping between threat and organization from two perspectives. First, the organizational target of the attack is weakly related to the threat topology, that is, an attack on a given organization may result in a set of consequences that span the threat spectrum. Second, there is no clean mapping between organizational responsibility and the threat topology. This is particularly true of the area identified as Potentially Strategic. It is always easier to solve problems with well-behaved or predictable objective functions or measures of value. As we have seen, the IW-D problem has situations where the relationship between events and variables behave in a chaotic manner. This introduces a large dose of uncertainty into the equation. If these first two characteristics of the IW-D problem did not present significant challenges in and of themselves, we are also faced with the fact that some of the key variables that have an influence on outcomes and the values of these outcomes are only partially controllable. For example, each of the following variables, if fully controllable, could significantly either reduce the number or severity of attacks and/or the impact of the attacks: proliferation of technology, level of awareness and training of personnel, availability of computer expertise, system defenses, and public perceptions. We have come to the end of the discussion of the nature of the problem and its characteristics that will drive the search for a solution. Next, a proposed solution approach is presented and discussed.

Proposed IW-D Strategy

The proposed solution to IW suggested here is a "Defense-in-Depth" strategy, a strategy that involves a series of successively stronger or "higher" defensive barriers that work together to decompose the spectrum of threats into manageable pieces. While implementing this concept still involves considerable challenges, it provides some structure for efforts to defend ourselves against information attacks. Following a discussion of this IW-D strategy, the nature of a division of responsibility, some of the critical prerequisites for progress, key challenges that lie ahead, and the elements of an action plan for organizations with IW-D responsibilities will be addressed.

Defense-in-Depth

The proposed "defense-in-depth" strategy, consists conceptually of three lines of defense. Each line of defense is designed specifically to counter the threats associated with a particular region of the threat topology. The first line of defense is to defend against Everyday attacks, which constituted most of the threat topology. Based upon the information available, the vast majority of these attacks can be handled with basic defenses.

The higher hurdles associated with the Potentially Strategic and Strategic attacks are then responsible for handling more sophisticated but far fewer attacks from fewer potential sources.

For example, attacks with strategic implications would need to get through the first two lines of defense that should filter out all but the most skilled, resourced, and persistent adversaries. This means we can concentrate our intelligence and monitoring efforts on a smaller population, which in turn increases the chances of successful defense. This defensive strategy also means that we can take different philosophical approaches with each line of defense depending on the nature of the threat. The two endpoints of the philosophical spectrum can be thought of as the "information first" and "security first" approaches. In the Everyday region of the threat topology our approach has been to emphasize access to information. In the Strategic region, we put security first by restricting access and connectivity to the point of degrading performance and efficiency.

Division of Responsibility

A suggested division of primary responsibility for IW-D between the public and private sectors as a function of the threat topology. The modifier "primary" is used to make the point that, despite the assignment of responsibility in a particular area to either the public or private sector, both public and private organizations have responsibilities in each area. The topological regions associated with either Everyday or Strategic threats are the most straightforward. Primary responsibility for the everyday threat should be the responsibility of the private sector. Handling such threats is simply the cost of doing business in the Information Age. With the availability of relatively low-cost defenses against these threats, the burden placed on the private sector is affordable. Furthermore, organizations are clearly in the best position to understand their own systems and the needs and concerns of their customers.

Responding to strategic threats is clearly the job of the public sector, although an adequate defense will involve some coordination with private sector and international organizations, particularly when it comes to the region of the threat topology that contains threats associated with attacks on the national information infrastructure or other institutions providing vital services.

Where to assign primary responsibility for defenses against threats in the Potentially Strategic region of the threat topology is less clear. This area could be called a "zone of collaboration," where the public and private sectors need to work closely together to understand the threat and develop mechanisms designed to counter it.

Perspectives on Information Security

Efforts to achieve effective collaboration will need to overcome the understandably different perspectives that organizations bring to the table. Commercial organizations traditionally treat events such as Everyday attacks as simply a cost of doing business not significantly different than pilferage euphemistically referred to as inventory "shrinkage." Countermeasures have a definite expected value and are employed when their costs are less than their expected value. Private sector organizations traditionally respond to relatively low probability events with potentially large costs by either purchasing insurance or providing self-insurance.

The perspective on information security taken by organizations entrusted with information and systems deemed vital to our national security is quite different. Unlike many information attacks on private sector systems, the cost of a breech in security of national security information can not easily be determined. Overshadowing the actual costs of a particular incident is the fact that the very protection of the integrity of national security information and the systems that handle it is considered to have intrinsic value in and of itself. Risk avoidance is the ingrained response in these situations.

Given the nature of the IW threat topology, national and private sector information security are now inexorably intertwined. Attacks on the national or global information infrastructure can seriously affect private sector organizations and attacks on key private sector organizations that provide vital services have definite national security implications. These situations are contained in the Potentially Strategic region of the threat topology. It is proposed that, in this region, rather than take a simple "dollars and cents" approach as in the Everyday region or a risk avoidance approach as taken in the Strategic region, we should take a collective risk management approach. This is clearly an area which requires defenses to be closely coordinated.

Managing the Solution

Given what we have seen about the nature of this problem as we have considered the different areas of the threat topology, it should be clear that any attempt to try to manage IW-D using a centralized approach is doomed to failure. If one has any doubt, they should be reminded of the weak threat to organizational mapping which prevents effective delegation of the problem with clean "chains of command" and the considerable limits on the ability of the Government or any single organization to control significant relevant variables. Given the urgency and importance of this problem, a proactive stance is required. Therefore, it should be equally obvious that a laissez-faire approach is also doomed to failure. A form of collective orchestration is needed to develop the degree of awareness and understanding of the threat and to develop the necessary defenses. The Government needs to lead by establishing what I have called a "framework for progress." The specific roles and responsibilities of the private and public sectors will vary as a function of the threat as we have seen in our brief look at each of the three major regions of the threat topology. While this discussion has focused on the roles, responsibilities and need for collaboration among U.S. players, the problem of IW-D transcends national boundaries. Without appropriate international agreements and cooperation among nations and international organizations, our collective ability to handle threats will be severely hampered.

Framework for Progress

While we have come a considerable distance in our journey to better understand the nature of this problem, many of us have been frustrated by the lack of a supportive environment for progress. Although we can continue to make progress, even on the rocky path we are currently forced to travel, progress in the six areas identified in the graphic will greatly smooth out our path and accelerate our progress. First, one of the key prerequisites for progress is to create awareness of the problem and its complexities, as well as to foster a climate that will facilitate discussion and cooperation among the many groups and organizations that need to be a part of this effort. Given recent events surrounding some aspects of information security, we need to start by rebuilding bridges between some public and private sector groups and organizations.

Second, it is important that we work toward a well-defined vision that clearly lays out what we are trying to achieve and the appropriate role of the Government.

Third, the "rules of the game" need to be developed and promulgated. Many of our current laws and regulations have not caught up with the realities of the Information Age. A set of rules needs to address the establishment of information security standards, or a minimum level of defense to be associated with different kinds of data and information services. These would be similar to the recent development of privacy standards.

Fourth, self-interest, even enlightened self-interest and the desire of individuals and organizations to be good citizens, are not enough to ensure that appropriate actions and defenses will be developed and employed.

Resources need to be provided for government organizations to help implement this framework for progress and to develop and implement the needed defenses. We also need to provide incentives that encourage public sector organizations to do what is collectively needed. In some specific cases, the Government will need to actually provide funds to private sector organizations to implement enhanced security.

Fifth, the solution to this problem depends on a great deal of cooperation among disparate groups and organizations. Mechanisms to facilitate and enhance cooperation (including the establishment of panels, groups, and clearinghouses) need to be developed.

Sixth, we need to fix responsibility for the many tasks involved in IW-D. We need to decide questions of jurisdiction. We need to make liabilities known and well defined. Finally, we need to clearly establish the responsibility of each organization. The nature of organizational responsibilities is discussed in more detail below.

None of these six aspects of the framework for progress is likely to be accomplished anytime soon. One only need review the legislative process and experiences with the translation of privacy concerns into a set of rules of the game to realize that it will be quite a while before each of these foundational pillars is in place. However, we must begin now to foster discussion of these issues and try to keep attention focused on this subject.

REVOLUTION OF THE INFORMATION WARFARE

Viewed from latter perspective, Information Warfare raises basic questions not only about how wars will be waged but who will wage them and for what purposes.

Such questions cannot, in turn, be separated from consideration of the larger changes that may flow from the ongoing "Information Revolution." If futurists like the Tofflers and John Naisbitt are right the global diffusion of new and emerging information technologies will have economic, social, cultural and political consequences as profound as any in human history. It is, of course, impossible to be sure about the direction of these changes, but they could involve dramatic shifts in political power and attitudes toward authority. now (Note 2)

A comparison with the political effects of the "First Information Revolution" in Early Modern Europe may be instructive. As J.M. Roberts points out, the invention of movable type and the subsequent diffusion of printed books and literacy gave rise to a "transformation of the European consciousness" after 1500 now (Note 3).

Among its other consequences, this transformation abetted the rise of nation-states by providing their rulers with opportunities to mobilize national loyalties and develop centralized administrations. The long-term political "losers" were subnational and supranational entities such as the Papacy and feudal authorities who proved less efficient at exploiting the new medium.

The present Information Revolution may be having precisely the opposite effect inasmuch as the globalization and personalization of electronic communications system appear to be undermining the authority of nation-states and facilitating a devolution of power to subnational and transnational movements, especially those that tap ethnic, religious or cultural loyalties. Naisbitt, who regards such movements as manifestations of a "new tribalism" speculates that traditional institutions of central government and representative democracy may become increasingly anachronistic even in Western societies as demands there for "self rule" and decentralization gain momentum now (Note 4).

One should not, of course, exaggerate the "empowerment" of the individual vis-a-vis the state. As David Ronfeldt notes, the Information Revolution "may give a state apparatus and its rulers powerful new means of control over their citizenry, with an official ideology determining what information is allowed now (Note 5)." This may be less of a concern in the United States and other countries where democracy has deep roots, but it is a distinct possibility elsewhere, particularly in the Third World where it is easier for charismatic leaders to generate a public consensus in favor of tyranny. The Information Revolution may promote either democracy or totalitarianism depending on the socio-political context.

It is likewise premature to conclude that the presumed decline of nationstates will inhibit conflict and war. Indeed, the Information Revolution may actually stimulate conflict by accentuating economic, cultural and political differences among peoples while at the same time binding together groups previously separated by geographic or national barriers. Benjamin Barber, for example, sees a threatened "Lebanonization" of many nation-states, in which culture is pitted against culture, people against people, tribe against tribe -- a Jihad in the name of a hundred narrowly conceived faiths against every kind of interdependence, every kind of artificial social cooperation and civic mutuality now (Note 6)."

While forecasts of a "coming anarchy" or "clash of civilizations" may be overdrawn now (Note 7), war in the Information Age could well spill outside of the Clausewitzian framework where it functions as a "rational' instrument of state policy. John Keegan reminds us that, historically, different cultures have shaped war into bizarre and self-destructive forms whose warrior practitioners, unlike modern soldiers, often looked upon combat as a means of self-expression, recreation or religious sanctification now (Note 8). In some parts of the world, the weakening of state authority and the eruption of violent sociopolitical conflicts are enabling such warriors to make a comeback. "as brutal as ever and distinctly better armed now (Note 9)."

In his chilling vision of war in a post-Clausewitzian world Martin van Creveld takes this line of reasoning a step further, speculating that modern high-tech armies are like to become obsolete. In his view, the relevance of these armies increasingly will be called into question because they will be unable to decisively defeat guerrillas and terrorists who operate beneath their "sophistication threshold" in low-intensity conflicts. Future wars, he suggests, will not be clean and short but "protracted, bloody and horrible" -- an affair of "listening devices and of car bombs, of men killing each other at close quarters, and of women using their purses to carry explosives and the drugs to pay for them now (Note 10). "

Van Creveld's work carries another interesting and, for professional soldiers, more disturbing implication: In order to wage low-intensity conflicts with any hope of success, conventional armies may have to adopt the organizational methods, and perhaps even the mentality of their opponents. Noting that war represents the most imitative activity known to man." van Creveld predicts that pervasive low-intensity conflict "will cause regular forces to degenerate into police forces or, in case the struggle lasts for very long, mere armed gangs now (Note 11)." Distinctions will thus erode between military and police forces, and ultimately between soldiers and the terrorists and criminals whom they are responsible for combating.

It might be objected that van Creveld and others who see non Clausewitzian war as the wave of the future underestimate the political dimension of the violence occurring in places like Bosnia. The systematic massacre or brutalization of non-combatants may affront "civilized" sensibilities and conceptions of warfare. If employed in the pursuit of political objectives such as the creation or defense nation-states, however, even "ethnic cleansing" can be seen as a continuation of politics. The problem, of course, is where to draw the line. Clausewitz himself recognized that war is at bottom an affair of "primordial violence" whose inherent tendency is to run to extremes of emotion and cruelty.

One can also question the strategic significance of many low-intensity conflicts, especially in the post-Cold War context. As appalling as their human costs may be, few of the small wars currently underway in the Third World and former Second World engage the vital interests of major powers or seem likely to bring about immediate changes in the international balance of power. The United States may choose to involve itself in military efforts to try to resolve or contain these struggles. With the disappearance of the Soviet Union as a global competitor however the geopolitical rationale for doing so has lost much of its former force, and the American interests at stake are often highly ambiguous.

"From a purely American point of view," as Eliot Cohen observes, "the world is, and for some length of time promises to be, a more secure place than it was during the cold war now (Note 12)." American statesmen now have, he notes "no dragons to slay, or even to tame; partners may be competitors, but no state poses a direct challenge to our security or that of our allies." Even with the current downsizing of the U S. military establishment, its Cold War "capital stock" of sophisticated military platforms, intelligence-gathering systems, military-technical infrastructure, and logistical assets, dwarfs that of any potential competitor and gives the United States unmatched global power-projection capabilities.

Although the external threats currently facing the United States are more diffuse and ill-defined than during the Cold War era, there is no lack of potential dangers and challenges. Clearly the most menacing contemporary development is the proliferation of weapons of mass destruction. Only slightly less worrisome, however, is the diffusion of long-range missiles, advanced aircraft, and other high-tech weaponry Both trends are likely to enhance the military capabilities of state and non-state actors, thus increasing the escalatory potential of ethno-sectarian and inter-state conflicts. These trends may also make it possible for even relatively weak powers to strike directly at the United States.

THE MILITARY-TECHNICAL REVOLUTION

The ongoing Information Revolution is having equally important, if less obvious effects on the post-Cold War security environment. There is, for example, broad agreement in the defense community that the 1991 Gulf War marked the early stages of a "Military-Technical Revolution" (MTR) which promises to transform the character of war as radically as did the advent of nuclear weapons fifty years age. Driving this revolution are advances in surveillance, communications, and information-processing technologies, which create the possibility of imbuing the "information loop of warfare" with unprecedented accuracy and speed, thereby achieving "information dominance" over less capable adversaries now (Note 13).

Information dominance, combined with cruise missiles and other precision weaponry, is expected to confer the ability to overwhelm virtually any opponent quickly, decisively and relatively bloodlessly. The key problem in this mode of warfare will be protecting one's own "centers of gravity" or vulnerabilities while striking those of an enemy. As was foreshadowed in the Coalition air campaign in the Gulf War, the solution to the latter problem is likely to involve "an improved ability to understand target systems and their relationship to operational and strategic objectives now (Note 14)," since knowing which targets to strike will be critical to the effective employment of large numbers of precision weapons.

Full exploitation of information technologies will, it is argued, necessitate major changes in "the ways militaries think about, organize themselves for, and wage combat now (Note 15)." Thus, reliance on sensors, computers and smart weapons points toward a reduced human role in decision cycles. Similarly, long-range strike capabilities will lessen the need for close-in combat and increase the importance of integrated air-land-sea-space operations. The extraordinary lethality of precision weapons and their ability to strike virtually anywhere will likewise require dispersed, independent combat units, and the replacement of present types of aircraft armored vehicles and surface ships by smaller and more stealthy platforms now (Note 16).

Beginning with then Undersecretary Perry's announcement in the aftermath of Desert Storm that the U.S. had achieved a revolutionary advance in military capability now (Note 17)," many U.S. military leaders have enthusiastically embraced the MTR idea. The main doctrinal construct for implementing it at operational level is the strategy of "Command and Control Warfare," which calls for "the integrated use of operations security, military deception, psychological operations, electronic warfare, and physical destruction, mutually supported by intelligence, to deny information to influence, degrade or destroy adversary C2 capabilities, while protecting friendly C2 capabilities now (Note 18)."

Enthusiasm within the U.S. military for the MTR is tempered by concerns about over-reliance on technology and the possible loss of traditional combat skills 19. But skepticism about the MTR in professional military circles has deeper roots.

As C. Kenneth Allard points out, the integration and information sharing required by emerging command and control technologies threatens to upset the "delicate balance" of service autonomy and, ultimately, the very notion of military hierarchy itself now (Note 20). Despite universal acceptance of the twin imperatives of "jointness and interoperability," service cultures and perspectives are therefore likely to act as a brake on institutional change.

For many MTR proponents, the U.S. military has barely begun the "intellectual revolution" necessary to realize the quantum leap in combat effectiveness potentially offered by information technologies. Dan Goure, for example, compares the present level of institutional adaptation to the U.S. Navy's initial efforts to develop carrier aviation in the 1920's. Absent a constituency for more radical doctrinal and organizational reforms, he predicts that U.S. military planners will "fall prey to the old tendency to look to technology as the solution to strategic and operational problems" and settle for the "fleeting advantage" conferred by "mere technological superiority now (Note 21)."

According to Goure and others, this piecemeal approach may create opportunities for more innovative competitors to vault ahead of the United States. Based on his study of previous military revolutions, Andrew Krepinevich warns that it is a "dangerous delusion" to assume that the United States will be able to control the direction of the current revolution now (Note 22). "Even when countries will not be able to compete in the full spectrum of military capabilities," he argues, "some of them, by specializing, will become formidable niche competitors." Moreover, they may find it easy to do so since the Information Revolution is lowering the cost of information technologies and increasing their availability.

In a similar vein Paul Bracken urges U S military planners to devote more attention to what he sees as the likely emergence 15 or 20 years hence of "Eurasian peer competitors." According to bracken, the rapid economic growth of countries like China will give them the means to field modern military forces based on advanced technologies and innovative operational concepts. Unless the United States begins now to think seriously about how to counter such challenges, it risks becoming "locked into" current force structures, concepts technologies and doctrines which -- although sufficient to deal with near-term contingencies -- may be inadequate to sustain the long-term U.S. competitive advantage now (Note 23).

A basic problem with these scenarios is that they rest on assumptions about the future shape of the international order, the nature of war, and the direction of technological change, none of which can be taken for granted. As Goure notes, military planners during the Cold War and interwar periods faced the task of bringing "known pieces of potential capability together in a fashion suited to an expected form of warfare against anticipated adversaries now (Note 24). Under current conditions of rapid technological change and the emergence of new subnational and transnational players, however, such certainties are denied planners who cannot be sure about the form or participants that will characterize future wars.

Since the MTR is seen as a long-term process and presupposes threats which have not yet materialized, its relevance to current defense needs is open to question. The basic rationale for reshaping the U.S. military now comes down to providing a hedge against the possible rise of future high-tech challengers. In addition, pushing ahead with the MTR is espoused as a way of increasing the effectiveness of U.S. forces in dealing with near-term, regional contingencies and conducting military operations short of war. Domestic, political, and budgetary constraints, which require the U.S. military to "do more the less" and minimize casualties on all sides, are also cited to justify this course now (Note 25).

The adequacy of current U S. military plans and programs to accomplish these objectives is a subject of controversy. The 1993 "Bottom-Up Review." DOD's blueprint for meeting the challenges of the post-Cold War security environment. emphasizes the need to maintain military capabilities sufficient to defeat regional aggressors in two "nearly simultaneous" conflicts. The areas of particular concern are the Korean Peninsula and the Persian Gulf, and the most likely aggressors are deemed to be North Korea, Iran or a resurgent Iraq. The kind of attack foreseen (an armor-heavy, combined arms offensive") and the forces considered necessary to defeat it are modeled on the 1990-91 Gulf conflict now (Note 26).

Many critics contend that the Bottom-Up Review falls into the familiar trap of "preparing to fight the last war" instead of the next one now (Note 27). They argue, for example, that regional aggressors are unlikely to repeat Saddam Hussein's blunders and will instead employ a range of strategies to deter U.S. military intervention, including "ambiguous aggression," guerrilla warfare, and threats to use weapons of mass destruction. It is also suggested that the kind of forces appropriate to counter threats from North Korea or Iraq are not suitable for meeting future challenges from more formidable peer competitors who may succeed in combining information technologies with innovative military doctrines.

Another focus of criticism is the force mix recommended by the Bottom-Up Review to maintain U.S. power-projection capabilities. Edward Luttwak is typical of those who see this mix as reflecting the success of the services in preserving their Cold War force structures rather than shifting to "low-casualty or noncasually forms of aerial and robotic military strength" more suited to the post-Cold War security environment now (Note 28). Luttwak and others are also concerned that the costs of supporting carrier battlegroups and heavy army divisions will consume an undue share of DOD's shrinking budget, allowing fewer resources for R&D and modernization programs necessary to sustain the U.S. comparative military advantage.

Some critics are also skeptical that it will be possible to reconcile the Bottom-Up Review's regional conflict strategy with the growing demands imposed on the U.S. military by peacekeeping, peace enforcement and other "operations other than war now (Note 29)." Since these operations tend to be manpower-intensive, expensive, and protracted, they drain resources needed to assure the readiness and modernization of forces which might be required to respond to major regional contingencies. Moreover, irregular operations, by their nature, offer fewer opportunities than conventional warfare to employ U.S. surveillance, command and control, and precision strike capabilities to achieve decisive military results.

The prescriptions for these problems offered by MTR advocates range from more rapid structural reform of the U.S. military to recasting American defense strategy. Krepinovich, for example, urges that higher priority be accorded to "preserving the long-term military potential of U.S. forces, as opposed to near-term capabilities now (Note 30)." This implies accepting a smaller force structure and devoting more resources to modernization. Such an approach also entails greater use of multinational coalitions to deal with regional contingencies, increased reliance on stand-off precision strikes to punish or deter troublemakers and more selective engagement of U.S. forces in peacekeeping and humanitarian ventures.

The emphasis put by Krepinovich and others on preparing for future high-tech conventional wars has not gone unchallenged. A.J. Bacevichi, for example, charges that the MTR idea is at bottom an exercise in "wishful thinking" designed to relieve U.S. military leaders of the burden of coming to grips with the realities of nuclear and unconventional war for which "they never devised an adequate response now (Note 31)." In a similar vein, Daniel Bolger, himself an infantryman, cautions that the "sanguinary shade" of Vietnam may rise again unless the US. Army "forsakes the seductive urge to keep refighting World War II" and devotes more attention to basic infantry skills needed to combat irregular opponents now (Note 32).

MTR theorists do not entirely ignore unconventional warfare but it is not central to their concerns. A recent study of the subject concludes that advanced surveillance and precision-strike systems can at present make only "limited contributions" to irregular operations, owing to the complexity of the human and natural environments in which such operations often must be conducted. While holding out the prospect that emerging sensor and non-lethal weapons technologies may change this situation in the near future, its authors recommend that priority should be given to "traditional combined-arms operations" which "pose the most serious risk to U.S. interests" over the next 10-15 years now (Note 33).

Several factors may, however, increase the relative importance of irregular warfare in the post-Cold War setting. As noted above U.S. dominance of the conventional battlefield is likely to encourage aggressive regional powers to eschew blatant adventurism in favor of indirect strategies, including sponsorship of low-intensify conflicts. Furthermore, cheap commercial information technologies such as satellite-based personal communications devices, encrypted fax machine, and global positioning systems will provide "force multipliers" for irregular forces. The availability of sophisticated weapons from the former Soviet bloc and other suppliers will also enhance the their capabilities. The growing dependence of modern societies on computer-controlled information infrastructures is opening up new areas for unconventional warfare. Recent intrusions into the U.S. civilian and military computer networks by hackers and criminals only hint at far more serious disruption that could be wrought by systematic electronic sabotage of national telecommunications systems power grids and financial institutions. As information security specialist Winn Schwartau suggests, such sabotage is a 'low risk/high reward endeavor" inasmuch as it can be conducted by "remote control" and offers the prospect of inflicting "indiscriminate damage on millions of people with a single keystroke now (Note 34)."

The advent of satellite-based global television broadcasting has created yet another arena for unconventional warfare. As was demonstrated in the Gulf War and the 1993 skirmishing in Somalia between UN forces and the clan warriors of General Aidid, live television coverage provides participants in armed conflicts with unprecedented opportunities to conduct military deception and shape the way distant audiences perceive events on the battlefield. Such "CNN Wars" are likely to become more common and to have disproportionately large political repercussions, especially in societies like the United Slates where policymaking is sometimes driven transitory public reactions to media images. The foregoing trends point to changes not only in the environment in which wars are fought but in the nature of warfare itself. Information technologies are enlarging the venue of conflict from the traditional "battlefield" to computer networks, electronic databases, television screens, and other unconventional settings. They are also expanding opportunities for waging war through sabotage, terrorism, propaganda and similar clandestine means. One possible consequence is that it may be increasingly difficult to draw a clear line between war and other forms of conflict. Another is that distinctions between military and civilian practitioners of war may become progressively blurred.

INFORMATION BASED WARFARE -THE NEW BATTLEFIELDS

Exiled to France, the Ayatollah Khomeni sought to maintain contact with the faithful. A cleric who espoused the return of his country to an Islamic theocracy-something: that many argued would move Iran back into the 16th century-the Ayatollah turned to 20th century tools to begin his crusade. Through the medium of cassettes, he began to record his message. After being mass-produced m 20th century studios, his 16th century message was smuggled back to Iran. Those tapes both planted the seed and inspired the flowering of a movement that brought Khomeni back to power m 1979.

For at least a decade, the American military had tinkered with devices for sabotaging enemy electrical systems. Some of the results were serendipitous. In the early 1980's, during a Navy exercise code-named Hey [Rube, long strands of rope chaff-glass filaments in which metal shards were embedded-had been dropped over the Pacific Ocean as part of a standard tactic to befuddle an opponent's radar. An unexpectedly skiff wind carried some of the chaff ninety miles to the coastline, where it got draped across power lines, shorting out transformers and causing power failures in parts of San Diego. The Navy quietly settled the damages- while carefully noting the effects of its unintended attack.

Information warfare has as many meanings as it has proponents, detractors and observers. Airpower theorists see it on the wings of Desert Storm; tank commanders see it in the American army's Force XXI; simulator designers see it in their virtual realities...and strategic-war planners see it as a way to lay waste to whole societies. Information warfare studies are proliferating within the American armed forces almost as quickly as the networks that carry them from desktop to desktop. The confusing planoply stems from the fact that the information revolution, whether it is in uniform or mufti, relies upon the fastest technology to do the oldest things. Thus it is always a peculiar mixture of the familiar and the shockingly new. In that war is all about strategies, command and morale, it has always been about information. All war is information war, and so every aspect of fighting wars in the information age can be called "information warfare" by someone. If information driven warfare means something new, it is the use of information as a substitute for traditional ways of fighting, rather than an adjunct to them. There are three ways that this might be achieved by:

- the high technology equivalent of brute force;
- subversion; and,
- a new form of deterrence.

For the purpose of this paper, we focus on the second element-subversion. It is our belief that because of the unique relationship between Americans and computers, IBW launched subversive acts-a prelude to, or the actual execution of "quiet wars"-may be accomplished.

The evolution and ultimate "blurring" of military and civilian sectors came about in large part because of the growth in hardware and software. It was not so long ago, in the early 1960's, that the

Pentagon provided the market for sophisticated electronics. Today, it makes up less than 1% of that market. In many ways, the military is following the revolution, not leading it. In 1962 Paul Baran of RAND developed a concept that permitted the linking of computers from distant locations. It was designed to preserve the integrity of the military command and control network in case of a nuclear attack. In 1969, the Defense Advanced Research Projects Agency (DARPA) funded the first test of the concept, and the first node was installed at RAND. The test consisted of scientists from remote locations passing findings and research notes back and forth. However, a year later it was being used like a mail box for the users and it proceeded to grow rapidly in use. In 1983, the military part and the nonmilitary part grew apart and finally split, the nonmilitary section grew up into what is now called the Internet.

For the first time in our nation's history, technology is no longer the sole domain of the military. The speed of the growth and application of technology is clearly a concern for defense planners. While the US used some of the world's most advanced weaponry and technology in the Gulf War (much of which proved inaccurate) it also used a great deal of older technology, some of which dated back to the 1960's. As B.R. Inman and Daniel F. Burton Jr. note in their article "Technology and US. National Security, "the 8088 microprocessor used in the Patriot missile was developed by the Intel Corporation fifteen years ago." This technology is not competitive today.

Opening and Closing Pandora's Box

In the center of Strike the battleship's commander, Captain David S. Bill, Ferched in his high backed padded chair. Although he occasionally glanced at the screens above, the captain s attention was largely fixed on the men clustered around four computers lining the far bulkhead. Something had gone awry with the ship's Tomahawk missile system.. For reasons no one could fathom, the Tomahawk computers seemed confused, refusing to transfer the necessary commands from the engagement-planning console to the launch console. The resulting impasse_"casualty" in Navy jargon_meant the missiles could not be fired...On Wisconsin, where the scheduled launch was now just moments away, the men in

Strike were running out of solutions...As the request for additional time flashed up the chain of command, an excited voice from one of the nearby ships crackled through Strike: "Alpha, alpha." This is the Paul F Foster. Happy trails." Happy trails: the code phrase for missiles away. Operation Desert Storm had begun without Wisconsin.

As the most technologically vulnerable nation, the US defense planners must recognize several concepts about the technical end of the IBW battlefield:

It must be assumed that everyone has access to technology, therefore the US is the most vulnerable to attack;

As the US's ability to wage IBW increases, so to do the IBW capabilities, and response capabilities, of other nation-states and non-state actors;

While at first glance it would appear that IBW is most effective against adversaries with like technological capabilities and infrastructure-the top end of the IBW target spectrum-it must be remembered that technology comes in two forms-high and appropriate-and it is the latter that will always defeat the former. Thus, the benefits of IBW in arena's of conflict as found in the Gray Areas are a target rich environment must be pursued alongside the force on force approach.

The technical realm of information based warfare can be split into two major areas: Netwar and Cyberwar. Netwar is the information related conflict between nations, societies, governments, or non-state actors with the targets being information systems and communications, and it consists of destruction of communications, acquisition of information, release of misinformation, and destruction or deletion of data. Cyberwar consists of militaries conducting their operations according to information based theories and principles. These terms can be broken down even further. Netwar can be broken into three main categories: Personal, Corporate, and Global.

We are constantly warned about the personal level of Netwar, we have passwords to computer accounts, never give our social security number over the telephone, and generally try to be careful about our own information. But protecting yourself from someone who genuinely wants to conduct information war against you is nearly impossible. Corporations are subject to a barrage of information security problems to an even greater extent. The stealing of company secrets is a new form of economic war that is plaguing many companies. It is also possible for one company to release false findings that indicate that a competitor has a poor or dangerous product. IBW spawned misinformation-a fertile area for denial and deception techniques-are very difficult to combat and correct. Finally, on the global level, Netwar can be waged against industries, economies, nations, or non-state groups. It ranges from intelligence and information leads, to the terrifying possibilities of terrorist groups breaking into such communications as an air traffic control system at a major US airport. The impact at the global level can be much more wide spread and all threatening than that of the personal or corporate levels of netwar.

On both sides of the war, Netwar and Cyberwar, the key to good protection and offense is good software to run the systems, encode the data, and peck holes in other's data. The vital link for the information and the technology is software, which relies heavily upon implanted logic. The newest and brightest theories and concepts of logic center around what is called 'fuzzy logic'. The name fuzzy logic makes one think of a system that is inexact, but that is not the case, instead it has an infinite exactness. Fuzzy logic expands our normal computer principle of 0 or 1, true or false, and in the place of this is infinite degrees between 0 and 1. Fuzzy logic is used every day in the development of everything from smart washers to train systems in Japan. With a smart washer, you merely press a start button and the machine figures the cycle, how much detergent, and the water use; the logic train systems are smooth as silk, quick, and always on time. The theory started with a few paradoxes one of which is The Paradox of Theseus' ship:

When Theseus returned from slaying the Minotaur, says Plutarch, the Athenians preserved his ship, and as planks rotted, replaced them with new ones. When the first plank was replaced, everyone agreed it was still the same ship. Adding a second plank made no difference either. At some point, the Athenians may have replaced every plank in the ship. Was it a different ship? At what point did it become one?

At different points in time the ship was certain degrees the original ship, for instance when half the planks were replaced, it was .5 the original ship. This same principle of degrees can be applied to many concepts around us, and what you end up with is a very exact and reliable process for computers. When you tie this concept into ideas such as artificial intelligence, you may obtain a computer that has the capacity to learn because it can start to work with more than 0 and 1.

Because of the importance of the technical tools of IBW-and their fragility-we list below the possible contents of an IBW techno "kit-bag":

Computer Viruses - A piece of code, or code fragment, designed to begin replicating itself when a host program begins to run. It's objective is to erase data, software programs, or memory in order to interrupt the action of the computer it infests. These can be loaded unwittingly by a user off the Internet or some other disk.

Worms - Instead of being just a code fragment, a worm is an entire program in and of itself. The code begins to replicate as soon as it touches a computer system, not dependent on the start of execution of any other program. Its aim is to eat up computer resources and/or delete data to result in a crippling effect on the host computer.

Trojan Horses - As the name would suggest, a Trojan horse is a program, or code fragment inside a program, that performs a function unbeknownst to the user. It usually performs a simple task on the outside, while unleashing a virus or a worm on the inside. It can also perform information retrieval while performing a task, leaving no trace.

Logic Bombs - Similar to a Trojan horse, a logic bomb is used to release a virus, worm, or complete some other secret task. These are usually planted by a programmer or system developer. This could be useful in US military strategy, instead of open bombs, the US could plant logic bombs to retrieve specific data from foreign users. This is plausible because many of the main software development in the world occurs in the US. Trap Doors - The use of this is similar to a logic bomb. It is a secret way back into a system left by a programmer or designer. Unlike a logic bomb that executes, a trap door is merely an unknown security flaw. Chipping - This is the term for doing any of the above to the hardware of a system instead of to the software. One can build in circuitry to a chip that performs specific functions.

Machines and Microbes - Although one thinks of Star Trek and other science fiction when the subject of nanny machines comes up, it is actually a feasible plan. machines and microbes are tiny machines, like a small insect, that "eat" electronic circuits, oil, plastics, etc. If unleashed on a computer center, the result would be total shut down.

Electronic Jamming, HERF guns, and EM bombs- These are all forms of electronic signal jamming. One can jam communications, stopping computer information flow; shoot radio signals at an electronic target to shut it down with a High Energy Radio Frequency (HERF) gun; or send out a high powered electromagnetic pulse, an EMP bomb.

Hitch-hiking- This is a group of people, a subsection of hackers, that merely sit on the net and wait. They wait for any information and interesting code to go by and then hitch a ride with it, they follow and delete it, or they simply copy and steal it. Thinking in terms of closing Pandora's Box, the following techniques will have to be considered as an IBW operational security plan is built:

Firewalls - A limited gateway to the Interment from a company or group. Only passwords and certain configurations can get in, and everything is checked for viruses, etc. Only privileged personnel, or personnel with certain system configurations can get out. If implemented correctly they can be useful.

Encryption - This growing area of interest consists on coding data so that others can not place bombs in or around it or read the data. This is growing more difficult as hackers and other groups become more efficient at breaking the codes. This is one of the areas that fuzzy logic could come into serious play. If, at first glance, the foregoing appears to be merely a "laundry list," a reading of the following paragraph will surely prove sobering to the IBW planner:

The Defense Information Security Agency (DISA) conducts vulnerability studies of military and government computer systems.

Their figures are truly alarming: 88% of defense computer systems are easily penetrated. Of the successful penetrations, 96% are not detected. Even worse, 95% of the detected penetrations are not reported or responded to. Even when an intrusion is detected, it is usually impossible to determine who did it. DISA studies indicate that there were possibly 300,000 intrusions into government computer systems in 1994 alone.

INFORMATION WARFARE AND DETERRENCE

It is clear that the information age has spawned new relationships and greatly expanded the range of possible interactions. It is no longer possible to separate and isolate military, national, public, and private systems. Thus, concepts of national security, to include protecting information systems and deterring attacks, need to be expanded to consider the full range of likely interactions. This would help to determine where the boundary between DoD and the rest of the national information infrastructure should lie. It was in this context that the workshop primarily addressed the relationship between information warfare and deterrence.

At the abstract level, the interface between these two concepts is dependent on setting the context clearly. First, deterrence is always from an actor toward a target. The very nature of the actor and target, as well as the degree of asymmetry between them is important. A nation state has much greater power than an individual hacker and has broad powers of law enforcement that can be brought to bear if the individual is within its borders or the reach of accepted international laws. However, two nation states are, at least in legal terms, equal and must exercise the international system (diplomacy, warfare, etc.) to influence one another's behavior.

Moreover, the nature of the relationship between the parties is important to the analysis. The use of deterrence is unlikely in cooperative arrangements, more likely in competitive ones, and most likely in conflictual patterns. Finally, substantive context may also make a difference. For example, deterrence is most likely in military arenas where the credibility of threats is greatest and easiest to assess. Hence, specification of the context (type of relationship, nature of the actors, substantive domain) is essential before any conclusion is possible about the effectiveness of deterrence.

The Steamroller and the Wrench

The most important insight arising from looking at the two concepts however, is the fact that they are only relevant to one another in highly selective contexts. The analogy that emerged was that of a steamroller and a wrench. Both are tools and depending on the situation, appropriate wrenches may be useful for, or even crucial to, the operation of the steamroller. However, most of the things the steamroller does are irrelevant to the wrench and most of the things the wrench can be used for do not involve a steamroller. In many cases, therefore, the workshop found itself venturing away from a pure consideration of the two concepts and into meaningful discussions in areas related to one or the other of the two central topics. These discussions revolved around the concepts, but kept slipping tangentially to more familiar issues such as command and control warfare (C2W), or IW in some other context such as retaliation in kind for an IW attack. It eventually became apparent that the main reason for frustration was that the related concepts and issues are grossly mismatched. IW is just too big and encompasses so much (particularly in the context of information dominance), while deterrence is limited and almost always case specific.

In retrospect, the revelation should not have been surprising. While workshop participants noted that certain IW actions are as old as warfare (a bluff for example), the exploding vistas of information technology and cyberspace are only beginning to be understood. Several of the participants were comfortable discussing deterrence as it might be related to command and control warfare (C2W). In this application there are five clearly defined "Pillars" which include Operational Security (OPSEC), Electronic Warfare (EW), Psychological Operations (PSYOPS), Military Deception, and Physical Destruction. The pillars are arrayed both offensively as "Counter-Command and Control" and defensively as "Command and Control Protection." Both arrays are dependent on and supported by intelligence. Any one of the pillars can have a deterrent effect. For example, in EW the presence of anti-radiation missiles may deter the use of air defense radar. Likewise, the adroit use of psychological operations might disrupt the enemy decision making process to the point where they are deterred from action, or at least their C2 process is greatly slowed.

While we believe that we understand C2W, the workshop brought into clear focus the fact that C2W is only a very small subset of IW, and it is that larger context that needs further exploration and analysis. Likewise, one size IW deterrence does not fit all. Equally important to the action itself is the intended recipient. Without getting into the adversary's mind and understanding his social, cultural, and religious values, as well as his education and past history, IW deterrence actions may be like the tree that falls in the forest and goes unheard. They may even be misunderstood and, therefore, have unintended consequences. The earlier discussion of deterrence stressed that creditable deterrence requires that the message be communicated clearly. Knowing how the adversary receives and understands messages is essential. It also became increasingly clear that IW deterrent actions must be part of an orchestrated and integrated effort. Seldom will an IW action in and of itself be a creditable deterrent. However, skillfully combined as part of an overall information dominance concept, some combination of IW and other actions may produce the desired deterrence.

How Might IW Attacks on the United States Be Deterred?

As information age technologies become more useful and valuable across all arenas and levels of interaction, vulnerabilities to disruption, deception, penetration, theft, and destruction increase as well. The vulnerabilities cluster around two basic areas: the computers that form the heart of most information systems and increasingly control operating systems, and the communication networks that tie them together. Workshop participants noted that recent studies indicate that all too often computer security is still given short shrift. Records that would be locked up if they were paper are often left unprotected in computers.

When computers are networked, they become even more vulnerable because information can be accessed from remote locations. Both locally and remotely, data can be manipulated, viruses inserted, and records stolen or destroyed. When the data being manipulated or moved represents money or other things of value, the manipulation is theft. Presently, the banking system is reportedly losing millions of dollars each year to computer theft. At the Department of Defense, hackers have penetrated DoD networks and systems (mostly unclassified). Moreover, recent tests indicate that only about five percent of attacks are detected, and of those detected, only five percent reported. If these figures are correct, the likelihood of knowing about an attack is .0025 (one-quarter of a percent) and the risk of being caught must be, by definition, even lower. Other military systems are likewise vulnerable. In many cases that vulnerability cannot be reduced by isolation because military systems depend on the national information infrastructure for about ninety percent of their traffic. Over ninety-five percent of all U.S. Government telecommunications within the U.S. travel on commercial circuits.

From the banking system to air traffic control, from military logistics to the telephone networks, from the stock exchanges to computer controlled trains, the United States, its economy, and its security are inexorably bound up in information technology. Many of the key systems lack safeguards or redundancy. Some, including some defense systems, are extremely fragile and easily disrupted. Most are vulnerable in one way or another. The U.S. information infrastructure is easily the world's biggest IW target.

Given these vulnerabilities, what can be done to enhance security and improve the likelihood that the United States can deter IW attacks? What are the DoD's responsibilities, and where are the boundaries of those responsibilities? Since U.S. forces cannot fight effectively without being well connected to the national information infrastructure, the responsibility would appear to go well beyond the protection of military systems alone. The workshop noted that this is a broad national security issue that the military cannot ignore. Since IW defense and deterrence are essential to military effectiveness, a crucial issue is to determine what role the professional military should have in this mission.

THE EVOLUTION OF INFORMATION BASED WARFARE

Therefore, at times of revolution, when the normal-scientific tradition changes, the scientist's perception of his environment must be re-educated-in some familiar situations he must learn to see a new gestalt.

The Structure of Scientific Revolutions

Whereas we had available for immediate purpose one hundred and forty-nine first-class warships, we now have two, these two being the Warrior and her sister Ironside. There is not now a ship in the English navy apart from these two that it would not be madness to trust in an engagement with that little [American] Monitor.. -The Times (London), 1862.

The most recent steps in that evolution can be found in the Military Technical Revolution (MTR) which may be attributed to Soviet Military thinkers; and, a recurrence of what is called the Revolution in Military Affairs (RMA).

In the early 1980's the Soviets noted that "the emergence of advanced non-nuclear technologies was engendering a new revolution in military affairs. They were particularly interested in the "incorporation of information sciences into the military sphere" and in the idea of a "reconnaissance-strike complex. The events in the Gulf War convinced them of their hypothesis (comparative strategies).

RMAs matter principally for two reasons. First, being second best may lead to catastrophic loss in future wars. Since the only objective benchmark for determining the relative effectiveness of forces (that is, success in combat) is unavailable in long periods of peace, there is great potential for asymmetries in combat effectiveness between militaries, observable only when the next war occurs. Secondly, as equipment life cycles, especially for platforms, steadily grow to encompass decades, many of the principal weapons systems of 2025 will likely be designed and built in the next few years. Since militaries are stuck with force structures they choose for long periods, it is more crucial than ever to think about them now, in peacetime, about the revolutionary changes in the nature of war and the about what will matter in winning wars in twenty or thirty years.

Today with the United States arguably the only superpower for the foreseeable future, one might ask why this issue is especially pressing. Replicating the US force structure is clearly beyond the reach of all but a few other nations, even in the long term. This may not be relevant. Even small-to medium sized powers may be able to exploit specific technologies for significant military leverage in certain areas. The current rate of change suggests that state of the art in any technological context will be an extremely short-lived phenomenon, particularly with respect to the technologies that were key to the success of Desert Storm: space systems, telecommunication systems, computer architecture's, global information distribution networks, and navigation systems. Future revolutions will occur much more rapidly, offering far less time for adaptation to new methods of warfare. The growing imperative in the business world for rapid response to changing conditions in order to survive in an intensely competitive environment is surely instructive for military affairs.

The present RMA entails a fundamental change in who, how, and, perhaps even why wars are fought. It is driven not only by new technologies but by new operational concepts, new tactics, and new organizational structures. The impact of the current confluence of social, political, economic, and technological forces on American society and armed forces may equal-or exceed-what occurred during the 1960's and 1970's during the turmoil associated with the war in Vietnam.

The question that must be asked as we attempt to understand this RMA, is what were the results of change wrought by past Revolutions in Military Affairs? It has been suggested that accelerated interservice rivalries and over-reliance on management systems marked the last RMA, driven by the advent of atomic weapons at the end of WW II and the relatively stable and sparse defense budgets of the 1950's.

The current RMA is characterized by four types of changes:

- extremely precise;
- stand-off strikes;

- dramatically improved command, control, and intelligence;
- information warfare; and
- nonlethality

Many analysts see a number of benefits from harnessing the current revolution in military affairs and using it to build 21st century US armed forces:

- rejuvenating the political utility of military power;
- delaying the emergence of a peer competition;
- providing a blueprint for technology acquisition and force reorganization;
- and inspiring conceptual, forward-looking thinking.

Looking ahead, many believe that the current RMA will have at least two stages. The first is based on stand-off platforms, stealth, precision, information domination, improved communications, computers, global positioning systems, digitization, "smart" weapons systems, jointness, and use of ad hoc coalitions.

The second may be based on robotics, nonlethality, pyscho-technology, cyberdefense, nanotechnology, "brilliant" weapons systems, hyperflexible organizations, and "fire ant warfare." Steven Metz and James Kievit of the Strategic Studies Institute argue that a cost /benefit analysis of the present RMA needs to be pursued. One the one hand, they argue that a case can be made that costs and risks of vigorous pursuit of the current RMA outweigh the expected benefits. These include the risk that:

- the current RMA will not generate increased combat effectiveness against the most likely or most dangerous future opponents;
- American pursuit of the RMA will encourage opponents or potential opponents to seek countermeasures;
- the current RMA might lead the United States toward over reliance on military power; and, vigorous pursuit of the current RMA might increase problems with friends and allies.

On the other hand, they argue that there are very pressing reasons for supporting the current RMA: it should bring significant increase in combat effectiveness against some mid-level opponents;

a force built around stand-off, precision weapons and disruptive information warfare capabilities would be more politically usable than a traditional force-projection military; the RMA could augment deterrence; and, the United States may need to pursue the current RMA to avoid stumbling into strategic inferiority.

Lastly, they posit-and we strongly agree-that if policymakers decide to pursue the present revolution in military affairs, strategy, rather than technological capability should guide force development. The key question is: What do we want the future US military to be able to do?

Unfortunately one finds little discussion of the foregoing ideas in the DOD's recently completed "Bottom-Up" Review. Former Secretary of Defense Aspin initiated the review with the laudable goal of rethink the basis for US defense planning. It placed emphasis in many of the right areas: readiness, keeping forces for more than one regional war, acquisition reform. This review built a substantial consensus in the Pentagon behind the new force structure. Nonetheless, the review offers a classic example of military leaders planning to fight the last war. The report's proposed force for a single regional contingency-four to five Army divisions, four to five Marine brigades, 10 Air Force fighter wings, 100 heavy bombers, and four to five carriers-mirrors almost exactly the forces deployed in Operation Desert Storm. The review offers few thoughts on new technologies or techniques that might change the nature of war in coming decades. Clearly, the challenge is to move beyond the last war-an undertaking that is fraught with peril and promise.

An Information Based Warfare Model

We are pilgrims, Master; we shall go

Always a little further...."

-Inscription on the Clock, Bradbury Lines, Hereford, Home of the Special Air Service Regiment J. F. Flecker

We believe that it is instructive to review the Program of Analysis for FY 1996 as set forth by the Directorate for Combat Support, National Military Intelligence Production Center, Defense Intelligence Agency. Entitled, Intelligence Support to Infrastructure

Warfare, the thrust of this paper is directed toward a new paradigm that is centered on the principal of attacking an adversary's infrastructure to degrade or deny mobility, support to combatants and leadership.

The paper sets forth valid arguments to support the thesis that to a large extent, recent advances in weapons and tactics were driven by the strategic objective of penetrating and rupturing the physical and psychological "centers of gravity" of the enemy warfighting capability. It is clear that new technologies have spurred an entire new generation of warfighting capabilities and, of equal importance, fundamentally altered the construct and performance of the modern nation-state.

Discrete centers of gravity are giving way to diversification and interdependence in the modern nation-state. Information is the raw material that fuels productivity and power. Critical systemic nodes in the dynamic flow of commodities-consumables, services, and information-are at the same time increasingly obscure, strategically important, and tactically vulnerable. Fine grain analysis [read Intelligence writ in large script] and precision targeting fin both the conventional and non conventional sense] of these nodes and their synergistic dependencies is the centerpiece of Infrastructure Warfare..

The primary elements of Infrastructure Warfare are:

- The nation-state as a System of Systems;
- Information as an Instrument of Power;
- Denial and Deception;
- Urban Infrastructure-The Operational Environment.

While the concept of Infrastructure Warfare is certainly a step in the right direction, we believe that this concept has several shortcomings that need to be addressed in order that it fully lead toward an answer to the strategic "bottom-line"-how do we win? We argue that the conflicts of the new world disorder will be largely fought on geography in the Third World (TW.) Driven largely by the chimera of the Gulf War, images of centers of gravity and smart weapons overshadow the tawdry back-alley settings in which actual conflict will take place in the future. In reviewing the "lessons learned" of recent wars in the Third World- where 95 percent of future conflicts will take place-a number of more accurate images appear:

First, the mix of forces facing each other has not been very different, regardless of the type of war being fought. Navies have been conspicuous by their absence or their modest role. Air forces have played a secondary role. Almost without exception, wars in the TW have been won or lost by ground troops.

Second, the type of war has not necessarily determined the tactics used; in fact, it has blurred the differences between them. Furthermore, as the frequent oscillations in tactics and strategy suggest, both irregular and regular armies in recent years have shared much in term of their ability to implement offensive doctrine. With the exceptions of campaigns involving an industrialized power, it seems that the defense has become the most effective form of warfare in the TW. With the exception of Israel and the war in Lebanon, none of the Third World combatants that have used an offensive doctrine has been able to effect a decisive breakthrough or cause the defenders to retire in disorder or retreat.

Third, the duration of recent wars have generally been protracted and have engaged large arrays of national and subnational forces. Most of the wars fought between regular lesser developed country army's have not been shorter.

Fourth, the involvement of external nation forces has been large. Of the wars fought between 1945 and 1976, 38 percent were fought with foreign participation.

Lastly, because guerrilla wars pose particularly difficult challenges for governments, they represent a new and difficult form of conflict.

If the foregoing is correct, then we believe that the Infrastructure paradigm must address the Gray Area Phenomena (GAP). GAP is defined as threats to nation-states by non-states actors and non-governmental processes and organizations. The Gray Areas at once appear to be strikingly new and uncomfortably old. Simply put, they are the most critical issues confronting the world community as we enter into the Century. Just beyond the horizon of current events lie two possible futures-both of which look bleak. The first is the retribalization of large swaths of humankind by war and bloodshed: a Lebanonization of national states in which culture is pitted against culture, people against people, tribe against tribe-a Jihad in the name of a hundred narrowly conceived faiths against every kind of globalization and interdependence.

The second is being borne by the onrush of technical, economic, and ecological forces that demand increased integration and uniformity. The planet, it appears, is both falling apart and coming reluctantly together at the very same time.

The GAP consists of the following "arena's of conflict":

- Ethno-religious-nationalistic conflicts;
- Weapons proliferation-both conventional and nuclear, biological and chemical;
- Conflict over scarce resources;
- AIDS and other infectious diseases;
- The globalization of Organized Crime;
- Drug Trafficking;
- Economic Warfare and conflict over technology;
- Emigration; and,
- Famine.

The United States today is involved to some degree in each of the aforementioned arena's. While we strongly believe that traditional force-on-force warfare will always be with us, in the main, we sense that the present and future world situation more than makes the case for a strategy that encompasses the full-range of conflict supported by the appropriate technologies. Thus, we would add the Gray Area "arenas of conflict" to the DIA construct, and in so doing, move the ongoing debate to the new plateau of Information Based Warfare.

Tomorrow

We should be seeking tentative answers to fundamental questions, rather than definitive answers to trivial ones. —James Billington

Before framing a new definition and model for Information Based Warfare, we turn to a nonwestern look at information and warfare. Shen Weiguang, a writer who appears to be at the forefront of PRC IW theorists argues that: in a military sense alone, information warfare refers to both sides' attempt to gain the initiative of the battle through their control over information and flow of intelligence. With the support of information, both sides intend to comprehensively apply military deception, operational secrets, psychological warfare, and electronic warfare to destroy the enemy's information systems, block the flow of the enemy's information, and create false information to affect and weaken the enemies command and control capability. At the same time, they must ensure that their command and control system is not damaged in the same way by the opponent.

Further addressing the issues, Shen Weiguang illuminates a number of thoughts that cut to the heart of the concept of Information Based Warfare.

He correctly argues that IBW in one sense is the "quiet battlefield," something we attempted to portray in our opening scenario. Turning toward the concept of "centers of gravity" we feel that his descriptions of "attacks on the enemies cognitive and trust systems" perhaps better portrays the idea of attacking C2 and C4I nodes.

This, he argues, is the main target of information warfare. The concepts of "hard attack" and "soft attack" with "soft damage" are noted as the two end-product manifestations of IBW; and, the concept of "war of structural damage" [read Infrastructure War] is thought to come into full play only when "it has absorbed the essence of information warfare."

Technology, he argues, does not determine superiority. It is determined by new tactics [in part this could be naval guerrilla warfare-PRC style] and "independent creations of commanders in the field. Information based warfare enables one to break with "traditional stylized engagement, " something we feel will give new impetus to the military arts.

Like a number of perceptive US thinkers, Shen Weiguang, has seized upon the Toffler' work to understand and further flesh-out the idea of "niche-warfare." And, he appears to understand that IBW will spawn special operating forces [differentiated from special forces] in the IBW setting.

His comments about command and control are perceptive:

The operational target of information warfare lies in control rather than bloodshed;

The key to victory lies in human policy decisions rather than technology [hopefully a lesson learned and re-learned in the Naval War College games]; genuine advantage does not necessary lie in the leading technology but the leading ideas. History has given evidence to the fact when some new technology brings mankind brightness, a shadow is cast simultaneously. Advanced electronic computers and information technology link society and the army to an integrated network; the result is very high efficiency and great fragility;

The input in grasping knowledge, costs far less than directly purchasing advanced weaponry [a Sun-tzuian slip, particularly in light of the fact that the PRC has taken this approach for years as it has covertly acquired primarily mid-level technology from the West, enabling them to jump the learning curve].

A Tentative Idea

Returning again to the working definition of Information Based Warfare we suggest the following changes as noted in italics:

Information-based warfare is an approach to [quiet war and] armed conflict focusing on the management and use of information in all its forms and at all levels to achieve a decisive military advantage especially in joint and combined environments [through the use of special operating forces that are an integral part of the overall force structure. capable of traditional force on force war and the execution of "quiet-war] Information based-warfare is both offensive and defensive in nature-ranging from measures that prohibit the enemy from exploiting information to corresponding measures to assure the integrity, availability, and interoperability elate of friendly information assets.

While ultimately military in nature IBW is also waged in political, economic. and social arenas and is applicable over the entire national security continuum from peace to war and from 'tooth to tail.' Finally. Information Based Warfare focuses on the command and control needs of the commander by employing state of the art information technology such as synthetic environments to dominate the battlefield.

We have added the concept of "quiet-war" because we believe that the information/communications tools that technology brings to the IBW table offers theoreticians strategists and tacticians the opportunity to plan and implement courses of action as exemplified by the opening scenario in this paper. We believe that it is this element- unattributable strikes which by their very nature preclude moving further up the conflict spectrum-is the concept that holds the most promise in the execution of Information Based Warfare.

Strategy

We argue that the very soul of strategic thinking is the search for the answer to the question: How do we win? That answer is to be found in the strategic principals:

- Ends-the protection of national interests
- Ways- the concept of how the job will get done
- Means-the resources that describe what it will take to support the concept.

Answers to applying the strategic elements-in any setting in the new world disorder, with any type of force structure-are to be found in five themes suggested by Colin Gray:

First, consider strategy as a mosaic, each of the pieces of which must be understood in terms of what the sum total means.

Second, geography is the most fundamental of the factors which condition national outlooks on security problems and solutions. Geography, treated properly in political and strategic analysis is not a rigidly determining factor. The influence of geography is truly pervasive, notwithstanding the fact that influence must vary in detail as technology changes.

Third, is the use, abuse and often simply nonuse of historical experience in strategic theorizing and strategic planning. The United States in the closing years of the twentieth century is a political culture characterized by a short attention span for difficult issues of international security; by a proclivity to seek pragmatic solutions to problems which may be conditions to be accommodated rather than puzzles to be solved; and by a very noticeable historical ignorance and general disinterest. Fourth, American strategists must begin to be aware of the influence of different national cultures upon choices for, and performance in, statecraft and strategy. Fifth, strategists must beware of the sin of technicism-the proclivity of a materialist school of thinking about defense questions to reduce issues of means and ends to the promise in particular new military machines. Technicism shows itself in an unbalanced interest in the machine in a man-machine system (i.e., in the crossbow as contrasted with the crossbowman). But technicism refers to the disorder when that which is only technical displaces, and effectively substitutes for, that which has to be considered tactically, operationally, and strategically in far more inclusive analysis.

Intelligence

Intelligence-in essence, evaluated information-is the lifeblood that courses through the strategic soul. While we could wax eloquent and long on the virtues of intelligence, it is our sense that the evaluated information that is the grist for Information Based Warfare is be found in what Sherman Kent called the "Substantive Content of Strategic Intelligence-The Speculative-Evaluative Element." This information is what the United States must know in order to be foresighted-what it must know about the future stature of other separate sovereign states [and non-state actors], the courses of action they are likely to initiate themselves [read applied alternative futures methodology], and the courses of action they are likely to take up in response to some outside stimulus.

Technological Tools Driven by a "Merkava" Frame of Mind

"Merkava"(chariot of fire) was the name given to an Israeli designed, fast prototype, tank. The essence of this type of technology is that it is driven by the state of mind that recognizes dramatic, fast-moving change, and attempts to support strategy by being capable of thoughtful design and rapid fielding. In US terms, it is the stuff of the "Skunkworks"-a similar belief that things can be accomplished quickly and made to work-on the battlefield.

4

Cyberspace Attacks

Cyberspace is constantly under assault. Cyber spies, thieves, saboteurs, and thrill seekers break into computer systems, steal personal data and trade secrets, vandalize Web sites, disrupt service, sabotage data and systems, launch computer viruses and worms, conduct fraudulent transactions, and harass individuals and companies. These attacks are facilitated with increasingly powerful and easy-to-use software tools, which are readily available for free from thousands of Web sites on the Internet.

Many of the attacks are serious and costly. The ILOVEYOU virus and variants, for example, was estimated to have hit tens of millions of users worldwide and cost billions of dollars in damage. Denial-of-service attacks against Yahoo, CNN, eBay, and other e-commerce Web sites were estimated to have caused over a billion in losses. They also shook the confidence of business and individuals in e-commerce. Governments are particularly concerned with terrorist and state-sponsored attacks against the critical infrastructures that constitute their national life support systems. The Clinton Administration defined eight: telecommunications, banking and finance, electrical power, oil and gas distribution and storage, water supply, transportation, emergency services, and government services.

There have been numerous attacks against these infrastructures. Hackers have invaded the public phone networks, compromising nearly every category of activity, including switching and operations, administration, maintenance, and provisioning (OAM&P). They have crashed or disrupted signal transfer points, traffic switches, OAM&P systems, and other network elements. They have planted "time bomb" programs designed to shut down major switching hubs, disrupted emergency 911 services throughout the eastern seaboard, and boasted that they have the capability to bring down all switches in Manhattan. They have installed wiretaps, rerouted phone calls, changed the greetings on voice mail systems, taken over voice mailboxes, and made free long-distance calls at their victims= expense — sticking some victims with phone bills in the hundreds of thousands of dollars. When they can=t crack the technology, they use "social engineering" to con employees into giving them access.

In March 1997, one teenage hacker penetrated and disabled a telephone company computer that serviced the Worcester Airport in Massachusetts. As a result, telephone service to the Federal Aviation Administration control tower, the airport fire department, airport security, the weather service, and various private airfreight companies was cut off for six hours. Later in the day, the juvenile disabled another telephone company computer, this time causing an outage in the Rutland area. The lost service caused financial damages and threatened public health and public safety. On a separate occasion, the hacker allegedly broke into a pharmacist=s computer and accessed files containing prescriptions.

Banks and financial systems are a popular target of cyber criminals. The usual motive is money, and perpetrators have stolen or attempted to steal tens of millions of dollars. In one case of sabotage, a computer operator at Reuters in Hong Kong tampered with the dealing room systems of five of the company=s bank clients. In November 1996, he programmed the systems to delete key operating system files after a delay long enough to allow him to leave the building. When the "time bombs" exploded, the systems crashed. They were partially restored by the next morning, but it took another day before they were fully operational. However, the banks said the tampering did not significantly affect trading and that neither they nor their clients experienced losses.

In another act of sabotage against a critical infrastructure, a fired employee of Chevron's emergency alert network disabled the firm=s alert system by hacking into computers in New York and San Jose, California, and reconfiguring them so they=d crash. The vandalism was not discovered until an emergency arose at the Chevron refinery in Richmond, California, and the system could not be used to notify the adjacent community of a noxious release. During the 10-hour period in 1992 when the system was down, thousands of people in 22 states and 6 unspecified areas of Canada were put at risk.

An overflow of raw sewage on the Sunshine Coast of Australia in June was linked to a 49-year-old Brisbane man, who allegedly penetrated the Maroochy Shire Council's computer system and used radio transmissions to create the overflows. The man faced 370 charges that included stealing, computer hacking, and use radio communications equipment without authority.

Government computers, particularly Department of Defense computers, are a regular target of attack. Detected attacks against unclassified DoD computers rose from 780 in 1997 to 5,844 in 1998 and 22,144 in 1999.

The most damaging and costly attacks have been conducted for reasons other than the pursuit of terrorism. As the above cases illustrate, they have been motivated by greed, thrills, ego, revenge, and a variety of other non-ideological factors. They are properly classifified as cybercrimes, but not cyberterrorism

Politically and Socially Motivated Cyberattacks

Terrorism is normally associated with attacks conducted in furtherance of political and social objectives. Numerous cyberattacks have been so motivated. For example, in 1998, ethnic Tamil guerrillas swamped Sri Lankan embassies with 800 e-mails a day over a two-week period. The messages read "We are the Internet Black Tigers and we=re doing this to disrupt your communications." Intelligence authorities characterized it as the first known attack by terrorists against a country=s computer systems.

Also in 1998, Spanish protestors bombarded the Institute for Global Communications (IGC) with thousands of bogus e-mail messages. E-mail was tied up and undeliverable to the San Francisco based ISP=s users, and support lines were tied up with people who couldn=t get their mail. The protestors also spammed IGC staff and member accounts, clogged their Web page with bogus credit card orders, and threatened to employ the same tactics against organizations using IGC services. They demanded that IGC stop hosting the Webs site for the *Euskal Herria Journal,* a New York-based publication supporting Basque independence. Protestors said IGC supported terrorism because a section on the Web pages contained materials on the terrorist group Fatherland and Liberty, or ETA, which claimed responsibility for assassinations of Spanish political and security officials, and attacks on military installations. IGC finally relented and pulled the site because of the "mail bombings."

During the Kosovo conflict in 1999, NATO computers were blasted with e-mail bombs and hit with denial-of-service attacks by hacktivists protesting the NATO bombings. In addition, businesses, public organizations, and academic institutes received highly politicized virus-laden e-mails from a range of Eastern European countries, according to reports. Web defacements were also common. After the Chinese Embassy was accidentally bombed in Belgrade, Chinese hacktivists posted messages such as "We won=t stop attacking until the war stops!" on U.S. government Web sites.

Since December 1997, the Electronic Disturbance Theater (EDT), a New York City based activist group, has been conducting Web sit-ins against various sites in support of the Mexican Zapatistas. At a designated time, thousands of protestors point their browsers to a target site using software that floods the target with rapid and repeated download requests. EDT=s software has also been used by animal rights groups against organizations said to abuse animals. Electrohippies, another group of hacktivists, conducted Web sit-ins against the WTO when they met in Seattle in late 1999. These sit-ins all require mass participation to have much effect, and thus are more suited to use by activists than by relatively small groups of terrorists operating in secrecy.

While the above incidents were motivated by political and social reasons, whether they were sufficiently harmful or frightening to be classified as cyberterrorism is a judgement call.

To the best of my knowledge, no attack so far has led to violence or injury to persons, although some may have intimidated their victims. Both EDT and the Electrohippies view their operations as acts of civil disobedience, analogous to street protests and physical sit-ins, not as acts of violence or terrorism. This is an important distinction. Most activists, whether participating in a street march or Web sit-in, are not terrorists.

However, there are a few indications that some terrorist groups are pursuing cyberterrorism, either alone or in conjunction with acts of physical violence. In February 1998, Clark Staten told the Senate Judiciary Committee Subcommittee on Technology, Terrorism, and Government Information that it was believed that "members of some Islamic extremist organizations have been attempting to develop a 'hacker network' to support their computer activities and even engage in offensive information warfare attacks in the future."

In November 1998, the *Detroit News* reported that Khalid Ibrahim, who claimed to be a member of the militant Indian separatist group Harkat-ul-Ansar, had tried to buy military software from hackers who had stolen it from Department of Defense computers they had penetrated. The attempted purchase was discovered when an 18-year-old hacker calling himself Chameleon attempted to cash a $1,000 check from Ibrahim. Chameleon said he did not have the software and did not give it to Ibrahim, but Ibrahim may have obtained it or other sensitive information from one of the many other hackers he approached. Harkat-ul-Ansar declared war on the United States following the August cruise-missile attack on a suspected terrorist training camp in Afghanistan run by bin Laden, which allegedly killed nine of their members.

The Provisional Irish Republican Army employed the services of contract hackers to penetrate computers in order to acquire home addresses of law enforcement and intelligence officers, but the data was used to draw up plans to kill the officers in a single "night of the long knives" if the British government did not meet terms for a new cease-fire. As this case illustrates, terrorists may use hacking as a way of acquiring intelligence in support of physical violence, even if they do not use it to wreak havoc in cyberspace.

Terrorists might also engage in computer network attacks as a way of financing physical operations. For example, they could penetrate an e-commerce Web site and steal credit card numbers, conduct fraudulent transactions against an Internet bank, or extort money from victims by threatening electronic sabotage.

Potential Threat

To understand the potential threat of cyberterrorism, two factors must be considered: first, whether there are targets that are vulnerable to attack that could lead to violence or severe harm, and second, whether there are actors with the capability and motivation to carry them out.

Looking first at vulnerabilities, several studies have shown that critical infrastructures are potentially vulnerable to cyberterrorist attack. Eligible Receiver, a Ano notice@ exercise conducted by the Department of Defense in 1997 with support from National Security Agency penetration testing teams, found the power grid and emergency 911 systems had weaknesses that could be exploited by an adversary using only publicly available tools on the Internet. Although neither of these systems were actually attacked, study members concluded that service on these systems could be disrupted. Also in 1997, the President=s Commission on Critical Infrastructure Protection issued its report warning that through mutual dependencies and interconnectedness, critical infrastructures could be vulnerable in new ways, and that vulnerabilities were steadily increasing, while the costs of attack were decreasing.

Although many of the weaknesses in computerized systems can be corrected, it is effectively impossible to eliminate all of them. Even if the technology itself offers good security, it is frequently configured or used in ways that make it open to attack. In addition, there is always the possibility of insiders, acting alone or in concert with other terrorists, misusing their access capabilities.

According to Russia=s Interior Ministry Col. Konstantin Machabeli, the state-run gas monopoly, Gazprom, was hit by hackers in 1999 who collaborated with a Gazprom insider. The hackers were said to have used a Trojan horse to gain control of the central switchboard which controls gas flows in pipelines, although Gazprom, the world=s largest natural gas producer and the largest gas supplier to Western Europe, refuted the report.

Consultants and contractors are frequently in a position where they could cause grave harm. This past March, Japan=s Metropolitan Police Department reported that a software system they had procured to track 150 police vehicles, including unmarked cars, had been developed by the Aum Shinryko cult. At the time of the discovery, the cult had received classified tracking data on 115 vehicles. Further, the cult had developed software for at least 80 Japanese firms and 10 government agencies.

They had worked as subcontractors to other firms, making it almost impossible for the organizations to know who was developing the software. As subcontractors, the cult could have installed Trojan horses to launch or facilitate cyberterrorist attacks at a later date. Fearing a Trojan horse of their own, last February, the U.S. State Department sent an urgent cable to about 170 embassies asking them to remove software, which they belatedly realized had been written by citizens of the former Soviet Union.

If we take as given that critical infrastructures are vulnerable to a cyberterrorist attack, then the question becomes whether there are actors with the capability and motivation to carry out such an operation. While many hackers have the knowledge, skills, and tools to attack computer systems, they generally lack the motivation to cause violence or severe economic or social harm. Conversely, terrorists who are motivated to cause violence seem to lack the capability or motivation to cause that degree of damage in cyberspace.

FUTURE PROSPECTS

In August 1999, the Center for the Study of Terrorism and Irregular Warfare at the Naval Postgraduate School in Monterey, California, issued a report titled "Cyberterror: Prospects and Implications." Their objective was to articulate the demand side of terrorism. Specifically, they assessed the prospects of terrorist organizations pursuing cyberterrorism. They concluded that the barrier to entry for anything beyond annoying hacks is quite high, and that terrorists generally lack the wherewithal and human capital needed to mount a meaningful operation. Cyberterrorism, they argued, was a thing of the future, although it might be pursued as an ancillary tool.

The Monterey team defined three levels of cyberterror capability. First is simple-unstructured: the capability to conduct basic hacks against individual systems using tools created by someone else. The organization possesses little target analysis, command and control, or learning capability.

Second is advanced-structured: the capability to conduct more sophisticated attacks against multiple systems or networks and possibly, to modify or create basic hacking tools. The organization possesses an elementary target analysis, command and control, and learning capability.

Third is complex-coordinated: the capability for a coordinated attacks capable of causing mass-disruption against integrated, heterogeneous defenses (including cryptography). The organization has the ability to create sophisticated hacking tools.

They possess a highly capable target analysis, command and control, and organization learning capability. The Monterey team estimated that it would take a group starting from scratch 2-4 years to reach the advanced-structured level and 6-10 years to reach the complex-coordinated level, although some groups might get there in just a few years or turn to outsourcing or sponsorship to extend their capability.

The study examined five terrorist group types: religious, New Age, ethno-nationalist separatist, revolutionary, and far-right extremists. They determined that only the religious groups are likely to seek the most damaging capability level, as it is consistent with their indiscriminate application of violence. New Age or single issue terrorists, such as the Animal Liberation Front, pose the most immediate threat, however, such groups are likely to accept disruption as a substitute for destruction. Both the revolutionary and ethno-nationalist separatists are likely to seek an advanced-structured capability. The far-right extremists are likely to settle for a simple-unstructured capability, as cyberterror offers neither the intimacy nor cathartic effects that are central to the psychology of far-right terror. The study also determined that hacker groups are psychologically and organizationally ill-suited to cyberterrorism, and that it would be against their interests to cause mass disruption of the information infrastructure.

Thus, at this time, cyberterrorism does not seem to pose an imminent threat. This could change. For a terrorist, it would have some advantages over physical methods. It could be conducted remotely and anonymously, and it would not require the handling of explosives or a suicide mission. It would likely garner extensive media coverage, as journalists and the public alike are fascinated by practically any kind of computer attack. Indeed cyberterrorism could be immensely appealing precisely because of the tremendous attention given to it by the government and media.

Cyberterrorism also has its drawbacks. Systems are complex, so it may be harder to control an attack and achieve a desired level of damage than using physical weapons. Unless people are injured, there is also less drama and emotional appeal. Further, terrorists may be disinclined to try new methods unless they see their old ones as inadequate, particularly when the new methods require considerable knowledge and skill to use effectively.

Terrorists generally stick with tired and true methods. Novelty and sophistication of attack may be much less important than assurance that a mission will be operationally successful. Indeed, the risk of operational failure could be a deterrent to terrorists. For now, the truck bomb poses a much greater threat than the logic bomb.

The next generation of terrorists will grow up in a digital world, with ever more powerful and easy-to-use hacking tools at their disposal. They might see greater potential for cyberterrorism than the terrorists of today, and their level of knowledge and skill relating to hacking will be greater. Hackers and insiders might be recruited by terrorists or become self-recruiting cyberterrorists, the Timothy McVeigh=s of cyberspace. Some might be moved to action by cyber policy issues, making cyberspace an attractive venue for carrying out an attack. Cyberterrorism could also become more attractive as the real and virtual worlds become more closely coupled, with a greater number of physical devices attached to the

Internet. Some of these may be remotely controlled. Terrorists, for example, might target robots used in telesurgery. Unless these systems are carefully secured, conducting an operation that physically harms someone may be easy as penetrating a Web site is today.

Although the violent pursuit of political goals using exclusively electronic methods is likely to be at least a few years into the future, the more general threat of cybercrime is very much a part of the digital landscape today. In addition to cyberattacks against digital data and systems, many people are being terrorized on the Internet today with threats of physical violence. On-line stalking, death threats, and hate messages are abundant. These crimes are serious and must be addressed. In so doing, we will be in a better position to prevent and respond to cyberterrorism if and when the threat becomes more serious.

COUNTERING THREATS TO CYBER SPACE

Other groups have worked to counter threats to cyber space. This includes efforts to investigate and analyse cyber attack incidents such as denial of service attacks and targeted use of malware. Founded in August 2008 by former intelligence analyst Jeffrey Carr, Project Grey Goose was an experiment in online, volunteer, open source intelligence (OSINT) aimed at investigating possible Russian government involvement in the large-scale cyber attacks that hit the country of Georgia during the Russian military invasion earlier that month. On August 22, 2008, Carr used his blog to announce the project and to put out a call for volunteers.

The final cadre of twelve that was listed in the group's October 2008 report was comprised primarily of current and former members of the intelligence community, academic researchers, and defence and security professionals. Contributors to a second Grey Goose report released in early 2009 largely fit the same demographic profile. The group has described their OSINT methodology as relying on "data mining" and "machine translation" of "foreign language forums and social media sites," technical analysis of "serverlevel data," "an examination of geopolitical events occurring around the time of the cyber attacks," and "a review of the Nation State's military doctrine related to Information Warfare." They believe that the open source nature of their work is a distinct advantage, allowing them to work more quickly and with greater participation from international volunteers.

The two Grey Goose reports have had a substantial impact on shaping perceptions of Russia's involvement in the 2008 Georgia cyber attacks, as well as shaping public debate about the threat of cyber war. Members and supporters of Project Grey Goose even believe that data that they turned over to authorities may have prevented some cyber attacks, as well caused the Kremlin "to reduce its support of various [hacker] groups". Jeffrey Carr has become a sought-after expert on issues of cyber war, resulting in his publication of the book *Inside Cyber Warfare* for O'Reilly Media in 2009. Carr's book is now on the Commander's recommended reading list for members of U.S., Strategic Command, the parent organisation of the newly-formed U.S., Cyber Command.

Once again, the case of Project Grey Goose indicates the ambivalence and ambiguities that often exist between producers and consumers of security. Like Rossmiller and others, Carr has argued that bureaucratic inefficiencies often prevent government from effectively countering "terrorism in cyber space". One of those limitations, he argues, is that state actors do not yet understand the power of either the Internet, open sources of information, or collaborative processes of knowledge production.

Thus, governments have proven ill-equipped for countering terrorists online or meeting the challenge of cyber attacks. He sees Project Grey Goose as exemplary of the value of applying the open source software development model to intelligence work and hopes that "it will prove that we do not have to wait for official channels to adopt innovative solutions". Carr and his supporters identify Project Grey Goose as an example of what they call a "security trust network" (STN). Michael Sinkowitch, an executive at Fujitsu Australia who specialises in national security and intelligence, has defined STNs as "expert affiliations of interested organisations and individuals that can investigate and mitigate cyber crime threats".

Alexander Klimburg, a fellow at the Austrian Institute for International Affairs and a contributor to Carr's 2009 book, defines them as the liberal, democratic, Western antithesis to Russian and Chinese "patriotic hackers." Where "patriotic hackers" are seen as beholden to or controlled by the state and composed of malicious actors with a dubious moral code, STNs are defined as free to "choose when and if" to support a government, as trustworthy and credible partners for government, and as "shar[ing] a common moral code" based in "doing the right thing" and "operating within the remits of the law". Carr, Sinkowitsch, and Klimburg all see STNs like Project Grey Goose as examples of the security-producing "informal groups and volunteer networks" that Klimburg speaks about in the epigraph to this chapter.

In the realm of cyber security in particular, Klimburg has claimed that most work is already being done by STNs and business with "government bringing up the rear". He has claimed that STNs are particularly good at addressing the "attribution problem" in cyber security—i.e., figuring out the origin of a cyber attack, which is "a notoriously difficult task". Sinkowitsch has gone so far as to claim that cyber security STNs are able to "defeat, or at the very least limit the damage of, these adversaries [i.e., cyber attackers of various sorts]". But like the other cases of convergence security examined here, STNs too are ultimately dependent upon their relationship to the state.

Even Sinkowitsch admits that "There is not much they [STNs] can do about stopping the threats". Though STNs are theoretically free to choose when and if they work with the state, in practice having an impact requires working with the state.

Since, the original call for volunteers for Project Grey Goose, Carr has solicited volunteers for a project he calls "Grey Balloons," which is an open-ended project to create a standing pool of volunteers that are ready and able to help the U.S., intelligence community with whatever challenges it might face. Grey Balloons is a reflection of Carr's "hope that a bridge could be established connecting intelligence community professionals with independent volunteers with the necessary expertise". Finally, as in the case of Rossmiller and cyber-counterterrorism, there is profit to be made in assisting the state.

In 2009, Project Grey Goose became Grey Logic, "a consultancy and information services provider to governments". It is perhaps unsurprising then that Sinkowitsch and Klimburg have encouraged Western governments to promote and support the formation of STNs as a necessary component of their national cyber security strategies. Finally, there are real reasons for concern when it comes to STNs. When questioned about the legal status of STNs and whether their work borders on vigilantism, Sinkowitsch claimed that there is no legal problem with what STNs do because they rely on information that is freely available on the Web; they are merely collecting and analysing it in a different, more effective way.

But recent scandals over advertiser use of social media content, as well as the case of a defence contractor mining and analysing social media content to smear supporters of WikiLeaks and political opponents of the U.S., Chamber of Commerce, indicate that there are legitimate privacy and legal concerns when volunteers begin doing their own online intelligence work on behalf of the state or powerful corporate interests.

ACTIVISM, HACKTIVISM, AND CYBERTERRORISM

The conflict over Kosovo has been characterized as the first war on the Internet. Government and non-government actors alike used the Net to disseminate information, spread propaganda, demonize opponents, and solicit support for their positions.

Hackers used it to voice their objections to both Yugoslav and NATO aggression by disrupting service on government computers and taking over their Web sites. Individuals used it to tell their stories of fear and horror inside the conflict zone, while activists exploited it to amplify their voices and reach a wide, international audience. And people everywhere used it to discuss the issues and share text, images, and video clips that were not available through other media. In April, the Los Angeles Times wrote that the Kosovo conflict was "turning cyberspace into an ethereal war zone where the battle for the hearts and minds is being waged through the use of electronic images, online discussion group postings, and hacking attacks."

Anthony Pratkanis, professor of psychology at the University of California, Santa Cruz, and author of Age of Propaganda: The Everyday Use and Abuse of Persuasion, observed, "What you're seeing now is just the first round of what will become an important, highly sophisticated tool in the age-old tradition of wartime propaganda.... The war strategists should be worried about it, if they aren't yet."

Just how much impact did the Internet have on foreign policy decisions relating the war? It clearly had a part in the political discoursetaking place, and it was exploited by activists seeking to alter foreign policy decisions. It also impacted military decisions. While NATO targeted Serb media outlets carrying Milosovic's propaganda, it intentionally did not bomb Internet service providers or shut down the satellite links bringing the Internet to Yugoslavia. Policy instead was to keep the Internet open. James P. Rubin, spokesman for the U.S. State Department, said "Full and open access to the Internet can only help the Serbian people know the ugly truth about the atrocities and crimes against humanity being perpetrated in Kosovo by the Milosevic regime." Indirectly, the Internet may have also affected public support for the war, which in turn might have affected policy decisions made during the course of the conflict.

The purpose of this paper is to explore how the Internet is altering the landscape of political discourse and advocacy, with particular emphasis on how it is used by those wishing to influence foreign policy. Emphasis is on actions taken by nonstate actors, including both individuals and organizations, but state actions are discussed where they reflect foreign policy decisions triggered by the Internet. The primary sources used in the analysis are news reports of incidents and events. These are augmented with interviews and survey data where available. A more scientific study would be useful.

The paper is organized around three broad classes of activity: activism, hacktivism, and cyberterrorism. The first category, activism, refers to normal, non-disruptive use of the Internet in support of an agenda or cause. Operations in this area includes browsing the Web for information, constructing Web sites and posting materials on them, transmitting electronic publications and letters through e-mail, and using the Net to discuss issues, form coalitions, and plan and coordinate activities. The second category, hacktivism, refers to the marriage of hacking and activism. It covers operations that use hacking techniques against a targets Internet site with the intent of disrupting normal operations but not causing serious damage. Examples are Web sit-ins and virtual blockades, automated e-mail bombs, Web hacks, computer break-ins, and computer viruses and worms. The final category, cyberterrorism, refers to the convergence of cyberspace and terrorism. It covers politically motivated hacking operations intended to cause grave harm such as loss of life or severe economic damage. An example would be penetrating an air traffic control system and causing two planes to collide. There is a general progression toward greater damage and disruption from the first to the third category, although that does not imply an increase of political effectiveness. An electronic petition with a million signatures may influence policy more than an attack that disrupts emergency 911 services.

Although the three categories of activity are treated separately, the boundaries between them are somewhat fuzzy. For example, an e-mail bomb may be considered hacktivism by some and cyberterrorism by others. Also, any given actor may conduct operations across the spectrum. For example, a terrorist might launch viruses as part of a larger campaign of cyberterrorism, all the while using the Internet to collect information about targets, coordinate action with fellow conspirators, and publish propaganda on Web sites. Thus, while the paper distinguishes activists, hacktivists, and terrorists, an individual can play all three roles.

The examples are drawn from the Kosovo conflict, cryptography policy, human rights in China, support for the Mexican Zapatistas, and other areas of conflict. The examples are by no means exhaustive of all activity in any of these areas, but intended only to be illustrative. Nevertheless, they represent a wide range of players, targets, and geographical regions.

The main conclusion of the paper is that the Internet can be an effective tool for activism, especially when it is combined with other communications media, including broadcast and print media and face-to-face meetings with policy makers. It can benefit individuals and small groups with few resources as well as organizations and coalitions that are large or well-funded. It facilitates activities such as educating the public and media, raising money, forming coalitions across geographical boundaries, distributing petitions and action alerts, and planning and coordinating events on a regional or international level. It allows activists in politically repressive states to evade government censors and monitors.

With respect to hacktivism and cyberterrorism, those who engage in such activity are less likely to accomplish their foreign policy objectives than those who do not employ disruptive and destructive techniques. They may feel a sense of empowerment, because they can control government computers and get media attention, but that does not mean they will succeed in changing policy. The main effect is likely to be a strengthening of cyberdefense policies, both nationally and internationally, rather than accommodation to the demands of the actors.

Activism

The Internet offers a powerful tool for communicating and coordinating action. It is inexpensive to use and increasingly pervasive, with an estimated 201 million on-line as of September 1999. Groups of any size, from two to millions, can reach each other and use the Net to promote an agenda. Their members and followers can come from any geographical region on the Net, and they can attempt to influence foreign policy anywhere in the world. This chapter describes five modes of using the Internet: collection, publication, dialogue, coordination of action, and direct lobbying of decision makers. While treated separately, the modes are frequently used together and many of the examples described here illustrate multiple modes.

Collection

One way of viewing the Internet is as a vast digital library. The World Wide Web alone offers about a billion pages of information, and much of the information is free. Activists may be able to locate legislative documents, official policy statements, analyses and discussions about issues, and other items related to their mission.

They may be able to find names and contact information for key decision makers inside the government or governments they ultimately hope to influence. They may be able to identify other groups and individuals with similar interests, and gather contact information for potential supporters and collaborators. There are numerous tools that help with collection, including search engines, e-mail distribution lists, and chat and discussion groups. Many Web sites offer their own search tools for extracting information from databases on their sites.

One advantage of the Internet over other media is that it tends to break down barriers erected by government censors. For example, after Jordanian officials removed an article from 40 print copies of the Economist on sale in Jordan, a subscriber found a copy on-line, made photocopies, and faxed it to 1,000 Jordanians. According to Daoud Kuttab, head of the Arabic Media Internal Network (AMIA), the government would have been better off leaving the print version intact. "We found this very exciting," he said. "For the first time the traditional censorship that exists within national borders was bypassed." Kuttab said AMIA opened Jordanian journalists to the non-Arab world and use of the Web as a research tool. "In the Jordanian media, we have been able to detect a much more open outlook to the world as well as to Arab issues," he said.

The Internet itself is not free of government censorship. According to Reporters Sans Frontiers, 45 countries restrict their citizens' access to the Internet, typically by forcing them to subscribe to a state-run Internet service provider, which may filter out objectionable sites.5 Authoritarian regimes recognize the benefits of the Internet to economic growth, but at the same time feel threatened by the unprecedented degree of freedom of speech.

Chinese authorities block access to Web sites that are considered subversive to government objectives. This has been only partially effective, however, and Chinese activists have found ways of slipping information past the controls. For example, the editors of VIP Reference, a Washington-based electronic magazine with articles and essays about democratic and economic evolution inside China, e-mails their electronic newsletter directly to addresses inside mainland China. The e-mail is sent from a different address every day to get past e-mail blocks. It is also delivered to random addresses, compiled from commercial and public lists, so that recipients can deny having deliberately subscribed. As of January, about 250,000 people received the pro-democracy publication, including people inside the government who did not want it. Chinese officials were not, however, complacent. When 30-year-old Shanghai software entrepreneur Lin Hai sold 30,000 e-mail addresses to VIP Reference, he was arrested and later sentenced to two years in prison. In addition, authorities fined him 10,000 yuan (HK$9,300) and confiscated his computer equipment and telephone. Lin was said to be the first person convicted in China for subversive use of the Internet. He claimed he was only trying to drum up business and was not politically active.

During the Kosovo conflict, people in Yugoslavia had full access to the Internet, including Western news sites. The Washington Post reported that according to U.S. and British officials, the government controlled all four Internet access providers in Yugoslavia and kept them open for the purpose of spreading disinformation and propaganda. The Post also said that Belgrade, with a population of 1.5 million, had about 100,000 Internet connections in mid-April. Individuals without their own connections could get access at Internet cafes.

Even though Serbs had access to Western news reports, both through the Internet and through satellite and cable television, many did not believe what they saw and heard from Western media. They considered coverage on Western television stations such as CNN and Sky News to be as biased as that on the Yugoslav state-run station, citing instances when Western reports of Serbian atrocities turned out to be wrong. Alex Todorovic, a Serbian-American who spent time in Belgrade during the conflict observed, "By and large, Serbs mistrust the rest of the world=s media. CNN, for example, is considered the official voice of Washington." Some Yugoslav surfers did not even bother looking at Western news sites on the Internet. When asked if she visited Web sites of Western news stations, one 22-year-old student replied, "No, I don=t believe in their information, so why should I upset myself?"9 Thus, it is not clear that the decision on the part of either Milosovic or NATO to keep the Internet open in Yugoslavia undermined Milosovics objectives. Further, given that people living in Yugoslavia personally witnessed and felt the effects of the NATO bombing and either disbelieved reports or heard little about Serb atrocities against the ethnic Albanians in Kosovo, it is not surprising that an anti-NATO discourse ran throughout Belgrade. As one pharmacist observed, "I have two children. The people who are bombing my kids are my only enemy right now."

In addition to information relating to a particular policy issue, the Web offers cyberactivists various information that can help them use the Net effectively. For example, NetAction offers a training guide for the virtual activist. The guide provides information on the use of e-mail for outreach, organizing, and advocacy; Web-based outreach and advocacy tools; membership and fundraising; netiquette and policy issues; and various resources.

Publication

The Internet offers several channels whereby advocacy groups and individuals can publish information (and disinformation) to further policy objectives. They can send it through e-mail and post it to newsgroups. They can create their own electronic publications or contribute articles and essays to those of others. They can put up Web pages with documents, images, audio and video clips, and other types of information. The Web sites can serve as a gathering place and source of information for supporters, potential supporters, and onlookers.

One reason the Internet is popular among activists is its cost advantage over traditional mass media. It is easier and cheaper to post a message to a public forum or put up a Web site than it is to operate a radio or television station or print a newspaper. Practically anyone can afford to be a publisher. In addition, the reach of the Internet is global. A message can potentially reach millions of people at no additional cost to the originator. Further, activists can control their presentation to the world. They decide what is said and how. They do not have to rely on the mass media to take notice and tell their story "right."

During the Kosovo conflict, organizations and individuals throughout the world used their Web sites to publish information related to the conflict and, in some cases, to solicit support. Non-government organizations with Kosovo-related Web pages included the press, human rights groups, humanitarian relief organizations, churches, and womens groups. Government Web sites on Kosovo tended to feature propaganda and materials that supported their official policies. An exception was the U.S. Information Agency Web site, which presented a survey of news stories from around the world, some of which were critical of NATO actions. Jonathan Spalter, USIA Chief Information Officer, commented that "The measure of our success is the extent to which we are perceived not as propaganda but anti-propaganda."

The British government's Foreign Office used their Web site, in part, to counter Serb propaganda. Concerned that the Yugoslav public was getting a highly distorted view of the war, Foreign Secretary Robin Cook posted a message on their Web site intended for the Serbs. The message said that Britain has nothing against the Serbs, but was forced to act by the scale of Yugoslav President Slobodan Milosevic's brutality. British Defense Secretary George Robertson said the Ministry of Defence (MoD) had translated its Web site into Serbian to counter censorship by Belgrade of the news.

The Yugoslav media was controlled by the Serbian government and served to promote Milosevic's policies. Yugoslavia had an independent, pro-democracy radio station, B92, but it was raided by the police in the early days of the Kosovo conflict and turned over to a government-appointed station manager. B92 had had a run-in with the government earlier in late 1996 when government jammers tried to keep it from airing news broadcasts. At that time, however, B92 prevailed, in part by encoding their news bulletins in RealAudio format and posting them on a Web site in Amsterdam. Radio Free Europe acquired tapes of the news programs and rebroadcasted them back to the Serbs, circumventing the jammers, who then gave up.

But when the government took over B92's facility in 1999, B92's then-managers ceded to the government and also discontinued posting materials on their Web site, which had offered viewers a reliable source of information about the conflict. This was considered a great loss to Yugoslavia's pro-democracy movement and general public, which had rallied behind Belgrade's top-rated news station.

A few individuals inside Yugoslavia posted to the Internet first-hand accounts of events as they were being witnessed or shortly thereafter. Their stories told of fear and devastation, the latter caused not only by the Serb military, but also by NATO bombs. By all accounts, the situation inside Yugoslavia was horrible for citizens everywhere, whether Serbian or ethnic Albanian. The stories may have inspired activists and influenced public opinion, but it is not clear what if any impact they had on government decision making.

New-media artists used to the Web to voice their opinions on the Balkans conflict. In late March, artist and high-school teacher Reiner Strasser put up a site called Weak Blood, which featured works of visual poetry, kinetic imagery, and interactive art, all making an anti-violence statement. Strasser vowed to add one or two pieces a day "as long as bombs are falling and humans are massacred" in the region.

Some Serbs with Internet access sent e-mails to American news organizations calling for an end to the NATO bombing. Many of the messages contained heated rhetoric that was anti-NATO and anti-U.S. One letter directed to the Associated Press ended, "To be a Serb now is to be helpless ... to listen to the euphemistic and hypocritic phrases as 'peace-making mission,' moral imperative." Other messages contained human stories about how their lives were affected. Tom Reid, London correspondent to the Washington Post, said he received 30-50 messages a day from professors at universities and activists all over Yugoslavia.

The general tenor of the messages was all the same, "'Please remember there are human beings under your bombs,'" he said.

The Serbs used e-mail distribution lists to reach tens of thousands of users, mostly in the United States, with messages attacking the NATO bombing campaign.

One message read AIn the last nine days, NATO barbarians have bombed our schools, hospitals, bridges, killed our people but that was not enough for them now they have started to destroy our culture monuments which represents the core of existence of our nation. Most recipients were annoyed by this unwanted "spam," which the Wall Street Journal dubbed AYugospam.

Dennis Longley, a professor in the Information Security Research Centre at Australia's Queensland University of Technology, said they received a suspicious e-mail from Serbia. The message had two paragraphs. The first was the usual friendly greetings, while the second was a rant about NATO that read like pure propaganda, characterizing NATO as a "terrorist organization" that "brought nothing but a gigantic humanitarian disaster to Kosovo," while attributing the cause of the problem to "albanian terrorist and separatist actions, not the repression by the government security forces." The second paragraph exhibited a style unlike the first and a standard of English well below that of the sender, leading them to speculate that Serb authorities had modified the e-mail. If that is so, one is left wondering how much other anti-NATO talk hitting the Net was the work of the government.

Of course, not all of the messages coming out of the Balkans were anti-NATO. Shortly after the Kosovo conflict began, I found myself on a list called "kcc-news," operated by the Kosova [sic] Crisis Center from the Internet domain "alb-net.com." The messages included Human Rights Flashes from Human Rights Watch, Action Alerts from the Kosova Task Force, and other appeals for support in the war against the Serbs. One message contained a flier calling for "sustained air strikes until total Serb withdrawal" and "ground troops to STOP GENOCIDE now." The flier included links to Web pages that documented Serb atrocities and aggression. Even though the Yugoslav government did not prohibit Internet activity, fear of government reprisals led some to post their messages through anonymous remailers so they could not be identified. This allowed for a freer discourse on Internet discussion groups and contributed to the spread of information about the situation inside Belgrade and Kosovo. Microsoft Corp. initiated a section called "Secret Dispatches from Belgrade" on the Web site of their online magazine Slate. An anonymous correspondent gives daily reports of both alleged Serb atrocities and civilian suffering inflicted by NATO bombs.

After human rights organizations expressed concern that the Yugoslav government might be monitoring Internet activity and cracking down on anyone expressing dissenting views, Anonymizer Inc., a provider of anonymous Web browsing and e-mail services, launched the Kosovo Privacy Project Web site. The site, which went on-line in April, offered surfers anonymous e-mail and instant, anonymous access to Voice of America, Radio Free Europe, and about 20 other Web sites. According to Federal Computer Week, Anonymizer planned to add NATO and other Western government information sites to the Kosovo list, and to launch similar projects for human rights situations in other parts of the world, for example, China. However, the effectiveness of the Kosovo project was never established. In August, USA Today reported that activists said the project was little noticed inside Kosovo, where traditional media seemed unaware while the fighting knocked out Internet trunk lines in short order.

The Internet has raised numerous policy issues in such areas as privacy, encryption, censorship, electronic commerce, international trade, intellectual property protection, taxation, Internet governance, cybercrime, and information warfare, all of which have a foreign policy dimension. As the issues surfaced and took on some urgency, existing industry and public-interest groups began to address them. In addition, both national and international advocacy groups sprung up specifically devoted to Internet issues. They all operate Web sites, where they publish policy papers and information about issues, events, and membership. Many also send out e-mail newsletters and alerts. In the area of encryption policy, for example, the major players include Americans for Computer Privacy (ACP), the Center for Democracy and Technology (CDT), Cyber-Rights & Cyber Liberties, the Electronic

Frontier Foundation (EFF), the Electronic Privacy Information Center (EPIC), the Global Internet Liberty Campaign (GILC), and the Internet Privacy Coalition.

The ACP has perhaps the largest group of constituents, being composed of 40 trade associations, over 100 companies, and more than 3,000 individual members. GILC is one of the most global, with member organizations from Europe, North America, Australia, and Asia. In July 1999, nine leading U.S.-based Internet companies joined forces to become the voice of the Internet on issues such as privacy, consumer protection, and international trade. The industry group, called NetCoalition.com, includes America Online, Amazon.com, eBay, Lycos, Yahoo!, DoubleClick, Excite@Home, Inktomi, and Theglobe.com. The companies represent 7 of the top 10 Internet sites and more than 90% of the world=s Internet users visit one of the sites at least once a month. The group plans to focus on 150 Internet-related bills that were introduced in Congress.

The Internet is used extensively as a publication medium by hackers (including hacktivists) and terrorists. Hackers publish electronic magazines and put up Web sites with software tools and information about hacking, including details about vulnerabilities in popular systems (e.g., Microsoft Windows) and how they can be exploited, programs for cracking passwords, software packages for writing computer viruses, and scripts for disabling or breaking into computer networks and Web sites. In March 1997, an article in the New York Times reported that there were an estimated 1,900 Web sites purveying hacking tips and tools, and 30 hacker publications.

Terrorist groups use the Internet to spread propaganda. Back in February 1998, Hizbullah was operating three Web sites: one for the central press office (www.hizbollah.org), another to describe its attacks on Israeli targets (www.moqawama.org), and the third for news and information (www.almanar.com.lb). That month, Clark Staten, executive director of the Emergency Response & Research Institute (ERRI) in Chicago, testified before a U.S. Senate subcommittee that "even small terrorist groups are now using the Internet to broadcast their message and misdirect/misinform the general population in multiple nations simultaneously." He gave the subcommittee copies of both domestic and international messages containing anti-American and anti-Israeli propaganda and threats, including a widely distributed extremist call for A jihad (holy war) against America and Great Britain. In June 1998, U.S. News & World Report noted that 12 of the 30 groups on the U.S. State Department=s list of terrorist organizations are on the Web. As of August 1999, it appears that virtually every terrorist group is on the Web, along with a mishmash of freedom fighters, crusaders, propagandists, and mercenaries. Forcing them off the Web is impossible, because they can set up their sites in countries with free-speech laws. The government of Sri Lanka, for example, banned the separatist Liberation Tigers of Tamil Eelam, but they have not even attempted to take down their London-based Web site.

Dialogue

The Internet offers several venues for dialogue and debate on policy issues. These include e-mail, newsgroups, Web forums, and chat. Discussions can be confined to closed groups, for example through e-mail, as well as open to the public. Some media sites offer Web surfers the opportunity to comment on the latest stories and current issues and events. Government officials and domain experts may be brought in to serve as catalysts for discussion, debate issues, or answer questions. Discussion can even take place on Web sites that themselves lack such facilities. Using Gooey software from the Israeli company Hypernix, for example, visitors to a Web site can chat with other Gooey users currently at the site.

Internet discussion forums are frequently used to debate, blast, and maybe even attempt to influence government policies. Encryption policy, for example, is discussed on the e-mail lists "cypherpunks" and "ukcrypto" and on several newsgroups, including alt.privacy and sci.crypt.

The ukcrypto list created was created in early 1996 by two academics, Ross Anderson (Cambridge) and Paul Leyland (Oxford), and one person then in government, Brian Gladman (NATO SHAPE), who was acting outside his official capacity. Motivated by a concern that a lack of public discussion and debate in the

United Kingdom on cryptography issues was allowing the government to set policies that they believed were not in interests of the United Kingdom and its citizens, they formed the list with the objective of impacting cryptography policy. They were concerned both with domestic policy, particularly proposals to restrict the use of cryptography by U.K. citizens, and on foreign policy, particularly export controls. As of May 1999, the list has 300 subscribers, including government officials responsible for U.K.policy and persons in other countries, including the United States. Many of the key contributors held influential positions in other policy making fora. Focus is on U.K. policy issues, but items of international interest are also discussed, including export controls adopted under the Wassenaar Arrangement (31 countries participate); policy changes adopted by France, the United States, and other countries; policy statements from the European Union and other organizations; and some technical issues.

Gladman believes the list has made four contributions:

(1) educating many about the policy issues and encouraging journalists and writers to write about them;

(2) bringing individual and industry views closer together and allowing U.K. industry to see more clearly that agreeing with their government may not be a good thing if private citizens do not support government policy;

(3) encouraging the more progressive voices in government to speak out and argue from within government that their views represent those of the public; and

(4) bringing groups together that were previously campaigning separately. "The most significant contribution of ukcrypto is not direct," Gladman said. "It is the contribution that it has made in promoting an educated community of commentators and a forum for the review of what government is doing that is fully open."

On the downside, some postings on ukcrypto may alienate the very government officials the authors hope to influence. According to Gladman, Adiscussions on the list can become slinging matches that quickly put those in government on the defensive and hence inclined to discount what is being said. It would be more effective if we had a way of focusing on the issues and not the personalities. But Andrew Brown gave ukcrypto high marks, crediting it with most of the thought and co-ordination behind the successful campaign to keep strong cryptography legal and widely available. "There, for the past two years, the civil servants responsible for policy have actually been available, more or less, to the people who disagree with them," he wrote in New Statesman. "They have had to justify their actions, not to the public, but to a small group of geographically dispersed experts ... It's a kind of updated version of Lions v Christians."

Nigel Hickson, one of the principal players in the policy debates from the U.K. Department of Trade and Industry, agrees the Internet and ukcrypto in particular have played a role in shaping U.K. cryptography policy. But he was also critical of the list: "Whilst ukcyrpto has undoubtedly had an influence on the development of UK encryption policy, it has tended to polarise the debate into extremes. This may be because there tends to be a large silent majority on the list who do not directly contribute because o f commercial or policy reasons." Besides participating in ukcrypto, the DTI has published draft consultation documents on the Web for comment. Many of the comments they receive arrive through electronic mail. DTI has also met with industry groups and participated in non-Internet forums such as conferences and seminars. These have also helped shape policy decisions.

There are Usenet newsgroups and other interactive forums that focus on practically every conceivable topic relating to foreign (and domestic) policy. Whether these are effective or not in terms of influencing policy is another matter. After studying the impact of the Net on the American political system, Richard Davis, a political science professor at Brigham Young University and author of The Web of Politics, observed that "In Usenet political discussions, people talk past one another, when they are not verbally attacking each other. The emphasis is not problem solving, but discussion dominance." Davis also found interactivity on the Internet to be primarily an illusion: "Interest groups, party organizations, and legislators seek to use the Web for information dissemination, but they are rarely interested in allowing their sites to become forums for the opinions of others."

CYBER-WAR ATTACKS

Beyond the attacks that one might envision in the context of classic IW and C2W, there are other vulnerabilities. For example:

- Attacks by creative individuals skilled and determined enough to exploit communications systems and computer networks for illegal gain or to disrupt society.
- Criminal organizations (terrorists, drug smugglers, illegal arms merchants, international poachers, and rogue banking groups) that sit across any one country's boundaries, move money or information from jurisdiction to jurisdiction, and all too often represent a poorly met challenge.
- Coalition warfare in which military cooperation and interoperability are essential, but political goals are not fully compatible and intelligence sources and methods must be protected.
- Psychological warfare waged against a general population in order to undermine confidence in leaders or the wisdom of their actions, often exploiting ethnic, social, or moral cleavages in the target society.

This wide range of possibilities caused considerable discussion before the group could agree on the various types of computer attacks that must be considered. Initially, some felt the discussion should focus only on protection of internal DoD systems, while others wanted to include broad strategic or operational attacks on the banking system or other commercial or quasi-governmental arenas. The workshop was aware, however, of an ACTIS analysis of Defensive Information Warfare the third and final part of the workshop read-ahead material) that differentiates attacks by their targets and implications into:

- Day-to-day or routine attacks with limited or diffuse impact on U.S. interests. These include "normal" hacking for fun and profit, typical white collar crime, and other attacks with discrete impact.
- Potentially strategic (catastrophic) attacks. These are limited attacks with unpredictable consequences that could, under some circumstances or in some combinations, have

catastrophic implications for U.S. interests. For example, an attack on a single bank, even if the losses are large (millions), is no threat to the U.S. banking system. However, an orchestrated and publicized series of successful attacks on individual banks could undermine confidence in the banking system and create a much more serious problem, even though the specific attacks were each quite limited.

- Strategic (catastrophic) attacks are those which, if successful, will in themselves do great harm to the United States. Destruction of the systems that control systems in key industries and leave them so they cannot be repaired promptly would fall into this category.

In addition, workshop participants stressed that not all information warfare attacks on computer systems need take the form of computer intrusion. Physical destruction of crucial telephone switching stations or other national information infrastructure assets would, in them-selves, be very damaging.

One significant finding was that the workshop participants consistently found themselves assuming that a visible set of defenses was the beginning point for deterring attacks on important computer systems. In essence, the argument was that attacks are instrumental acts and will not occur if the attacking party perceives little opportunity for success.

At the same time, the workshop also noted that "success" has very different meaning for different types of actors. Some individuals, particularly those with "typical" hacker attitudes, would be likely to perceive a more robust defensive posture as a challenge, not as discouragement. This, of course, is a lesson in the need for specific contexts when discussing deterrence and IW. What works in some circumstances may be very wrong for others.

Regardless of whether good defenses necessarily deter attacks, there was consensus that the set of defenses now in place is inadequate for discouraging any but the least well prepared intruder. As mentioned earlier, many systems are poorly protected, very few intrusions are detected, and very few of those detected are actually reported. Improved indications and warning, as well as improved reporting of detected attacks, are essential elements of improved defensive systems. In essence, the workshop concluded that assessing the ability of DoD or others to deter attacks will require much better documentation and understanding of the pattern of attacks being experienced.

Deterrence of cyber-attacks was also understood to depend on the nature of the attacker. On one level, deterrence requires identification of the values held by the potential attacker as well as the capacity to communicate with that attacker. Neither is possible without information about the nature of the person, group, or entity to be deterred. The variety of potential attackers is vast, which makes it impossible to create a "one size fits all" deterrence policy that will be effective. However, cyber-attacks and physical attacks on key computer systems can be prevented or discouraged by aggressive, visible, effective defensive systems. Analogies were drawn to terrorists, who also act from a variety of motives against a wide range of targets (including information domain targets), but who have been deterred in selected instances by explicit threats and retaliatory actions implying future threats unless the terrorists cease to attack some types of targets.

There is no single, simple solution. However, combinations of defensive measures are important initial building blocks. Further, defense against information attacks should be viewed as a continuing process rather than a "finishable" project. The process begins with awareness of the issues and problems and proceeds to indoctrination, education, training, and physical defensive measures. Awareness, education, and security training are being taught within the DoD but need to be improved across all levels. It would also appear that DoD should reach out further and address the issues to other government agencies and relevant non-governmental organizations through interagency seminars, vulnerability analysis, and training.

Systems vulnerability analysis is a critical first step. We should lay out our potential target sets and interconnecting networks and look for actual and potential vulnerabilities. Defensive nodal analysis (like that conducted in offensive command and control warfare) is particularly important. Once the weaknesses are identified, defensive measures should be put in place. Table 1 lists some of the common and accepted system defenses.

Information Systems Defensive Measures

- Systems Vulnerability Analysis
- Systems Hardening
- Security Training
- Redundancy and Backup
- Aggressive Law Enforcement
- Tagging Hardware and Software with Electronic ID
- Embracing (Systems Interdependency with Potential Attackers)

Systems vulnerability analysis and improved design can yield three positive results. Besides the obvious result of reducing vulnerability, the systems can be made less attractive targets; that is, successful attacks would yield less damage and publicity. As stated by VADM Cebrowski (the JCS J-6, and workshop luncheon speaker), decoupling IW attacks from their objectives is an effective deterrent technique. Since IW attacks, like almost all types of attack, are assumed to be conducted for instrumental purposes, he argued that de-coupling the attack from its goal was an important way to ensure such attacks were unsuccessful and also to deter the attacks themselves because the attackers saw little opportunity for success. Good design can also raise the potential costs of attacking in terms of time and equipment needed to penetrate. This also has a deterrent effect. Hardening and protective measures should be designed into all systems. This is an enormous field that spans the spectrum from satellite antenna design to electrical protection of personal computers and workstations.

Security training is absolutely essential at all levels, and without it other defensive measures are less effective. Password protection, for example, can make information systems less accessible, but bad procedures can defeat its purpose. One of the workshop participants described security exercises where he was able to penetrate password-protected computer networks by manipulating the password protection system itself. Perhaps more important, almost every penetration and technique tried on that exercise and those in the experience of other workshop participants had been successful in the vast majority of cases. Hence, the need for basic system security design, improved security procedures, and better training within DoD.

Other key steps include redundancy and backup. These methods reduce or limit the harmful effects of an attack or system penetration. Frequent backup can minimize the damage caused by lost, stolen, or disrupted data, and information can be rapidly restored or reconstituted. Redundant baseline data can also be used to check against unwanted changes or clandestine data manipulation.

Aggressive domestic and international law enforcement can certainly have a deterrent effect on potential adversaries. Since cyberspace recognizes no borders, international agreements and laws are necessary. This is particularly important because many information systems are not only national, but also worldwide. Telecommunications and international banking systems are prime examples. Further, hackers appear motivated by the challenge of defeating defenses. Defenses alone apparently just make hacking more enjoyable. To deter hackers, there must be a realistic threat of capture and punishment.

Tagging information systems hardware and software with electronic IDs can also deter would-be penetrators and attackers. The analogy is similar to caller ID, where those who penetrate systems are identified, and a record of the penetration is made.

"Embracing" is a concept that engages potential attackers by including them as stakeholders in the information system. By embracing and educating these possible adversaries, they may be less likely to consider attacks that could potentially cause self-harm. The concept is already in effect since many systems are worldwide, and an attack by one nation on another could have cascading effects beyond those intended. An attack on the banking system in one nation, for example, could have unintended consequences and cause disruptions around the world. Embracing would appear to have deterrent effect only on rational nation-states. There are two weaknesses to the concept. First, it is doubtful that cyber-terrorists would be deterred in such a scenario; rather, cascading consequences might actually make the attack more attractive. Second, what may be viewed as embracing by one party may instead be an opportunity for infiltration by the other. Again no "one size fits all" deterrence policy is available because of the range of motives that may be encountered.

Finally, we must develop an effective system of IW attack indications and warnings (I&W). The adage of "forewarned is forearmed" is particularly relevant here. Indications of attack can come from traditional intelligence sources, monitoring of events and activity, and perhaps other cyber-tags that we have yet to discover. Penetration warning systems should be designed and built into critical information networks, nodes and stations. Cyber I&W is an area that needs much more careful study, analysis, and debate.

Many of the defensive measures discussed are not unique to the deterrence arena, but rather reflect the workshop participants' assumption that some attacks will be deterred by effective defenses. The technical representatives in the workshop also stressed that for the foreseeable future the advantage will lie with the offense in the cyber-war arena. Hence, building defenses does not guarantee success, and creating redundancy as well as the capacity to contain, recover from, and reconstitute in spite of successful attacks are essential elements of a successful strategy.

An interactive exercise scenario introduced the topic of "SOFTWAR," which is a trade name for one concept of media war. This concept involves the use of television images to change or modify the political will of an opponent. SOFTWAR was defined as "the hostile utilization of instantaneous global television to shape another nation's will by changing its view of reality." The main technique of SOFTWAR is to unglue the adversary government's hold on the unifying national mass communications system, the most powerful medium of which is television, and distribute alternate video productions (or some other form of video manipulation) in its place. The speaker asserted that the controlled projection of video information has joined economic, political, and military power as a pillar of national security and that it will become a co-equal power by the year 2020.

The exercise scenario involved a campaign aimed initially at public attitudes in friendly and other regional countries whose cooperation is essential to major U.S. operations in and around the Persian Gulf, and later at public attitudes in the United States. In the demonstration scenario, the U.S. was the victim of a carefully orchestrated television campaign aimed at both the U.S. TV audience and at a selected Middle East and North Africa audience within the footprint of a direct broadcast satellite. The thrust of the argument was that prudent, even essential, military actions could well be called into question through media attacks with primarily political messages.

Some workshop participants were skeptical about the impact such a campaign might have on U.S. resolve and action. There are, however, past examples of how TV has affected U.S. political action going back to the Vietnamese War when rather primitive TV reporting (by today's standards) brought bloody battlefield images into U.S. homes for the first time. There is little doubt that television coverage of Vietnam changed or eroded the will of the U.S. population to sustain the conflict. Likewise, TV images of the bombing of the U.S. Marine Barracks in Lebanon tested our resolve and hastened our departure.

More recent examples include the Somalian relief mission where graphic, quite gruesome TV images of relatively light U.S. casualties soured the support for continued presence and led to an early U.S. pullout. In Haiti, TV images of U.S. soldiers standing by while Haitian police beat innocent people celebrating the arrival of U.S. forces caused an overnight change in policy as to how Rules of Engagement (ROE) were interpreted. The workshop agreed that indeed, television is an extremely effective, and potentially dangerous, medium for propaganda. Given the ability of modern technology to manipulate images, it becomes an even more powerful IW weapon. Several other conclusions emerged from the media war discussions:

- First, because of its democratic traditions and freedom of speech considerations, the United States will almost certainly be placed in a reactive mode if a hostile media war campaign is launched.
- Second, foreign powers will find it difficult to intimidate U.S. leaders or to put forward obviously false information

toward the U.S. public without effective U.S. media responses, but may be able to communicate quite inaccurate images to selected foreign publics who are predisposed toward them.

- Third, the infrastructure to deliver television images into distant regions may not be readily available within DoD, particularly in a non-warfare situation where the sovereignty of foreign states must be respected. Review of the hardware requirements for flexible responses that give the National Command Authority a rich set of options appears to be wise. Equally important, the workshop concluded that the creation of reserve units or other mechanisms to ensure the availability of the human capital needed for commercial quality television production on a sustained basis, also appears wise.
- Fourth, wargames and seminars involving not only DoD, but also the range of civilian agencies and industry representatives necessary for effective television imagery in media wars, appear to be needed. Incorporation of meaningful media attacks into appropriate military exercises is an important first step, but would be inadequate in itself over the long run.
- Fifth, media warfare can put enormous time pressure on U.S. and allied decision making, particularly when the adversary is an authoritarian state with little or no necessity for either internal or international consultation. With proper preparation and effective technical support, however, this time pressure can be managed.

Policy Issues

Many of the workshop discussions naturally evolved into policy explorations. Two of the most prominent were: one, "Should the United States have a declarative policy about its response to IW attacks?" and two, "Should information be viewed as a separate element of national power?" Opinion was divided on both issues. The workshop participants were strongly in favor of a declared policy, with 70 percent voting for such a policy, 17 percent against, and 13 percent ambivalent. A declared policy was considered essential if there was to be any deterrent effect. Further, without a policy, there is no direction for the government, and many agencies are going their own ways and establishing their own policies. If we are to have cooperative international agreements and treaties, a declared policy is an essential starting point. The policy should be coordinated with industry and public debate encouraged to secure support and resources required to protect our interests. The overall workshop consensus was that there should be a broad, publicly stated, general policy phrased in terms of effects rather than method or type of attack (e.g., economic, military, social, political). One recommended statement was: "Attacks on the U.S., its infrastructure, or other interests (by whatever means) will receive an appropriate response using the fullest range of U.S. capabilities."

Those who were ambivalent or opposed to a declared policy were generally concerned that such a policy was premature, that we lacked sufficient understanding of IW attacks and their effects and consequences. By not stating a specific policy, we create ambiguity, which some felt was useful in terms of deterrence. There is much to think through before declaring an IW policy particularly in terms of the international implications and complications. Finally, and somewhat in agreement with those who advocated a formal policy, one reason not to have a policy is simply that there is no need to separate IW from other kinds of attacks.

On the second issue, whether information should be viewed as a separate element of national power, opinion was also divided; however, most participants viewed information as a separate element of national power.

All participants agreed that information was an essential element of power. The debate ranged around whether that should be stated explicitly or not. Those in favor (80 percent) cited the growing importance of information and information age technologies, and how information is creating a cultural revolution and changes in the behavior processes between nation-states. For those who voted "no" (20 percent), the major consideration was that they viewed information as ubiquitous and pervasive in each element of power, and not an independent element.

One participant made the analogy that information was like "electricity." It is subsumed in other elements and systems.

There were numerous other questions with policy implications and these included:

- What is (what constitutes) an information attack?
- When is an information attack an act of war?
- How do we verify an attack?
- How do we determine or confirm the attacker?
- Does penetration into an information system equate to an attack?
- Can one develop a concept of hostile intent for IW?
- Are there reasonable or potential tripwires?
- How do we respond, and who should respond?

Since at present no one has the charter for IW (in the larger context -- beyond C2W) responses will be ad hoc at best. The boundary between DoD and the rest of the national infrastructure is blurred and undefined. The workshop reached no consensus as to where that line should be or what DoD's role should be within the larger context.

IW policy issues emerged as the area that needed much further study. Without policy definition, concepts like IW and deterrence can't be fully explored. Policy is essential and the workshop participants recommended a follow-on roundtable to explore policy issues. Basic policy statements have begun emerging, but final work appears necessary.

The Role of DoD

Given the low rate of reporting system penetrations and other security problems, the U.S. presently lacks the data needed to know just how serious the unauthorized penetration problem might be. Are we hemorrhaging or simply suffering "duck bites"? Better reporting is essential.

The starting point for DoD should be to raise the level of awareness, not only within the Department, but also throughout the national information infrastructure upon which it is so vulnerably dependent. Developing and implementing cyber I&W should also take high priority. One note of concern voiced was that the DoD procurement cycles and information technology growth cycles are greatly mismatched.

That is, several technology cycles occur within one DoD procurement cycle. This can result in DoD developing yesterday's solutions for tomorrow's problems.

DoD's next priority should be a comprehensive vulnerability analysis, first of DoD systems and later expanded to the national infrastructure upon which they depend. At present, vulnerability is usually assessed for only a particular system or subsystem. Future vulnerability analyses should expand the studies to examine interrelated systems, and systems of systems. In due course, the analyses should be expanded to include all U.S. systems. We should implement defensive and deterrent actions as soon as vulnerabilities are uncovered.

Beyond DoD, there is a need for a national level, strategic debate to formulate a coherent IW policy and a determination of DoD's boundaries and responsibilities. Neither DoD nor the Federal Government can do this alone; all relevant public and private sectors should be included. But until there is policy about IW defense and deterrence, DoD still has the responsibility to protect its strategic, operational and tactical systems. The strategic systems appear reasonably well protected and redundant through hardening, elaborate security procedures, and multiple backups. Operational and tactical systems appear far less protected and need additional emphasis.

Core Conclusion

While recognizing that the variety of potential attackers, attack contexts, and arenas where information warfare attacks can occur is vast and too complex for simple solutions, the workshop participants were confident that the U.S. already has basic policies in place that serve as effective deterrents in many circumstances. In essence, information warfare attacks on the United States are deterred by the same policy that deters other types of attack.

Acting under its rights as a sovereign state, the U.S. stands ready to respond to any attack on its interests with all appropriate means, including law enforcement as well as military capacity. As discussed in the workshop:

- Individual hackers and white collar criminals are liable when they break the law and can be prosecuted within a legal system that takes into account both their motives and the degree of harm that they cause.
- International criminal enterprises, such as drug cartels, terrorist groups, or interest groups willing to engage in illegal information attacks or manipulation, are liable under the legal system and also pursued under international law and treaties that govern their behavior and specify both the jurisdictions and processes for determining their punishment if caught.
- Nation states are restricted by the rights of others and liable for a range of political, economic, diplomatic, or military sanctions if they undertake information operations that harm U.S. interests. As in other arenas, the U.S. reserves the right to undertake actions it perceives to be both appropriate and proportional.

There was also consensus that information attacks may well pose some unusual challenges that may make them more difficult to deter. For example, information warfare attackers will likely seek to be anonymous, thereby making it impossible for the U.S. to punish them. Cyber-attackers, in particular, have a variety of mechanisms by which they can hide their identity. Since certainty of punishment is a prerequisite for deterrence, anonymity is an effective counter-strategy.

Moreover, information attacks can be hidden or made to look like natural events. In media war, this may be a half-truth fed to an aggressive reporter. In cyber-war it can be a destructive attack made to look like a system error or design flaw. Disguised attacks are also effective countermeasures for deterrence, regardless of the capability and will of the actor. Hence, while significant, overall U.S. capability and will do not guarantee deterrence of information attacks.

Finally, the workshop recognized that considerable legal work needs to be completed in this arena. First, U.S. law (both state and federal) needs to be clear about the definition of crimes in the information arena. Second, international agreements and treaties are needed to ensure that information criminals can be prosecuted effectively.

Cases in which lack of appropriate law limited or prevented prosecution were easy for participants to recall. The Departments of Justice and State are generally aware of these needs and interagency working groups have been making some progress on them, but this area will require continued effort for some time to come.

5

Intelligence for Cyber Space

Although many of the intelligence methodologies and principles remain the same, new ways of thinking appropriate to the cyber-domain are essential. The lack of borders in cyber-space is a critical difference from the more familiar domains of intelligence. Indeed, geography and political borders often aided traditional military intelligence analysis-it is a simple thing to develop threat scenarios if the potential enemy can only use certain terrain or sea lines of communication and then, only at certain times of the year-while simple factors of physics such as time and distance also provided opportunities for warning. Within the Internet, however, these limiting factors are absent, (although other limiting factors, such as geometry of network connectivity, might exist in a form useful to be incorporated into intelligence analysis), contributing to what can appear to be “instantaneous threats”.

Assessment of cyber-space threats requires not only a merger of old methodologies and new modes of thinking but also analysts willing and able to approach the art of threat assessment and warning from new perspectives. Only with a distinctive blend of the traditional and the new will it be possible to obtain real understanding of threats and vulnerabilities, to differentiate among types of intrusions and to forecast or anticipate specific incidents or clusters of incidents in ways that lengthen warning time. Enhancing the ability to identify perpetrators is also highly desirable: removing the cloak of anonymity would make perpetrators more concerned about the potential costs and risks of their actions and could have an important deterrent effect. In short, there are several fundamental questions at the heart of the intelligence process. They consist of variations on the who, what, when, where, why and how questions that are familiar parts of most research and analysis.

Security Challenging

Efforts to identify intruders are critical both to the assessment of the challenge and the nature of the response. Potential intruders run the gamut from young hobbyists engaged in the equivalent of joy riding to terrorist organizations and nations that are intent on maximizing damage to the target. The problem of identification is particularly difficult in a domain where maintaining anonymity is easy and there are sometimes time lapses between the intruder action, the intrusion itself, and the actual disruptive effects. Moreover, the consequences are not always commensurate with the objectives, in some cases falling short of what the intruders hoped to achieve, and in others going well beyond what they had envisaged.

There is a broad spectrum of potential intruders on the Internet and an almost equal number of motives for intrusions against organizations. Not surprisingly, this includes perpetrators conducting operations against other perpetrators. As enticing as this prospect is, it does not mitigate the effects of such internecine rivalry. New and more sophisticated tools are often the result of such interplay. This sort of jousting can also provide valuable insights to analysts once it is recognized, but does not simplify the analytic task and puts an incredible strain on limited analytic/ warning resources. With the continuing proliferation of sophisticated computer technologies into the mainstream population, attribution for an intrusion becomes more difficult by the day.

The dynamism of the intruder population is itself a problem. On the one hand, success breeds imitation and the sophistication of readily available tools means that even those with limited skills can become intruders.

On the one hand, there is a certain degree of attrition in the intruder community. Indeed, there are many reasons why intruders might cease their activity, including increased maturity, a need to find gainful employment, and a perception of the rewards of working to increase network security rather than attack it. The implication, of course, is that the mix of agents threatening network security is changing as the nature of the Internet changes.

The vast majority of the intrusions are probably being conducted by nuisance hackers or "ankle-biters" who have limited objectives and are usually satisfied with the actual penetration of the system or conduct relatively harmless cyber-vandalism such as the defacement or alteration of web-sites. While aggravating to the target, no significant or lasting damage occurs. The more serious problem occurs when an intrusion is carried out by a more sophisticated intruder (either an individual or a group) whose objective is better defined and involves malicious intent. Motives for these sorts of intrusions are also as varied as the persons carrying them out. They range from greed to defined military strategy and doctrine, and all that falls in between.

Four of the more dangerous, and less well defined categories of intruder are governments conducting operations against other sovereign states, the organized terrorist group, insurgency or revolutionary groups, and organized crime. All these entities are beginning to appreciate the potential power, anonymity, and effectiveness of the Internet. There are myriad examples of governments instituting programmes for Computer Network Warfare. In the case of Russia, policy-makers consider the security of their information infrastructure so critical that–rhetorically at least-they equate an attack against it with a strategic nuclear strike (and have promised an appropriate response). As a result of the realization of the criticality of information infrastructures, computer warfare is now a part of the formal Russian Military Strategy and Doctrine. The same is true of organized terrorist groups. In fact, "most of the 30 top terrorist organizations identified by the U.S. government have web pages and use e-mail, and are ``fairly well developed'' at using the Internet."[Casciano] In many cases, dependence on technology is viewed as an Achilles Heel to be exploited by terrorist organizations.

Within the U.S., many of the more militant indigenous groups have discovered the power of the Internet and have well designed and effective Web sites. Indeed, militia and supremacist groups have had significant increases in membership since developing their Web pages. It is a natural progression from using the Internet for propaganda and recruiting to exploiting its potential as a weapon. There is also growing evidence that some of the active insurgency groups around the world are discovering the potential of the computer. It is just a matter of time until they discover the effect of a computer-generated attack against the infrastructure of the government they are fighting. Once that realization is made, cyber-attacks will likely become a weapon of choice for organizations intent on overthrowing an existing government. Disturbingly, Aum Shinrikyo, the group responsible for the Sarin gas attack on the Japanese subway, has increasingly been involved in the Japanese software industry!

Organized crime probably was the first of the sophisticated intruder threats to realize the power and value of the computer. In 1995, it was discovered that the Cali cartel had sophisticated state-of-the-art equipment for electronic eavesdropping, while smaller drug trafficking organizations in Colombia are using the Internet to pressure the Colombian government to change the policy of extraditing traffickers to the United States. Furthermore, the use of computers by organized crime organizations to garner illicit profits is well documented. However, some criminal efforts have gone beyond simple siphoning of funds and money laundering. Extortion of money from financial institutions by threatening to destroy or modify their computer databases is also evident. It is probable that at least some of these extortion operations are conducted by transnational criminal groups. Some of the extortion efforts go wrong–as did the effort to extort Bloomberg. In other cases, however, large payoffs are almost certainly made to the extortionist. It seems likely, therefore, that larger and potentially more dangerous operations should be anticipated.

The obvious challenge is to develop a capacity to identify and track the activities of these potential intruders with the goal of being able to provide predictive analysis and warning of intrusions. Some of the traditional intelligence techniques should apply to these threats, but new methodologies and the ability to contemplate new and complex concepts have to be developed concurrently. This will become even more important (and difficult) as perpetrators of increasing sophistication operate on the Internet. As motivations vary, so will the efforts of the individuals behind malicious operations to either conceal or reveal their responsibility. All of this complicates efforts to track responsible parties determine attribution. Nations and transnational criminal organizations, by their nature, will be diligent in their efforts to maintain anonymity. In some of these cases, identifying the intended victim may give valuable insight into tracking the intruder. Sometimes the target of an intrusion allows the analyst to rule out certain possible perpetrators. A multi-million dollar extortion plot against a major financial institution is probably not the work of a 13-year-old hacker working out of his bedroom. At the same time, however, many victims, especially within government or sensitive industries such as banking or insurance, often complicate the effort to track intruders because of their reluctance to report the incident. In other cases, such as politically motivated attacks, the perpetrators may want their identity known, but not their location. As such operations become more sophisticated, tracking the attack back to its point of origin will be a major challenge to the intelligence analysts involved. What is clear from all of this is that tracking intruders and gaining attribution is much more than just a technical challenge.

One difficulty, of course, is that there are legal constraints on intelligence collection, especially by the military and the national security establishment. Traditionally the focus of intelligence has been on foreign threats, and there are restrictions on intelligence activities directed against individuals or groups that are domestic in nature. Insofar as these groups are the focus of government attention, it is from the law enforcement community. This points to yet another problem: that of coordination and information sharing between the traditional national security agencies and the law enforcement community. Generally law enforcement focuses on individual cases and wants evidence that stands up in court; intelligence agencies in contrast are concerned with protecting the sources of their information so that they can continue to use them.

The problem with cyber-threats is that they fall in the gray area where crime and national security merge into one another.

Forms of Intrusion are Occurring

It is tempting to see intrusions in terms of a pyramid that goes from transient vulnerability probing and defacing web-sites at the base to large scale efforts to undermine the critical missions of an organization or the critical functions of a nation at the top-and to suggest that there is an inverse relationship between frequency and significance, with many trivial incidents and comparatively few of the more serious incidents. There are several difficulties with this however. The first is that probes that appear relatively insignificant could be a harbinger of more serious intrusions. The second is that there is sometimes a gap between intent and consequences–the effects and impact of an incident can either fall far short of what was intended, or far exceed what the perpetrator initially envisaged. This lack of congruence between limited intent and far-reaching consequences stems from the capacity of worms and viruses for infinite replication and multiplication combined with the seamless inter-connectivity of systems. Incidents such as the Love Bug cross the public-private divide and have an indiscriminate impact on corporations, governments, and private individuals irrespective of the initial target. In cases such as this, the consequences have less to do with targeting than with the ubiquity of a particular programme such as Microsoft Outlook that is used as the vector of transmission. In effect, the incident takes on its own momentum.

When the consequences are widespread, of course, the incident becomes very public and is the subject of much media and official commentary. In many other cases, however, there is far greater reticence about the scale, type and targets of attack. The analytic effort must successfully build a trust relationship for the collection of data across a broad variety of organizations. This trust relationship allows for observation of incidents from early probing and experimentation through widespread deployment of automated forms of intrusion. For example, in recent months (June and July 2000) CERTÒ/CC has received reports of intrusions involving a wide variety of automated tools, ranging from simple viruses and system corruption toolkits through complex viruses designed to attack relatively hardened sites with low probability of detection and distributed tools designed to crash network infrastructure. Roughly 10%-25% of the CERT/CC reports involve viruses. Roughly 20%-40% are intrusions where the victim site cannot discern the type of the intrusion from available data. The remaining intrusions are a large number of other forms of intrusion, including compromise of system administration accounts, web defacements, reconnaissance attempts and misuse of computing resources.

Being intruded Upon

Determining who are the victims of intrusions is, in some respects, an enormously significant part of the intelligence process. It is important-at least in those cases where attacks are not indiscriminate-to differentiate between public and private targets, to distinguish infrastructure targets from individual targets, to distinguish between intrusions that focus on targets of convenience and those that are much more precise and calculated. For example, existing analysis has shown a link between port scanning and certain types of later intrusions, but this needs to be more fully explored to provide for effective warnings. Profiling victims can sometimes play a critical role in determining the nature of the intrusion and the nature of the intruders. For this to be done, understanding is needed of the level of "background noise", probes and intrusion attempts occurring across the Internet. Once understood, it may be possible to isolate this activity from the more significant activity directed at a particular victim.

Victim profiles will be just as important, in terms of strategic intelligence analysis of the Internet, as profiling potential intruders. The more serious the intrusion, the more critical this sort of profiling will be. One of the potential hurdles to this effort, however, will be the natural tendency of the victim, whether private or public, to withhold sensitive or proprietary information. A few examples of this kind of reticence would be financial institutions withholding information about loses due to intrusions; companies failing to divulge the nature of an intrusion due to proprietary corporate data; or a government agency protecting information that is sensitive or even classified. Beyond simply protecting proprietary or sensitive data, there are also serious legal questions that have not yet been resolved in the courts or in the legislature. These include constitutional guarantees of privacy; contradictory national laws (or lack of laws) as perpetrators use the global network; laws limiting various governmental agency's efforts to track down the source of an intrusion, and the need to determine what is domestic and what is foreign.

If these barriers can be overcome, critical information will become available. Details of the victim's infrastructure, the nature of the intrusion, identity clues left by the intruder, network traffic flow as observed by the victim site, and intrusion tools left as artifacts on the victim hosts can all provide indispensable clues. Without such information, motivation becomes more difficult to define and profiling efforts will be seriously flawed. Some work has already been accomplished in this area by organizations involved in incident monitoring, including the members of the Forum of Incident Response and Security Teams (FIRST) community. Much more remains to be accomplished, however, as new cooperative agreements are forged and additional analytic efforts and methodologies are developed. Furthermore, while it is true that some of the legal restrictions are avoided by the voluntary nature of the cooperative relationships, they are by no means completely overcome. The keys to success seem to be twofold. First, the analytic organization has to prove itself to be a highly secure confidant, never disclosing victim identities while working to assist victims in recovering from intrusions. Second, it must return information that is of value to the victims, including information that might place the intrusion in a larger context as well as providing assistance in dealing with vendors or other sites. More simply put, the exchange of information must be in both directions. Experience with other organizations has shown that neither trustworthiness nor returned value alone is sufficient, but both appear to be required for effective information gathering with victims.

Beyond their reticence, victim organizations are often unaware of critical parts of their security stance. Available data suggests that victims are often not aware that their networks have been intruded upon. The effectiveness of installed security measures is often overestimated. Levels of trust given to users by computing practices are often unwarranted. All of this hampers both analysis and defence.

One of the reasons that profiling the victims is so critical is that it provides insights in to motivations that can greatly assist analysts in predicting future intrusions under similar circumstances. This insight will need to incorporate identification of circumstances that facilitate or hamper intrusion. For example, K-12 educational institutions might offer a significant opportunity for intruders to stage their attacks, since many such institutions lack knowledgeable system administrators. However, such hosts may be removed from the network during summer break and other times when school is not in session. During the Year 2000 rollover, conditions for system intrusion were relatively poor not only because of the active presence of a large number of system administrators, carefully monitoring their systems, but also the significant number of alternative activities available to potential intruders. These examples serve to identify that there exist time-varying circumstances; further analysis is required to delineate these factors more fully.

THE CYBER INTELLIGENCE COMMUNITY

This unique, currently ad hoc, community is made up of government, telecommunication and internet providers, CERTs, and other formal information security entities, specialty companies, and vendors. The members of this community engage in a myriad of activities that could be the potential victim of a cyber threat. This "Cyber Intelligence Community" is currently an informal coalition of the willing that collects and analyses unclassified and classified cyber intelligence data and trends. There is no formal mechanism across industry and government cyber intelligence entities that successfully collects, processes, and analyses all identifiable key cyber threat behaviour and reports it at an unclassified or reasonable classification level to all appropriate customers. An effective connection between intelligence provider and the customer means that the customer has understood and internalized the intelligence resulting in action to work the intelligence and mitigate the threat. Good intelligence professionals relentlessly pursue interactions with customers to ensure that: the data is collected, analysed, and conveyed; the intelligence serves customers' purposes; and some action is being taken (or deliberately not taken). This cycle can be referred to as a constant process of story-finding, storytelling, story-updating, storylistening, and story-heeding. A concept to institutionalize this ad hoc community is currently missing.

Investing in Cyber Intelligence Tradecraft

A substantial and continuing investment in cyber intelligence should be a strategic imperative in the information age. It is also imperative to use that intelligence to safe guard our ability to maintain security. We must ensure that stable domestic and international economies are not jeopardized by possible conflict with rival powers, rogue states, failing or failed states, modern terrorists and thieves, and WMD proliferators.

All formal and informal intelligence disciplines contribute to these imperatives, including Signals Intelligence (SIGINT), Human Intelligence (HUMINT), open Source Intelligence (OSINT), geospatial and Measurement Intelligence (GEOINT), and the volumes of unclassified network data and behaviour being watched by global CERTs.

Continuous liaison among all related parties is critical so that sharing is seamless. This ensures an evolving, improved level of insight and reporting to an increasingly secure and highly performing cyber environment for all.

This evolving cyber intelligence tradecraft requires deep and powerful technical and analytic expertise at all levels. Such technical talent and related capabilities remain ill-defined and in short supply across government and industry.

An institution that has made some headway in this regard is the Information Assurance Directorate (IAD) at the national Security Agency.

IAD is the front line of the defensive cyber mission. It commands substantial resources, high performing talent, strong processes, and informed outreach.

It also works hand in hand with military, public, and private partners to ensure that our cyber capabilities and intellectual property are defended and that our defence is informing offence and vice versa. IAD is a good start, but we must emulate their good practices and innovativeness in defining professional attributes, associated education, and training goals for the unique career fields associated with the cyber realm.

THE NATURE AND LEVELS OF INTELLIGENCE ANALYSIS

Intelligence analysis requires many of the same analytical methods and techniques, irrespective of domain. From this perspective, intelligence analysis for Internet security is no different from the intelligence task in any other area of national and international security.

The commonality is the concern with those who want to inflict harm and the vulnerabilities they can exploit to do this. Threats can come from many sources: the military activities of hostile nations; inimical economic strategies pursued by adversarial or even allied states; the activities of terrorist groups intent on inflicting harm on society in order to achieve political objectives; transnational criminal organizations pursuing the acquisition of large profits through illegal activities, violence, and corruption; and groups (including any of those just mentioned) and individuals with the ability and desire to distort, disrupt, degrade or destroy information and communications systems.

Whatever their source, threats are inextricably linked to vulnerabilities. Indeed, absolute security could only be achieved if there were no vulnerabilities to be exploited. It is crucial, therefore, not only to identify vulnerabilities but also to understand how hostile groups or individuals might exploit them. Strictly speaking, real security threats only come from those with a combination of hostile intent (*i.e.* a desire to do us harm) and the capacity to inflict harm (*i.e.* exploit vulnerabilities in ways that transform intent into reality).

In the realm of cyber-space, vulnerabilities are inescapable. There are many reasons for this, ranging from the inherent weaknesses in complex systems to specific problems in the creation of software code.

Even if protective security measures were an integral part of information systems rather than being subsequently grafted onto them, problems would remain. Some vulnerabilities stem from the underlying protocols used to communicate on the Internet, which were formulated when the Internet was a relatively small community of trusted systems, with connectivity determined by government contract.

Other vulnerabilities stem from development practices, which may ignore validation of input (or even length checking) and avoid controlling the environment in which programmes execute. Finally, vulnerabilities stem from the rapidly evolving use of software, in which programmes meant for a limited purpose are applied in ways not anticipated by their developers. The intruder community is constantly seeking to find interesting (and, from their point of view, profitable) ways to discover and exploit vulnerabilities.

This behaviour tends to be quite trend-driven. A newly discovered interesting vulnerability exploit in an application will spawn both intensive interest in other vulnerabilities in that application and an intensive search for similar vulnerabilities in other applications.

This results in waves of discovered vulnerabilities that impact both specific vendors and the community in general.

At the same time, the recognition that there are measurable trends in vulnerability exploitation are at least a temporary advantage to intelligence analysis efforts. From a tactical perspective, the recognition of a trend in intrusion tools and their applications may well allow for at least short-term predictive analysis and the potential for limited warning.

One of the greatest challenges to system owners and administrator is determining how much security is enough. Managing risks inherent in information systems is problem that changes as fast as new technologies are brought online.

Intelligence analysis of the threats to information systems should, by definition, be a major component of the risk management process. Without application, intelligence analysis efforts are merely an intellectual exercise and have no value. It is only when the results of that analysis, the assessments derived from the analytic process, are provided to operators that they begin to have value.

Obtaining prior knowledge of both threats and vulnerabilities– as well as sensitivity to possible opportunities to exploit the vulnerabilities-is essential. Intelligence analysis, of course, operates at different levels, ranging from the specific to the general, and from short-term incidents and operations to long term patterns and challenges. Each form or level of analysis is crucial, and complements and supplements the others. Nevertheless, it is important to distinguish them from one another and to be clear at which level the activities are taking place.

It is also important to recognize that the most critical insights will be obtained from fusion efforts that combine these different levels. The several complementary levels of intelligence analysis are strategic analysis, tactical analysis and operational analysis. In practice, these categories shade into each other and are not always sharply differentiated, and differing definitions for these terms exist in the intelligence community. Nevertheless, they offer a useful framework within which intelligence tasks and requirements can initially be delineated.

Strategic Intelligence Analysis

Strategic analysis is perhaps the most important form of intelligence. It provides a framework within which other forms of intelligence collection and analysis take place, offers an overall assessment from the top down rather than from the bottom up, and helps to provide a basis for policy formulation, strategic planning, and resource allocation. Its weakness is its focus on macro-level issues rather than the more detailed levels of analysis.

On the Internet, such analysis is even more problematic, due to the rapidly evolving nature of Internet usage. Prior to 1994, for example, Internet commerce was illegal. Today it is a multi-billion dollar economic force. New methods of organizational and economic cooperation are constantly evolving, with greater or less security.

Maintaining continuity on this constantly shifting environment is one of the greatest challenges to conducting effective strategic analysis of cyber-threats. Furthermore, for many consumers, strategic intelligence is irrelevant to day-to-day tasks and needs. At the end of the day, however, the importance of strategic intelligence analysis is undeniable. Such an effort helps to discern and make sense of trends, to identify and extract patterns that would otherwise not be visible, and to provide an overall picture of the evolving threat environment and the level of damage that might be occurred in certain specified contingencies.

Analytical initiatives that would fall under the rubric of strategic intelligence analysis include:

- *Overall threat assessments*. These include in the analysis the vulnerabilities of critical missions (including levels of dependence), the kind of disruption and damage that could be caused to the implementation of these missions, the kinds of weapons/instruments that could be used to cause such disruptions, and the likelihood of such attacks and intrusions taking place
- *Sector threat assessments*. Such analyses focus on vulnerabilities and threats either in particular areas such as national infrastructure, or in particular sectors of the economy such as banking or e-commerce. In effect, a strategic analysis of this kind has to take account of changes in what can be a very dynamic environment.
- *Trend Analysis to highlight changing threats and vulnerabilities*. These might include base-line assessments so as to better recognize departures from the baseline. Alternatively, they might focus on future threats and vulnerabilities in an effort to determine in what ways the problem is evolving– and what can be done to anticipate and contain future challenges. The way in which e-commerce has become a major issue suggests that the pace of change in the cyber-space environment is posing novel challenges that can best be understood through strategic intelligence analysis that is very forward looking. Indeed, trend analysis is likely to be most effective when it is linked with careful attention

to drivers, *i.e.* fundamental trends in the political, economic, social and technological sectors that will shape the future threat and vulnerability environment of the future.

- *Potential Damage Assessments.* Because of the macro-level view taken by strategic analysis, it also offers the best approach for assessing potential cascade effects of intrusions. The specific target of a an intrusion might be a regional electric power grid, but the effects of a failure to that system can cascade to include telecommunications, public emergency services, water systems, etc. The potential for such wide-spread effects will be recognized most readily as a result of in-depth strategic analysis–which in turn would offer opportunities to develop both defensive and mitigation strategies. Crisis management, contingency planning, mitigation strategies, and disaster management would all be enhanced by strategic analysis of potential damage assessment. Indeed, the capacity for effective and rapid reconstitution might depend on such analysis.
- *Categorizing and differentiating attacks and attackers.* Intrusions in cyber-space can emanate from individuals, whether insiders or outsiders; from hacker groups intent on displaying their skills and capabilities; activist groups using direct action on the Internet to publicize their political cause; terrorist organizations using intrusions to create massive disruption or other forms of large-scale harm, and seeking to obtain widespread publicity and create a climate of fear; transnational criminal organizations responding to law enforcement pressure with cyber-retaliation, and states using attacks on, or through, information systems as a form of asymmetric warfare. One of the most important tasks of intelligence analysis for the Internet is to discover ways of differentiating among intrusions from these various sources. This will be especially true as groups or individuals develop intrusion strategies that mimic other forms and thereby lessen their chances of identification or, in the case of nation states, provide plausible deniability of their actions. From the perspective of strategic intelligence

analysis, this is critical in efforts to determine appropriate responses that might go beyond simply defensive or mitigation strategies. How specific attacks are categorized, of course, will also be an issue at the tactical and operational level. But the differentiating and categorization methodologies, initially at least, are a matter for strategic analysis.

- *Identification of Anomalies.* Searching for anomalies that provide indicators of emerging threats and problems is an important task of strategic intelligence analysis (albeit one that both feeds into and relies on tactical and operational efforts). Anomalies in this context can be understood as developments or events that do not fit typical or known patterns. The detection of anomalies or novel patterns can be a major element in anticipating new methods of intrusion, new targets, or even new classes of intruders. It is a macro-level task that requires careful and systematic "environmental scanning" as well as the coalescing of tactical and operational intelligence reports that identify and highlight specific aberrations from the norm.
- *Analysis of Future Net Environments.* The greatest constant about the Internet is change. Strategic intelligence analysis must take that into account and attempt to provide assessments of potential future environments on the Net and the potential impact of malicious activity within those environments. Given the dramatic changes in technology within the recent past, and seeing the rapid pace with which innovation continues to grow, it seems a reasonable assumption that the Internet (in one form or another) will become more and more integrated into the fabric of society. As this occurs, intrusions or attacks will have far more wide-ranging consequences. Considerations of social as well as political and economic impacts will have to be factored into intelligence assessments.

It is clear from this discussion that not only does strategic intelligence analysis provide a framework for tactical and operational assessments, but that work done at these levels in turn helps to shape the strategic intelligence focus. As for the strategic assessments themselves they should be useful for consumers, providing forecasting estimates that help to reduce uncertainties in ways that feed into policy processes, providing a basis for more informed decision-making and more effective resource allocation.

As strategic analytic methodologies mature, they will also offer the basis for predictive or anticipatory assessments that can serve to provide warning of potential hostile operations. In effect, strategic intelligence assessments provide a basis for the development of high-level policy and strategy and for strategic responses to vulnerabilities, whether actual or potential.

Tactical Intelligence Analysis

Tactical analysis is a necessary and important complement to work done at the strategic level. It is the natural linking element between macro-level analysis and the micro-level focus on individual cases.

Among the kinds of studies that come under the level of tactical analysis would be:

- Cluster and pattern analysis designed to discern temporal patterns, the use of particular intrusion methods, commonalities of targets, and attempts to build profiles of perpetrators, whether hackers or insiders.
- Stimulus-response analysis designed to identify potential actions that could be taken by intruders in response to specific known or predicted events. This analysis could be used both proactively in development of warnings or reactively in lending significance to otherwise-unrecognized activity.
- Network environmental analysis methods will have to be developed. It is probable that in-depth analysis of the Internet will reveal patterns similar to those in the physical world. Net weather is already being discussed, and network terrain is a viable concept. Unlike physical environments, however, the Internet environment will probably be subject to much more rapid shifting. That places this sort of analytic effort squarely in the realm of Tactical Analysis.

In physical space, geography helps to differentiate tactical from strategic, but on the Internet this component is lacking, an absence that makes the distinction between strategic and tactical somewhat more tenuous than in other domains. At the same time, the strategic and tactical levels are mutually reinforcing: although strategic intelligence analysis provides the framework for tactical assessments, these assessments in turn help to feed strategic analysis. With a highly dynamic inter-relationship among the various levels of analysis, each level is strengthened by and strengthens the others.

6

Strategic Development of Special Warfare in Cyber Space

Why are regional powers such as Iran and Russia better prepared for cyber-enabled special warfare operations than the United States? How do Iran and Russia empower their tactical operators, while the United States masses its cyber-authorities and cyber-capabilities at the strategic level? Why are U.S. policies, authorities, and doctrine for cyber-enabled special operations so immature despite their first announcement over 20 years ago? Although these are serious questions, what is even graver for the Nation is addressing the root question: How does the United States develop a strategic cyber-enabled special warfare capability? Philippine special operations forces soldier fast ropes out of SH-60 Sea Hawk during training with U.S. and Australian SOF soldiers at Fort Magsaysay, Philippines, May 2014 (U.S. Marine Corps/Pete Thibodeau) As far back as 1993, cyber-thinkers John Arquilla and David Ronfeldt in their seminal study *Cyberwar Is Coming!* foreshadowed recent cyber–special operations forces (SOF) actions by Iran and Russia.

The prescient notion that "numerous dispersed small groups using the latest communications technologies could act conjointly" to master networks and achieve a decisive advantage over their adversaries has been played out repeatedly. As predicted by Arquilla and Ronfeldt, "We're no longer just hurling mass and energy at our opponents in warfare; now we're using information, and the more you have, the less of the older kind of weapons you need." As senior leaders have recently recognized, groups of special operators armed with asymmetric cyber tools, irregular warfare tactics, and mass disinformation can have strategic effects. This article argues that Iran and Russia have already successfully employed cyber-enabled special warfare as a strategic tool to accomplish their national objectives.

Both countries have integrated cyber-SOF that clearly demonstrate they understand how to leverage this tool's potential within the asymmetric nature of conflict. The countries' asymmetric innovations serve as powerful examples of an irregular pathway for aspiring regional powers to circumvent U.S. military dominance and secure their strategic interests. The diffusion of inexpensive yet sophisticated technology makes it easier for potential adversaries to develop significant capabilities every year. Thus, the time has come for the United States to make a strategic choice to develop cyber-enabled special warfare as an instrument to protect and project its own national interests.

IRAN

The Iranian regime strangled the Green Movement with the very tools that were supposed to liberate it: information and communication technologies (ICTs). The regime exploited "emancipating" ICTs to target activists, induce fear, and expand military and paramilitary suppression of cyberspace. Shortly after the Green Movement began, the government dispatched its Islamic Revolutionary Guard Corps (IRGC) to break the "counter-revolutionaries." Charged with fighting domestic and foreign threats to the regime, the IRGC mobilized its subordinate Basij cyber units and its notorious clandestine paramilitary wing, the IRGC–Quds Force (IRGC-QF).

The IRGC commander, Major General Mohammad Ali Jafari, quickly restructured and integrated Iran's cyber, paramilitary, and clandestine capabilities into a brutal national tool to terrorize Green Movement dissidents into "inaction and passivity." The Basij used various devious cyber-intimidation methods against activists, such as sending threatening emails and Internet messages, publishing activists' photos and offering rewards for their capture on government Web sites, infiltrating social media networks, seeding disinformation, sowing leader mistrust, and staging false events to arrest people who showed up. The Basij also institutionalized cyber skills on "blogging, social networking sites, psychological operations, online spying . . . mobile phones and their capabilities, and computer games with the aim of targeted entry in the virtual world." In concert with Basij cyber-targeting activities, the IRGC-QF tracked, imprisoned, tortured, or assassinated regime threats. Iran had set in motion a new symbiotic cycle of misattributable/nonattributable cyber-targeting activities married to old-fashioned brute force. Iran would subsequently strengthen its marriage of counterinsurgency (COIN) and cyber activities in Syria.

RUSSIA

Russian Chief of the General Staff Valery Gerasimov published an article titled "The Value of Science in Prediction" in the obscure military journal *Military-Industrial Courier*. In the article, General Gerasimov heralded a game-changing new generation of warfare whose strategic value would exceed the "power of force of weapons in their effectiveness." He called for widespread asymmetric actions to nullify enemy advantages through "special-operations forces and internal opposition to create a permanently operating front through the entire territory of the enemy state, as well as informational actions, devices, and means that are constantly being perfected." In spring 2014, Russia successfully demonstrated its new understanding of how to integrate asymmetric technology into unconventional warfare (UW) operations by supporting paramilitary separatists in eastern Ukraine.

Russia dispatched small teams of unmarked *Spetsnaz,* or special forces, across the Ukrainian border to seize government buildings and weapons armories, and then turn them over to pro-Russian separatist militias. Concurrently, Russia disconnected, jammed, and attacked digital, telephone, and cyber communications throughout Ukraine. Russia enlisted virtual "privateers" and bounty hunters to conduct cyber attacks against Ukrainian government information and logistic infrastructure, from

Internet servers to railway control systems. Russia bankrolled a "troll army" to wage *deza*, a Russian hacktivist term for disinformation, paying millions for each troll to post 50 pro-Russian comments a day on social media, blogs, and news sites that were critical of Russia's actions. Russia surged epic streams of disinformation, both inside and outside Ukraine, not only to obscure its cyber-enabled UW campaign, but also to create complete political illusions: "Russia doesn't deal in petty disinformation, forgeries, lies, leaks, and cyber-sabotage usually associated with informational warfare. . . . It reinvents reality, creating mass hallucinations that translate into political action." In response, during a North Atlantic Treaty Organization (NATO) security summit in September 2014, the Supreme Allied Commander Europe, General Phillip Breedlove, USAF, proclaimed that Russia's "hybridized" UW in eastern Ukraine represented "the most amazing information warfare blitzkrieg we have ever seen in the history of information warfare."

General Breedlove urged the Alliance to develop new capabilities to counter Russia's mastery of UW, propaganda campaigns, and cyber assaults immediately. NATO and the West were caught off guard by Russia's ability to advance its political objectives using nontraditional means in a manner once "not even considered warfare by the West." Russia did not use Spetsnaz, information operations (IO), or cyber capabilities in a piecemeal manner to accomplish its objectives.

Instead, as General Gerasimov described, "Wars are no longer declared"; they simply happen when SOF armed with advanced technology and mass information create the conditions for conventional forces to achieve strategic objectives "under the guise of peacekeeping and crisis." In other words, choreographed cyber disinformation and cyber attack bought time and space for laptop-carrying Spetsnaz to conduct unconventional warfare "between the states of war and peace." Russia's cyber-enabled UW was a brilliant success, not simply for its cyber-SOF hybridization, but also for successfully invading a signature partner nation of the European Union without sparking any meaningful Western military response.

SYRIA

Iran dispatched IRGC-QF operators and ICT experts, who had mastered their craft in breaking the Green Movement, to Syria to advise pro–Bashar al-Asad forces. Iran sent "several hundred members of the Revolutionary Guards al Quds force" to Syria armed with domestic COIN expertise, money, arms, and advanced equipment "designed to disrupt communications, the Internet, email, and cell phone communications." Operations in Syria fell under the command of Major General Qasem Soleimani, an infamous figure described by General David Petraeus as "truly evil" and characterized by a senior Central Intelligence Agency officer as the "single most powerful operative in the Middle East." Under Soleimani's authority, Quds Force operators trained proxy Hizballah and Syrian elements in Iranian camps such as Amir Al-Momenin and integrated themselves into key command and control centers across Syria.

According to Dexter Filkins, "To save Assad, Soleimani called on every asset he had built since taking over the Quds Force: Hezbollah fighters, Shiite militiamen from around the Arab world and all the money and materiél he could squeeze out of . . . Assad's own besieged government." Inside Syrian operation centers, Quds Force operators initially provided advice on techniques for suppressing social media and deterring civil disobedience, but soon escalated "with all kinds of kinetic options" to crush the rebellion, just like they had done at home. The Quds Force showed a ruthless understanding of cyber-enabled COIN using "their intelligence networks to train the Syrian army how to fight people without killing; how to use force to cause injury, without being accused of a massacre . . . teaching them how to control Web sites and social media and how to jam television channels."

As with the 2009 attacks on the Green Movement, the Quds Force backed up its cyber-targeting activities with brute force. By this time, however, operatives had learned to distance themselves from the Iranian-trained Syrian, Iraqi, and Hizballah proxies doing the dirty work. As a RAND paper pointed out, "Iran has skillfully employed its own special warfare capabilities as part of a long-term regional strategy, using state and nonstate proxies to advance its regional interests." At the same time, the Syrian Electronic Army (SEA) benefited from Iranian expertise, money, and technology to attack anti-Assad social media and Web sites. The SEA "aggressively engaged in a wide range of online activities to punish perceived opponents and to force the online narrative in favor of the Assad regime." The SEA used distributed denial-of-service attacks, jammed online portals, overloaded networks, and used malware to thwart opponents' messages and actions. Supporting the efforts from Iran, the Basij actively disseminated propaganda, developed increasingly advanced cyberspace capabilities, and professionalized offensive paramilitary hacker field training. It seems that the Basij inundated the Internet with disinformation to obscure Iran's true complicity in Syria and redirect any blame as a Western conspiracy to overthrow Assad.

Iran succeeded against the Green Movement and anti-Assad forces by interweaving ICT efforts to identify key human and information networks with brute force. Beginning with Jafari's reorganization of the IRGC, Iran's cyber-enabled COIN was later perfected with Soleimani's operations in Syria. Throughout both campaigns, the Basij cyber force was a "core state instrument of suppression," honing its techniques to provide cover for Iran's ruthless actions. Iran's cyber-enabled COIN is a stunning success, not only for its cyber-SOF hybridization but also for crushing two separate rebellions and never triggering any meaningful Western military response.

Lessons Learned

There are four primary lessons learned from the actions of Iran and Russia that inform a conceptual framework for aligning cyber capabilities to U.S. special warfare operations.

1. There is a distinction between the offensive cyber tools the IRGC-QF and Spetsnaz employed at the tactical level and those that exist at the strategic level. Iranian and Russian operators targeted tactical-level "circumscribed or closed networks," such as local communications, social media, and regional Internet and logistic infrastructure, while seemingly keeping their more sophisticated open network tools in reserve.

2. Cyber-enabled special warfare is primarily a proxy-executed endeavor that values minimal source attribution. As described by General Gerasimov, "Long-distance, contactless actions against the enemy are becoming the main means of achieving combat and operational goals." Cyber-enabled SOF generally avoid direct force-on-force engagement and strive to operate in the gray areas between peace and war. As observed in Ukraine and Syria, cyber-enabled violence seeks to retain a modicum of deniability, letting proxies execute the dirty guerrilla tactics of assassination, sabotage, and ambush. Russia and Iran retained the strategic flexibility to cut and run should things go awry.
3. ICT exploitation, cyber attack, and IO play significant roles in cyber-enabled irregular campaigns. Properly conducted, traditional special warfare campaigns extend to far more than SOF; "they involve the comprehensive orchestration of broader capabilities to advance policy objectives." Likewise, for these campaigns to work, expertise from other arenas must be integrated and synchronized.
4. Cyber-enabled special warfare could both deter conflict and be applied throughout the spectrum of conflict because it "is well suited to all phases of operation, from shaping the environment through intense warfare through reconstruction." Even though Iran and Russia have operated at the malicious end of the spectrum, cyber-enabled special warfare has a constructive side, too. The proliferation of low-cost information and communication technologies benefits partner nations in the building of security, thereby helping to keep conflicts from breaking out.

CLOUD-POWERED FOREIGN DOMESTIC DEFENSE

Cloud-powered foreign internal defense (FID) is both a technical computing concept and a metaphor for building partner capacity and trust through virtual means. Although not yet fully defined, FID clouds link cross-disciplined communities together to better understand human, geographic, and virtual arenas, and then act conjointly on targeted overlaps. Technically speaking, FID clouds strengthen partner relationships through federated architectures that share data in real time, enhance automation, and diffuse analytic processes. Clouds have adjustable configurations that can take the shape of private, public, community, and hybrid models, each characterized by different software, platform, and infrastructure architectures. FID clouds power encrypted mobile applications, analytic tools, and pooled data through smart technology in the hands of those involved with building security. Although data are virtually tethered to a cloud, the real value lies in enabling the diffusion of timely information to elements at the tactical level. FID clouds are also a metaphor for persistent and vibrant partnerships because, like the technology, the data never rest and the networks do not go idle. This technology is simply a vehicle to empower a deeper, broader, and more contextual community of understanding for the sociocultural, political, and historical factors that all too frequently fuel strife. Instead of reactive relationships characterized by intermittent FID deployments, which achieve a spotty understanding, FID clouds are metaphors for building a more persistent form of capability, capacity, and trust between partnered nations.

FID clouds lay a virtual foundation for future growth of diverse institutions, centers, and laboratories that can help close the seams between U.S. interagency community interests in a country. From a strategic U.S. Government perspective, FID clouds are a pragmatic "partner-centric approach to design campaigns around a partner's core interests, rather than hoping to transform them in ways that have frequently proved to be ephemeral." FID clouds also provide strategic discretion "when a public relationship of a U.S. partner state is problematic because of the partner state's domestic politics."

FID clouds provide other opportunities as well. The technology and relationships that they foster across communities can be quickly scaled up to respond to sudden emergencies such as humanitarian assistance/disaster relief operations, counter-genocide, or noncombatant evacuation missions. They can save money, time, and manpower by feeding information to decisionmakers when time is of the essence. For partner-building efforts, FID clouds can store information hosted by indigenous non-U.S. social media platforms, enriching social network analysis, sociographic mapping, and behavior and sentiment trend analysis. Most importantly, FID clouds spread trust in a creative and super-empowered way that helps to establish long-lasting influence with allies, coalitions, and other partners.

Counternetwork COIN

Counternetwork COIN (CNCOIN) is a simple concept aimed at leveraging, harnessing, and exploiting social media networks. Designed to break an adversary's asymmetric information advantage, CNCOIN employs nontechnical attacks against people to manipulate their perceptions, behaviors, and actions. It puts a military twist on many of the ill-defined yet ubiquitous anti–social networking tactics practiced across cyberspace. Although these tactics are not clearly defined, this article characterizes them as actions that obscure a perpetrator's true identity while he manipulates social media for reasons other than what is stated. Although social media pose a wide array of opportunities for any anti–social network, ranging from criminally exploitative to benignly misrepresentative, from a military perspective, social media present a rich array of information on ways to influence psychological vulnerabilities and an ideal attack platform from which to do it.

There are three broad functional categories for classifying CNCOIN: operations, intelligence, and IO. There are also several techniques within each functional category that help highlight its practice rather than define it outright. These techniques are by no means all encompassing or without overlap.

The first CNCOIN category is operations. It includes but is not limited to cyber-pseudo and cyber-herding operations. A *cyber-pseudo operation* is a classic COIN strategy "in which government forces and guerrilla defectors portray themselves as insurgent units" to infiltrate enemy networks and apply advanced tradecraft inside the network to destroy it. A *cyber-herding operation*, on the other hand, "is the action by which an individual, group, or organization drives individuals, groups, or organizations to a desired location within the electronic realm." The beauty of both techniques is that they drive invisible wedges between insurgents and their command and control by exploiting the inherent weaknesses of communication and communication platforms within every network. Cyber-pseudo and cyber-herding operations. prey on an enemy network's natural need to maintain a low signature to survive. Both techniques target intermittent and decentralized insurgent leader communications, manipulating or replacing them, which synergistically leads to growing opportunities for the cyber counterinsurgent. The virtual world simply amplifies the environmental factors because personalities are harder to authenticate as real or fictitious. The lack of command and control authentication, communication frequency, and platform availability are key cyber-pseudo and cyber-herding pressure points to manipulate, misinform, or drive targets toward desired outcomes.

The second CNCOIN category is intelligence, which includes but is not limited to crowdsourcing and social networking analysis (SNA) exploitation techniques. *Crowdsourcing*is a practice that taps into large pools of diverse knowledge willingly provided by participants to solve problems with new ideas, services, or observations and quickly broaden the organizer's perspective. *SNA* visually depicts and measures relationships, their density, and the centrality of social links in order to illuminate social network structures. The social network visualizations, or sociograms, provide a unique window to assess, map, and even predict the intensity of relationship events over temporal, geospatial, and relational horizons.

During the September 2013 Zamboanga City crisis in the Philippines, rogue Moro National Liberation Front (MNLF) forces, dissatisfied with the state of national reconciliation, mobilized a force that seized over 200 civilian hostages, raided businesses, and burned buildings throughout the city. During the crisis, both crowdsourcing and SNA exploitation were successful techniques. Although inadvertently at first, Philippine security forces (PSF) used crowdsourcing techniques to encourage Zamboanga residents to spot and report information on rogue MNLF locations throughout the city. The PSF fused crowdsourced information with intelligence analysis, informing both security and humanitarian operations. The PSF used SNA exploitation to assess populace support for rogue MNLF, as well as to counter and discredit rogue MNLF statements on social media by taking down propaganda Web sites that violated social media user agreements. The PSF also used crowdsourced information to cordon pockets of rogue MNLF forces and raid ad hoc command posts. Although less sophisticated than Iran's cyber-enabled COIN, the PSF thwarted rogue MNLF asymmetric advantage by using social media to target key information and leadership nodes, following up with physical force to defeat them.

The third CNCOIN category is IO and includes but is not limited to cyber aggression, sock-puppeting, and astro-turfing techniques. All three techniques exploit social media anonymously to misrepresent, misinform, and manipulate behavior, sentiment, and actions. Advanced by Diane Felmlee, *cyber aggression* "refers to electronic or online behavior intended to harm another person psychologically or damage his or her reputation" by using "email, instant messaging, cell phones, digital messages, chat rooms, as well as social media, video, and gaming Web sites" and is wider in scope than common cyber bullying. Its anonymous application could cause substantial psychological harm and negative consequences as messages are repeatedly viewed by the target or forwarded across social media sites. Its value to CNCOIN is in exploiting sensitive digital information that could shame, demoralize, or traumatize targets into taking psychologically impaired actions. These deliberate cyber aggression operations could undermine the target's credibility, influence, and power to the point of triggering the target to neutralize himself or other insurgents.

The other techniques, *sock-puppeting* and *astro-turfing,* are defined as fictitious online propaganda tools that disseminate contrived views to fabricate a broader illusion of support or nonsupport. Astro-turfing is the same concept as sock-puppeting, but it is more sophisticated and organized and is undertaken on a larger scale than sock-puppeting. Both astro-turfing and sock-puppeting use virtual personas and "bots" to pump false information across cyberspace to incite reaction or mobilize mass action. As witnessed with Russia's army of trolls, botnets, and hired hackers in Ukraine, astro-turfing networks are awash with an arsenal of propaganda, pictures, and videos stoking conflict and obscuring actions on the ground. Counternetwork IO becomes even more effective when combined with deliberate and misleading cyber-targeting activities, such as IRGC activities during the 2009 Green Movement.

Cyber UW Pilot Teams

The third way to advance U.S. cyber-enabled special warfare is the Cyber UW Pilot Team, a capability meant to harness social media networks to shape a physical environment, establish regional mechanisms, and stitch together area complexes prior to executing UW operations. Cyber UW Pilot Teams are purpose-built around the nucleus of a Special Forces Operational Detachment Alpha, augmented with interagency and technical support, whose mission is to digitally prepare an area for UW operations.

The teams undertake the same traditional pilot team tasks that previously were accomplished upon infiltration in the physical domain, but do it through virtual means before they ever put boots on the ground in sensitive, hostile, or denied areas. By operating virtually, Cyber UW Pilot Teams could decrease the time, risk, exposure, and attribution to the U.S. and partnered resistance forces because most of their activities would have been digitally accomplished prior to physical infiltration.

Conceptually, Cyber UW Pilot Teams build human, physical, intelligence, and information infrastructures on social media platforms with cyber tools and advanced techniques. The teams could sharpen their localized language and cultural skills while deepening their understanding of the local human terrain. They could also identify resistance leaders, assess motivations, evaluate resistance capabilities, and assess overall support for U.S. Government objectives while simultaneously evaluating informal hierarchies, psychology, and behavior. In addition, the teams could blend into the white noise of the Internet by tapping into social media networks to "improve U.S. contextual understanding of potential partners and the situation on the ground before the United States commits to a course of action."

Every Cyber UW Pilot Team would have tailored execution authorities and acceptable levels of UW infrastructure development. Once those levels are reached and authorities given, the same team that established the infrastructure virtually would ideally execute its own plan on the ground with the area complex and resistance forces they nurtured online. Cloaked in dual-purpose technology, indigenous equipment, and mobilized networks, these teams would digitally initiate and then physically execute their assigned UW operations from beginning to end.

While there has long been recognition of the strategic role of cyber operations in U.S. national security, this awareness has not fully translated into the development of clear strategic-level thinking and operational capacity. For example, the *Department of Defense Strategy for Operating in Cyberspace* offers few solutions or specifics, but rather reiterates earlier cyber themes in a five-point outline. The lack of well-defined ideas creates a vacuum in cyber strategy that puts the United States in danger of ceding its superior cyber-technological advantage to potential adversaries. In contrast, the asymmetric innovations demonstrated by Iran and Russia present a template for other aspiring regional and global powers to imitate as an irregular pathway to circumventing U.S. military dominance and securing their strategic interests. Moreover, the diffusion of inexpensive yet sophisticated technology increases this potential every year. Iran and Russia have made the American lack of specificity in strategic-level cyberspace documents irrelevant, as the country does not need simply to write about strategy, but must now catch up.

Cyber-enabled special warfare is a strategic-level offensive capability gap that must be filled. Clearly, the United States must aggressively pursue a form of special warfare that integrates cyber operations into tactical-level irregular operations. A recent RAND report on special warfare concluded that "the United States needs to employ a more sophisticated form of *special warfare* to secure its interests . . . and given recent trends in security threats to the United States and its interests, special warfare may often be the most appropriate way of doing so." Cyber-enabled special warfare is the answer in an increasingly interconnected global environment in which physical infrastructure is rapidly being assigned Internet Protocol addresses for assimilation into an "Internet of things." By the year 2020, over 50 billion machine-to-machine devices (compared to 13 billion today) will connect to cyberspace through "the embedding of computers, sensors, and Internet capabilities." Cyber-enabled special warfare bridges the gap between the virtual and the physical by harnessing modern-day information networks and melding them with old-fashioned, face-to-face SOF partner engagement.

Today's global environment impels the United States to adopt cyber-enabled special warfare as a strategic tool of national military strategy. The devastating examples of integrating offensive cyber capabilities into irregular tactics as demonstrated by Iran and Russia pave the way for other U.S. adversaries to soon follow. This article offers the Nation three new options for aligning emerging technology to special warfare missions: cloud-powered FID, counternetwork COIN, and Cyber UW Pilot Team operations. Developing these three concepts to their fullest transcends simply maintaining a U.S. cyber-technology edge; their development projects revolutionary influence across the globe to build critical partnerships and shape issues across the spectrum of conflict. If successfully developed, cyber-enabled special warfare will become a powerful new strategic option for the Nation.

CYBER-WARFARE TACTICS

Other cyber tactics are less sophisticated. The attack that temporarily brought down Estonian networks began with a flood of bogus messages targeting government servers, called a "denial of service" attack. The approach harnesses "botnets"—massive networks of interconnected computers—to bombard targeted networks with information requests while masking the location of the primary attacker. James Lewis, a security expert with the Center for Strategic and International Studies (CSIS), says hackers in the Estonia example likely took control of tens of thousands of computers around the world without the knowledge of their owners and directed them at the government's servers. The result, he says, was a relatively minor attack that was nearly impossible to trace.

Another technique is the use of "malware," "spyware," and other malicious programs imbedded into computer systems to steal information without user knowledge. The software is designed to hide undetected and siphon information from its host—everything from secrets stored on personal computers to Pentagon military mainframes. A December 2007 analysis of U.S. Air Force cyber vulnerabilities notes much of the Pentagon's operating systems are off-the-shelf components manufactured overseas, due to cheaper costs. But pinching pennies has potentially opened U.S. military networks to intrusion. "Foreign countries could place hidden components inside the computers, making the computers vulnerable for attack and/or spying," the analysis concludes.

> *"Our ability to penetrate into enemy computer networks, our ability to exploit communication networks, to manipulate digital information, is real." –Defense Analyst William M. Arkin*

Less common but far more worrisome are cyber attacks aimed at critical infrastructure—like nuclear-power-plant control systems, banks, or subways. In March 2007 the Department of Energy's Idaho Lab conducted an experiment to determine whether a power plant could be compromised by hacking alone.

The result—a smoking, self-combusting diesel generator incapacitated by nothing more than keystrokes—sent shivers (CNN) through the private sector. The worries were apparently well-founded.

In January 2008 a CIA analyst told U.S. utilities that hackers had succeeded in infiltrating electric companies in undisclosed locations outside the United States and, it at least one instance, shut off power to multiple cities. The hackers then demanded money (AP). "The [U.S.] government is scrambling to try and protect its own systems, to try and check the Chinese from reading government email," says economist Scott Borg, director of the U.S. Cyber Consequences Unit, a nonprofit research institute that studies cyber threats. "But the focus probably needs to be critical infrastructure. That's what we need to defend."

Patching the Holes

On paper the U.S. government appears to agree. For over a decade government-sanctioned studies have delved into the subject; the Pentagon published a report on "Information Warfare-Defense" (PDF) in 1996, when public use of the Internet was still in its infancy. Saydjari says all of these studies reached the same conclusion: "The threat and vulnerabilities to our national infrastructure is serious, it's getting worse, and it's getting worse at an increasingly fast rate."

But only recently has the concern been a constant focus of attention for the security and intelligence communities. Part of the attention deficit lies with the difficulty in defining the cyber threat. A 2006 Air Force task force termed cyberspace "a warfighting domain bounded by the electromagnetic spectrum," but air force officials acknowledge "a full understanding of the domain is years away."

What is understood is how potentially devastating the loss of cyberspace dominance could be to U.S. interests. In his annual threat assessment to Congress delivered in February 2008, Director of National Intelligence Michael McConnell discussed "cyber threats" before talking about the war in Afghanistan.

"Our information infrastructure ...increasingly is being targeted for exploitation and potentially for disruption or destruction by a growing array of state and non-state adversaries," McConnell said. "We assess that nations, including Russia and China, have the technical capabilities to target and disrupt" the United States' information infrastructure.

> *"Chinese [cyber warfare] capabilities have evolved from defending networks from attack to offensive operations against adversary networks." –U.S. Deputy Under Secretary for Defense Richard P. Lawless*

The Pentagon, too, has acknowledged the threat to its infrastructure. The Defense Department is considering banning nonofficial traffic (Federal Computer Week) from its servers, and the U.S. Air Force is creating a Cyber Command to defend Pentagon networks. "When we talk about the speed range and flexibility of air power, the thing that enables this for us is the fact of our cyber-dominance," Air Force Gen. Robert Elder told United Press International.

The recent flurry of high-level pronouncements also comes amid a renewed funding commitment from Washington. In November 2007 the Bush administration called on the National Security Agency to coordinate with the Department of Homeland Security to protect government and civilian communication networks from hackers. The $144 million plan, unveiled quietly in White House budget documents (PDF), aims to enhance "civilian agency cybersecurity and strengthen defenses to combat terrorism."

In January 2008 President George W. Bush signed two presidential directives calling for the creation of a comprehensive national cybersecurity initiative. According to an article by the Wall Street Journal, the White House's 2009 budget request takes the program exponentially further, with an estimated $6 billion request to build a secretive system to protect U.S. communications networks. Details of the proposed program remain classified, angering some civil libertarians who fear monitoring of civilian networks could infringe on privacy rights. Rep. Bennie G. Thompson (D-MS), chairman of the House Homeland Security Committee, has called for the program to be put on hold (PDF) until Congress can adequately review it.

Measuring the Threat

Cyber experts don't dispute that electronic espionage is a vexing problem, or that the United States is a prime target. But they do disagree on how pervasive such attacks are, who is behind them, and how disruptive they may prove to be.

According to a tally by the Heritage Foundation, a conservative Washington think tank, the hackers may already be winning: In 2007 the Department of Homeland Security logged an estimated 37,000 attempted breaches of private and government computer systems, and over 80,000 attacks on Pentagon systems. Some hacks "reduced the U.S. military's operational capabilities," the report says. Economist Borg says the biggest threat from cyber attacks may be economic. He estimates a shutdown of electric power to any sizable region for more than ten days would stop over 70 percent of all economic activity in that region. "If you can do that with a pure cyber attack on only one critical infrastructure, why would you bother with any traditional military attack?" CSIS' Lewis takes a less alarmist view.

"The U.S. is a very big set of targets, and some of our important networks are very secure. So you could inflict damage on the U.S. but it wouldn't be crippling or decisive," he says. "I've seen people who say a cyber attack could turn the United States into a third-world nation in a matter of minutes. That's silly. We have to be realistic about this."

CASUALTIES OF CYBER WARFARE

That the United States and China have engaged in skirmishes in the cyber domain is no secret. Since the beginning of the 21st century, targeted cyberattacks, often with signs of Chinese origin, have attempted to penetrate the computer networks of U.S. corporations and government agencies in search of potentially valuable information. In response to this new strategic threat, the U.S. Military's Strategic Command commissioned the creation of a sub-unified Cyber Command in 2009, with one of its stated objectives being the "defense of specified Department of Defense information networks."

U.S. President Barack Obama very clearly defined the threat that cyberattacks pose to the economy, in both the public and private sectors, when he said that the "cyber threat is one of the most serious economic and national security challenges we face as a nation." Indeed, conflict in the cyber domain is still having some serious repercussions for the business world.

Civilian Involvement in Cyber Warfare

The characteristic of cyber warfare that makes it so uniquely dangerous to the corporate sector is that military power in the cyber domain must be extended through computer networks provided and maintained by non-governmental bodies. The use of these networks for cyberattacks or defense requires the conscription or cooperation of civilian resources. This creates extreme liabilities for the corporations that provide these networks, as they will quickly become the targets of suspicion and possible retaliation from the enemy state. In recent years, both Chinese and American companies have been caught in just this situation.

On October 8, 2012, the U.S. House of Representatives' intelligence committee released a report that warned of potential national security threats posed by Chinese telecommunication giants Huawei and ZTE. After conducting a year-long investigation of the suspect companies, the intelligence committee found serious vulnerabilities caused by hidden "backdoors" worked into the companies' technologies that would allow access to U.S. government and business networks.

The report advised against the purchase of products manufactured by Huawei or ZTE, and suggested that policymakers block any mergers between either of the two companies and U.S. telecommunication corporations.

These accusations have seriously hurt consumer confidence in the two companies, to the extent that in December of 2013, Huawei's executive vice president dramatically declared"we are not interested in the U.S. market anymore." While Huawei has managed to hold on to a small market share in America, the company's association with Chinese state-sponsored cyberattacks has devastated its ability to operate in the United States.

It became clear last year, though, that the United States was a perpetrator of cyberattacks as well as a victim. In June 2013, former U.S. National Security Agency contractor Edward Snowden provided the world with a look into the intelligence apparatus of the NSA, releasing thousands of classified documents to the media. The released documents revealed that the U.S., like China, was using domestic tech firms (in many cases without their knowledge or consent) as conduits for intelligence gathering cyberattacks. In May 2014, the Chinese government announced that it would no longer purchase or use two of Microsoft's main products, the Windows 8 operating system and the Microsoft Office 365 Suite. Then, in late July and early August, Chinese officials from the State Administration for Industry and Commerce (SAIC) raided multiple offices owned by Microsoft and its contractors in China. While vague statements about an anti-monopoly probe were made, the company's decision to end support for the Windows XP operating system – a move that would expose the many Chinese computers that use the operating system to security risks – was also cited as a factor in the raids.

While it is likely that the ban and subsequent raids were also intended to pave the way for new operating system technologies created in China, the Snowden revelations allowed potential U.S. espionage activities to be cited as a justification. Just as Huawei and ZTE suffered for their association with espionage activities of the Chinese government, Microsoft took a major hit because of the provocative actions of its government.

An Undefined Battlefield

On both sides of the Pacific, it is clear that both U.S. and Chinese tech firms are being caught in the crossfire of these cyber skirmishes between the two countries. Any escalation in tensions in the cyber domain could be disastrous to the private sector. Unfortunately, despite the risks that future cyberwars hold for multinational corporations, there is a marked absence of legislation, precedent, and international norms that could govern the relationships between private companies and the governments looking to use them as avenues through which cyberwar could be conducted.

For as long as these ambiguities exist, corporations that deal in the communication technology industry will exist in the gray area of an unregulated cyber battlefield devoid of any policies meant to protect the assets and infrastructures of civilian actors. It is in the interests of both countries to more clearly define, through domestic cooperation with corporate partners and with bilateral international discussion and agreement, the boundaries between civilians and the military in cyber warfare. Failure to do so could severely hamper the economic interaction that has been so lucrative for both countries and further destabilize an already fragile Sino-American relationship.

Government's Role in Domestic Cyber Security

While organizations have taken extensive measures to provide security against cybercrime, the challenges of a larger cyberwar against a capable and persistent foe require greater national organization and civilian-government cooperation. Unfortunately, in the United States, government responses to engagements in the cyber domain have been slow at best, but more often nonexistent. The cause of this is commonly the difficulty in identifying attackers and the lack of procedures in place for how a national response can and should be mobilized to address an attack on a civilian target. This lack of definition creates additional liability for the civilian counterpart because the opposing state (in this case China) does not know to what extent the civilian is involved with the defense and possible subsequent counterattacks. The lack of clarity directly increases the probability that the civilian will be the target of general suspicion and will suffer financial damage, as was seen with Huawei, ZTE and Microsoft. In broad terms, foreign attacks on domestic civilian targets can be placed in one of two categories: those that pose a national security threat and those that cause potential financial harm to the recipient of the attack. These two types of attacks require specific responses that have not yet been clearly defined by the U.S. government and the business community.

A cyberattack that directly threatens the national security of the United States might require the temporary direct use, or even the partial or complete conscription, of a civilian network. Disruptions of public utilities, theft of sensitive information from a security contractor, or the sabotage of civilian networks necessary for the operation of the military are examples of intrusions that might necessitate such a response. However, the documents released by Edward Snowden revealed that civilian networks were commonly conscripted for foreign surveillance activities, often without the knowledge of their owners. One of the largest barriers that conscription faces to becoming a transparent counter-cyberattack strategy is the ambiguity surrounding the cyber domain in warfare. Because no legislation exists that explicitly defines cyberattacks as acts of war and because the Supreme Court has never ruled on the constitutionality of conscription in any form during peacetime, no precedent has ever been set that would instruct the government on how to publicly organize a defense in the case of a cyberattack against a civilian target that threatened national security. While this does not excuse the NSA of its secrecy, it does indicate the need for legal clarification on the matter of cyber warfare. A decisive answer to the question of the legality of government conscription of civilian network assets in the interests of national security would allow a transparent strategy that involved input from both civilian and government representatives to be formed.

If a cyberattack is not a national security threat, but only threatens the financial health of the victim, the procedures for a government response are even more unclear. With traditional cybercrime, civilians are responsible for their own cyber security and the liability of unsuccessfully defending against an attempted network penetration falls on the civilian's security provider or the civilian's own security measures. However, it seems unreasonable to assume that a civilian would be able to successfully defend against the cyberattacks of a foreign state, which presumably would have greater access to technology, talent and funding.

Say, for example, a cyberattack of Chinese origin manages to steal sensitive information relating to a patented product of an American company. What response could that company expect to receive from the government? The answer to that question has yet to be explicitly defined through any official legislation or successful precedent. However, the Cybersecurity Act of 2013, which was recommended for further consideration in July 2013, might be a step in the right direction. The bill directs the Secretary of Commerce and the Director of National Institute of Standards and Technology to work toward the, "development of a voluntary, industry-led set of standards and procedures to reduce cyber risks to critical infrastructure." While the bill does not specifically say what measures can be taken to address the problem, a dialogue between the government and the civilian sector is a necessary first step toward assuring that the government will take an active role in preventing damaging cyberattacks on civilian targets.

A Line in the Cyber Sand

The lack of adequate procedural preparation for cyber warfare and ambiguity about the government's role in protecting its civilians from cyberattacks represents a real strategic threat to the United States as well as a financial liability for civilians. Before the release of the NSA documents last year, the U.S. government was acting unilaterally to address the problems presented by aggression from the Chinese in the cyber domain. The nature of cyber warfare, however, necessitates civilian cooperation. Now there is an opening to create a partnership to more clearly define the lines between state actions that might be internationally provocative and civilian resources that, while necessary to the state's actions, do not represent the civilian's participation as an aggressor. Not only will this protect civilian assets that are not directly involved in cyber warfare efforts, it will also create procedures that will allow for a more effective and efficient strategy for the conduct of cyber warfare.

Given the very real risk that conflict between China and the U.S. in the cyber domain could escalate in the future, we need to find ways to isolate it from the vibrant economic exchange that have benefited both countries. The worst-case scenario would be the disintegration of the line between warfighting assets and civilian assets, such that the intentional targeting of noncombatants becomes a viable strategy. Both China and the U.S. need to act to ensure that their civilians do not become casualties of cyber warfare.

7

Defamation in Cyber Space

The Internet is a cheap, fast means of international communication of text, sound or image. In other words, an information resource without political or content boundaries; limited only by the extent to which the information providers are willing to disclose their materials and the fruits of their own writing and research. In the present day, web sites displaying information of all kinds are proliferating. These sites are established and controlled by Internet Service Providers (ISPs) or, sometimes, by the company's information technology department.

These sites can be accessed through suitable search engines, which will trace and display information to suit the requirements of the searcher. However, not many of the companies are aware of the risks attached with the hosting of a Web site. Who would be held liable, for instance, if an employee clandestinely posts racist, sexist, or defamatory allegations about a competitor on the company's official web site?

It is to be remembered that a number of features unique to the internet distinguishes it from any other medium. These features have led to the current re-examination of existing laws relating to defamation, to allow for their possible evolution and ultimately their application in cyberspace. A key feature of the internet is its highly interactive nature. The ease with which users of the internet can access information and communicate with each other has engendered in its users a false sense of freedom in their communications. Accessibility is another feature of the internet, which distinguishes it from traditional print or broadcast media.

The relatively low cost of connecting to the internet and even of establishing one's own website means that the opportunity for defamation has increased exponentially. Now, on the internet everyone can be a publisher and can be sued as a publisher.

Another key feature of the internet is that users do not have to reveal their true identity in order to send e-mail or post messages on bulletin boards. Users are able to communicate and make such postings anonymously or under assumed names. This feature, coupled with the ability to access the internet in privacy and seclusion of one's own home or office and the interactive, responsive nature of communications on the internet, has resulted in users being far less inhibited about the contents of their messages resulting in cyber space becoming excessively prone to defamation.

Defamation can be understood as the intentional infringement of another person's right to his good name. It is the wrongful and intentional publication of words or behaviour concerning another person, which has the effect of injuring that person's status, good name, or reputation in society. Libel is written defamation and slander is oral defamation. The primary difference is that in libel, damages are presumed, whereas in slander actions, unless the slander falls into a certain category, called slander per se, the plaintiff must prove actual or quantifiable damages.

A person's good name can only be damaged if maligning statements are made to someone other than that person; that is, the defamatory statement must be disclosed to a third person, thereby satisfying the requirement of publication. When determining whether or not defamation has taken place, the only issue to consider is whether a person of ordinary intelligence in society would believe that the words would indeed injure the person's reputation.

Thus the law of defamation places a heavy burden on the defendant. All that a plaintiff has to prove, in a defamation action, is the publication of defamatory matter. The onus then lies on the defendant to prove innocence. Once again, most people are unaware of this burden.

In essence, the law on defamation attempts to create a workable balance between two equally important human rights: The right to an unimpaired reputation and the right to freedom of expression. In a cyber society, both these interests are increasingly important. Protection of reputation is arguably even more important in a highly technological society, since one may not even encounter an individual or organization other than through the medium of the internet. The elements of a defamation action can be summarized as follows:

- The plaintiff must prove publication of the defamatory statement;
- The plaintiff must prove that the defamation refers to the plaintiff; and
- The plaintiff must prove that the statement is defamatory.

Upon proof of publication, the law makes several presumptions in favour of the plaintiff:

- That the statement is false;
- That it was published with malice; and
- That in the case of libel or slander per se, the plaintiff has suffered damage.

Defences that can be raised against such a defamation action are as follows:

- Truth.
- Fair comment: The defendant is allowed to comment on facts truly stated, as long as the comment is fair and the defendant is not motivated by actual malice.
- Privilege: On certain occasions, the courts have held that policy and convenience require that a person should be free from responsibility for the publication of defamatory words. These occasions constitute privileges. Privilege may be absolute, such as statements in the House of Commons or the Courts. It may be qualified, in that it may be lost if the publication is unnecessarily wide or made with malice.
- Innocent dissemination: This last defence is potentially very important in cyber libel.

If a defendant proves that his statements were true and in public interest, then his conduct is regarded as lawful. In addition, if the defendant can show that he had no intention to defame (the plaintiff), then he could avoid liability.

This paper seeks to throw light on the law relating to cyber defamation and to suggest a legal framework to handle such situations, which is inevitable, especially in the light of the present IT boom in India.

CYBER DEFAMATION: A SOCIO-ECONOMIC OFFENCE

Cyber law encompasses cyber crimes, electronic commerce, freedom of expression, intellectual property rights, jurisdiction issues and choice of law, and privacy rights. Cyber crimes involve activities like credit card fraud, unauthorized access to computer systems, child pornography, software piracy and cyber stalking. Freedom of expression includes defamation, obscenity issues and censorship. Jurisdiction issues focuses on who makes and enforces the rules governing cyber space.

The definition of what constitutes a crime in cyber space is still being developed. In the past, the states and federal government defined cyber crime activities to include the destruction or theft of computer data and programs. More recently the definition has expanded to include activities such as forgery, illegal gambling, cyber stalking, cyber defamation etc.

There are several areas on the internet where there is a real risk of liability for defamation. The fact that a user is "alone" with his computer and distanced from other users creates a sense of intimacy. There is no spoken/telephonic conversation or dictated correspondence that would normally instill some caution. In addition, the notion that the internet is a "free-for-all" cyberspace where there are no limits or boundaries results in a user's sense of social norms and propriety generally getting blurred.

The Web results in an instant global publication of information at a very low cost. Information, which would not normally have been revealed prior to the dawning of the internet, can now be unearthed by practically anyone. Intranets are intended to be exclusively used by a company. However, information from an intranet can be easily downloaded and forwarded by e-mail or otherwise to third parties. Information posted to a bulletin board can be accessed by anyone. This means that anyone can place defamatory allegations on the bulletin board. E-mail users generally tend to treat their correspondence as a kind of conversation rather than a written interaction. Users forget that e-mails are stored and can be retrieved as hard copies and that their contents then cannot be disputed. One message can be circulated to literally hundreds of people. As a defamatory allegation need only be disclosed to one person for publication to be proved, every time e-mail is forwarded to another person, it is published again and an additional cause of action for defamation arises.

The scope of every firm having a cyber presence to liability for defamation is global. Internet sites can be accessed in most countries throughout the world; huge amounts of data can be transmitted simultaneously to several different destinations; and e-mail can be forwarded to an indefinite number of recipients without the original author having any control over the transmission. While a legal action based on defamation is usually aimed at stopping the defamatory allegations, the harm in most cases has already been done. Consequently, the most important relief claimed in a defamatory action is damages. The amount of damages granted will depend on the nature of the defamation sought and the extent of publication.

Furthermore, a defamation claim can be instituted in any jurisdiction in which a cause of action arises. In theory then, a potential defendant to a defamation suit could be sued in respect of a particular defamatory statement in a number of different countries with which it has no connection under any number of different laws with which it is totally unfamiliar. Indeed, a potential plaintiff can choose to litigate in whichever country has the most favourable laws. Theoretically, every time a third party accesses a defamatory posting on the Internet, publication has occurred.

The global nature of the Internet also raises some interesting procedural questions for the libel lawyer. In traditional libel law there are three different types of defamatory statements:

(i) The first is a statement that is defamatory on its face and which is obviously defamatory.

(ii) The second is a statement, which contains false innuendo. False innuendo is a defamatory statement that has an inferential meaning, therefore only persons with the necessary contextual knowledge appreciate that the statement is defamatory. Since statements on the internet are published globally, their inferential meanings may vary depending on the geographic or cultural location of the reader or the newsgroups or the Usenet group involved.

(iii) The third category is legal innuendo. While not defamatory on their face, these statements are defamatory when viewed together with extrinsic circumstances. Once again, contextual knowledge may render a statement defamatory in one jurisdiction but not in another.

Cyber defamation need not necessarily be directed against an individual victim, but it could be harmful to the whole society. No doubt, at times, it could be directed against an individual ('victim'), but the criminal act is potentially capable of harming a large number of persons and that is the principal object behind punishing it.

In short it is an offence, which affects the health or material welfare of the community as a whole and not merely of the individual victim. Similarly it is also an offence, which affects the country's economy and not merely the wealth of an individual victim, since defamation of a corporate house could even adversely affect its share value.

Two very significant aspects of such a social and economic offence are:

(i) the gravity of the harm caused to society; and

(ii) the nature of the offence.

The gravity of the harm is not easily apparent, but is nevertheless, undeniable. The nature of the offence is peculiar, in the sense that they are planned and executed in secrecy by shrewd and dexterous persons with sophisticated means. The public welfare is gravity affected; but detection is unusually difficult.

Cases of cyber defamation do not fit neatly in the accepted categories of crimes. They represent harm of greater magnitude than the traditional crimes and of a nature different from them.

Unlike the traditional crimes, they are not in the shape of positive aggressions or invasions. They may not result in direct or immediate injury; nevertheless, they create a danger, which the law must seek to minimise. Hence if legislation applicable to such offences, as a matter of policy, departs from legislation applicable to ordinary crimes in respect of the traditional requirements as to mens rea and the other substantive matters as well as on points of procedure, the departure would be justified.

Position in Other Countries

Defamation laws vary from country to country and in countries such as the Canada, Australia and the United States, it can vary from province to province and state to state. Therefore, plaintiffs may have the luxury of "forum shopping" or choosing the jurisdiction with the laws most favourable to him/her.

Position in US

In the United States, about 75% of defamation lawsuits are filed in state courts, and the remaining 25% in federal courts. A comprehensive discussion of what is and is not libel or slander is difficult, because each state's definition differs. Some states lump slander and libel together into the same set of laws. Some states have criminal libel laws on the books, though these are old laws, which are infrequently prosecuted. Most defendants in libel lawsuits are newspapers, which are involved in about twice as many lawsuits as are TV stations. Most plaintiffs are corporations, business people, entertainers and other public figures, and inmates. Most states do not allow defamation lawsuits to be filed if the allegedly defamed person is already deceased. None of the states allow the plaintiff to be a group of people.

In the various states, whether by case law or actual legislation, there are generally several "privileges" that can get a libel case dismissed without proceeding to trial. These include the allegedly defamatory statement being one of opinion rather than fact; or being "fair comment and criticism", as it is important to society that everyone be able to comment on matters of public interest. If a defamation lawsuit actually gets to trial, truth is an affirmative defense. Further, if the allegedly defamatory statement is not actually capable of being defamatory, i.e., an insulting statement that does not harm someone's reputation is prima facie not libelous.

New York Times Company v. Sullivan was a U.S. Supreme Court case which established the actual malice standard before press reports could be considered to be defamation and libel; and hence allowed free reporting of the civil rights campaigns in the southern United States. It is one of the key decisions supporting the freedom of the press. The actual malice standard requires that the publisher knows the statement is false or acts in reckless disregard of the truth.

The decision established that for a plaintiff to win a libel ruling against a newspaper, "actual malice" or "reckless negligence" must be proved on the part of the paper if the statement in question is about a public official or public figure. In the case of a private figure, the plaintiff must merely prove negligence.

Prior to the enactment of the Telecommunications Act of 1996, the position in US with regard to cyber defamation was such that the Courts applied the common law definition of "publisher," which held liable anyone who exercised a substantial degree of editorial control over the distributed product. This definition distinguished between a distributor, such as a newsstand or a library, and a publisher, such as a newspaper or book author. Distributors were not to be held liable for the information they disseminated, while those who reviewed content before publication would be held liable. Courts generally analyzed ISP liability under the same standards applied to newspapers and other media.

Data Security

Data security is the means of ensuring that data is kept safe from corruption and that access to it is suitably controlled. Thus data security helps to ensure privacy. It also helps in protecting personal data.

8

Network-centric Warfare

INTRODUCTION

Network-centric warfare, also called network-centric operations or net-centric warfare, is a military doctrine or theory of war pioneered by the United States Department of Defence in the 1990s. It seeks to translate an information advantage, enabled in part by information technology, into acompetitive advantage through the robust Computer networking of well informed geographically dispersed forces.

WHY NETWORKING?

Much has been written and said over the last decade as to why networking is essential, and how it improves warfighting capability. Unhappily, not all of the publications present robust arguments, and much of what has been written has been accepted as fact, rather than critically analysed.

At the most fundamental level networking aims to accelerate engagement cycles and operational tempo at all levels of a warfighting system. This is acheived by providing a mechanism to rapidly gather and distribute targeting information, and rapidly issue directives. A high speed network permits error free transmission in a fraction of the time required for voice transmission, and permits transfer of a wide range of data formats.

In a more technical sense, networking improves operational tempo (optempo) by accelerating the Observation-Orientation phases of Boyd's Observation-Orientation-Decision-Action (OODA) loop. Identified during the 1970s by US Air Force strategist John Boyd, the OODA is an abstraction which describes the sequence of events whihc must take place in any military engagement. The opponnent must be observed to gather information, the attacker must orient himself to the situation or context, then decide and act accordingly. The OODA loop is thus fundamental to all military operations, from strategic down to individual combat. It loop is an inevitable part of reality and has been so since the first tribal wars of 25,000 years ago, as it is fundamental to any predator-prey interaction in the biological world. Sadly, its proper understanding had to wait until the 1970s.

At a philosophical and practical level what confers a key advantage in engagements is the ability to stay ahead of an opponent and dictate the tempo of the engagement - to maintain the initiative and keep an opponent off balance. In effect, the attacker forces his opponent into a reactive posture and denies the opponent any opportunity to drive the engagement to an advantage. The player with the faster OODA loop, all else being equal, will defeat the opponent with the slower OODA loop by blocking or pre-empting any move the opponent with the slower OODA loop attempts to make.

The four components of the OODA loop can be split into three which are associated with processing information, and one which is associated with movement and application of firepower. Observation-Orientation-Decision are information centric while Action is kinematic or centred in movement, position and firepower.

If we aim to accelerate our OODA loops to achieve higher operational tempo than an enemy, we have to accelerate all four components of the loop. Much of twentieth century warfighting technique and technology dealt with accelerating the kinetic portion of the OODA loop. Mobility, precision and firepower increases were the result of this evolution.

There are practical limits as to how far we can push the kinetic aspect of the OODA loop - more destructive weapons produce collateral damage, faster platforms and weapons incur ever increasing costs. Accordingly we have seen evolution slow down in this domain since the 1960s. Many weapons and platforms widely used today were designed in the 1950s may remain in use for decades to come, the B-52 being a good case study.

Observation-Orientation-Decision are all about gathering information, distributing information, analysing information, understanding information and deciding how to act upon this information. The faster we can gather, distribute, analyse, understand information, the faster we can decide, and arguably the better we can decide how and when to act in combat. Networking is a mechanism via which the Observation-Orientation phases of the loop can be accelerated, and the Decision phase facilitated.

Well implemented networking can contribute to improved effectiveness in other ways. One such technique is 'self synchronisation' which permits 'directive control'. Rather than micromanage a warfighting asset with close control via a command link tether, warfighters are given significant autonomy, defined objectives, and allowed to take the initiative in how they meet these objectives. A fighter pilot who receives continuous updates from an AEW&C aircraft over a network can make his own tactical decisions, exploiting the situational picture broadcast from the AEW&C aircraft. This is of course not a new model, but networking facilitates it in ways difficult to match - compare this example with the AM radio broadcasts issued in 1943-1945 by Luftwaffe air defence nodes to permit night fighters to autonomously hunt for Allied bombers. Both amount to a 'self synchronisation' scheme, but the underlying technology is five decades apart.

Networking is not a panacea, nor can it be. The ultimate limits on the combat effect produced by a warfighting system, and thus is capability, are bounded by the Action or 'kinetic' phase of the loop. Bombs or missiles delivered is the bottom line, and networking is a tool to facilitate this effect, it is not a sustitute for bombs and missiles on target as some proponents of NCW publicly advocate.

Until recently the mathematics underpinning capability gains in large networked warfighting systems had not been studied closely. Many scholars of NCW simply borrowed the well established Metcalfe's Law from the commercial domain and simply declared it to be valid for military systems. Metcalfe's Law states that the 'utility' of a network increases with the square of the number of nodes in the network - ten nodes (platforms) permit a hundred possible connections, a hundred nodes ten thousand. Unfortunately the mathematics of web site driven sales statistics are not particularly revelant to the behaviour of networked military forces. What we now understand is that Metcalfe's Law presents a possible best case scenario for distribution of information collected by sensors on platforms in a military system. At best it is an indicator of gains in situational awareness, assuming the data being distributed is valid, timely and relevant. The real limits to capability gains in networked systems arise from the Decision-Action phases of the OODA loop.

The Decision phase sees a commander exploiting knowledge acquired in the Observation-Orientation phases, and conferring as required with his superiors and subordinates to determine what is the best choice of action. In the Action phase the commander must deploy his assets and effect the engagement. Both of these phases of the loop, in mathematical terms, are queuing systems. The commander must wait for others to respond, and must marshal and position assets to engage. All of these events involve one entity waiting for another, in effect queueing up.

The mathematical model which contrains such systems is Amdahl's Law, like Metcalfe's Law a defining equation in the computer industry. The reality Amdahl defines is simple - increasing the number of assets in the system increases the achieved work or effect at best only by the number of assets added. The actual improvement is limited by the queuing effects seen in marshalling and positioning assets to perform engagements.

The mathematical bottom line in NCW is a very simple one: networking can permit a significant improvement in operational tempo, where a shortage of targeting information is the bottleneck to achieving a high operational tempo, but networking itself has very little impact on the absolute ability of a force to deliver weapons against targets, that being constrained by the capabilities and number of combat platforms in use.

A good example is the classic Desert Storm scenario of an air force attacking strategic targets and in situ battlefield targets like deployed armoured divisions. With ample targeting information, especially for fixed targets, networking of the attacking force would not have dramatically increased combat effect.

Accordingly we have seen networking produce its greatest gains in combat effect during battlefied strike and close air support operations, especially against highly mobile and fleeting ground targets. In such an environment, where the opponent is continuously on the move, networking can produce spectacular gains since the bottlneck limiting force capability lies in the flow of targeting information to strike aircraft.

No less interesting are the effects observed in demand for specific types of assets to support networked interdiction and strike operations. Short targeting cycles in strike operations require that the bomber be orbiting in close proximity to the intended target - this is persistent strike formally now labelled a killbox interdiction. In practice this has driven up the demand for tanker sorties and the demand for B-52H, B-1B and F-15E - all at the expense of the smaller F-16C and F/A-18 variants. Bigger is better in the networked strike game, so much so that a recent discussion piece by US analyst Price Bingham in the ISR Journal predicted the demise of the classical battlefield interdiction tasked fighter-bomber, in favour of larger bombers and UCAVs. This is a direct challenge to the basic rationale for the Joint Strike Fighter family of battlefield interdiction and close air support fighters, and the longer term use of legacy designs like the F-16 and F/A-18 variants.

Networking has produced other useful benefits. One is combat identification and deconfliction, where the JTIDS/Link-16 system has been used very effectively as a more capable substitute for conventional IFF, capable of supporting air, land and sea assets.

A key issue for all networking is the Intelligence-Surveillance-Reconnaissance capability supporting it. Networks like all computing systems obey the Garbage-In Garbage-Out rule - without accurate high quality ISR systems feeding the network, it is little more than high speed digital plumbing between platforms, with nothing useful to carry. In the US force structure, the pressure to introduce network developed mostly due to bottlenecks in pushing ISR derived targeting information out of existing ISR systems like AWACS, JSTARS and Rivet Joint.

Networking capabilities are not confined to Western nations. The diffusion of commercial computing and networking systems globally has contributed to a growing in focus by non-Western militaries. Russia has capitalised on this by aggressively marketing ISR platforms like the A-50 AWACS, digital datalinking products - the Soviets were deeply enamoured of digital air defence networks - and counter ISR systems. The latter include long range AAMs like the R-172, R-37 and Kh-31 variants, as well as airborne and land mobile high power jamming equipment, and very long range SAMs like the S-400 and Imperator series.

THE UNDERLYING TECHNOLOGIES HAVE CHANGED

Information technology is undergoing a fundamental shift from platform-centric computing to network-centric computing. Platform-centric computing emerged with the widespread proliferation of personal computers in business and in the home. The significant investment the IT sector makes in research and development and product development (in some cases up to 18% of sales) has led to key technologies that have created the conditions for the emergence of network-centric computing.

This shift is most obvious in the explosive growth of the internet, intranets, and extranets. Internet users no doubt will recognize transmission control protocol/internet protocol (TCP/IP), hypertext transfer protocol (HTTP), hypertext markup language (HTML), Web browsers (such as Netscape Navigator, and Microsoft's Internet Explorer), search engines, and JavaTM Computing. These technologies, combined with high- volume, high-speed data access (enabled by the low-cost laser) and technologies for high- speed data networking (hubs and routers) have led to the emergence of network-centric computing. Information "content" now can be created, distributed, and easily exploited across the extremely heterogeneous global computing environment.

Network-centric computing is governed by Metcalfe's Law, which asserts that the "power" of a network is proportional to the square of the number of nodes in the network. The "power" or "payoff" of network-centric computing comes from information-intensive interactions between very large numbers of heterogeneous computational nodes in the network. Sun Microsystems may have been the first to point out that it is not so much about the computer as it is about the computer in the networked condition. Under fierce competitive pressure, and sensing a strategic opportunity in this fundamental shift in computing, IBM Chairman Lou Gerstner announced that IBM was moving to network-centric computing. The compelling business logic for this shift in strategy was the opportunity for IBM to link its heterogeneous computing lines more effectively and provide increased value for its customers. This is the same value proposition we seek in warfare.

The Business of America Has Changed

The emergence of the dynamic and unstable Economy B has changed the American way of business significantly. First, many firms have shifted their focus to the much larger, adaptive, learning ecosystems in which they operate. Not all actors in an ecosystem are enemies (competitors); some can have symbiotic relationships with each other. For such closely coupled relationships, the sharing of information can lead to superior results. Second, time has increased in importance. Agile firms use superior awareness to gain a competitive advantage and compress timelines linking suppliers and customers. Even firms that operate in Economy A have found ways to harness Economy B technologies and techniques to increase efficiency and productivity. Central to these developments is the shift to network-centric operations, which are characterized by information-intensive interactions between computational nodes on the network. Whether these interactions are focused on commerce, education, or military operations, there is "value" that is derived from the content, quality, and timeliness of information moving between nodes on the network. This value increases as information moves toward 100% relevant content, 100% accuracy, and zero time delay—toward information superiority.

Dominant competitors across a broad range of areas have made the shift to network- centric operations—and have translated information superiority into significant competitive advantage—but the benefits are particularly apparent in transaction- intensive operations, such as retailing and securities trading. Wal-Mart and Deutsche Morgan Grenfell are two firms that have made the shift to network-centric operations. Both have gained tremendous competitive advantages by co-evolving their organizations and processes to exploit information technology. Characteristic of big winners, they employ network-centric operational architectures that consist of a high-powered information backplane (or information grid), a sensor grid, and a transaction grid. These architectures provide the ability to generate and sustain very high levels of competitive space awareness, which is translated into competitive advantage.

Leading U.S. firms have come to understand and employ this network calculus well.

- The shift from platform to network is what enables the more flexible and more dynamic (and profitable) network-centric operation. Therefore, the construction of high-quality networks is their top priority.
- The shift from viewing partners as independent to viewing partners as part of a continuously adapting ecosystem increases speed and profitability in both sales and production. Therefore, they have developed high-speed sensor grids and automated command-and-control systems closely coupled with their transaction grids.
- The key to market dominance lies in making strategic choices appropriate to changing ecosystems. Simply pursuing operational effectiveness while adhering to an obsolete strategy is a formula for failure.

How Can the Military Not Change?

Network-centric operations deliver to the U.S. military the same powerful dynamics as they produced in American business. At the strategic level, the critical element for both is a detailed understanding of the appropriate competitive space—all elements of battlespace and battle time. Operationally, the close linkage among actors in business ecosystems is mirrored in the military by the linkages and interactions among units and the operating environment. Tactically, speed is critical. At the structural level, network-centric warfare requires an operational architecture with three critical elements: sensor grids and transaction (or engagement) grids hosted by a high-quality information backplane. They are supported by value-adding command-and-control processes, many of which must be automated to get required speed.

Network-centric warfare enables a shift from attrition-style warfare to a much faster and more effective warfighting style characterized by the new concepts of speed of command and self-synchronization. Attrition is the traditional "Economy A" analogue because it yields decreasing returns on investment. Reversals are possible, and frequently the outcome is in doubt.

Network-centric warfare, where battle time plays a critical role, is analogous to the new economic model, with potentially increasing returns on investment. Very high and accelerating rates of change have a profound impact on the outcome, "locking-out" alternative enemy strategies and "locking-in" success. There are two complementary ways that this is accomplished:

- Network-centric warfare allows our forces to develop speed of command.
- Network-centric warfare enables forces to organize from the bottom up--or to self-synchronize—to meet the commander's intent.

Speed of command has three parts: (1) The force achieves information superiority, having a dramatically better awareness or understanding of the battlespace rather than simply more raw data. Technologically, this will require excellent sensors, fast and powerful networks, display technology, and sophisticated modeling and simulation capabilities. (2) Forces acting with speed, precision, and reach achieve the massing of effects versus the massing of forces. (3) The results that follow are the rapid foreclosure of enemy courses of action and the shock of closely coupled events. This disrupts the enemy's strategy and, it is hoped, stops something before it starts. One of the strengths of network-centric warfare is its potential, within limits, to offset a disadvantage in numbers, technology, or position.

Speed of command facilitates the lock-out phenomenon observed in Economy B, but with even more powerful effects. Lock-out often takes years to achieve in business, but in warfare it can be achieved in weeks or less.

The joint suppression of air defence mission provides an example at the tactical level of how the increased combat power associated with network-centric operations can contribute to speed of command and lock-out. The High-speed Anti-Radiation Missile (HARM) is used to suppress or destroy enemy surface-to-air missile (SAM) sites. When we employ platform-centric operations in this scenario, we achieve virtually no kills.

The HARM still will suppress the SAM sites—because site operators realize that these missiles are out there and so adjust their behaviour--but those sites will stay there through the duration of the war. Consequently, aircraft that carry HARM missiles have to fly throughout the entire campaign, and all strike aircraft continue to be at risk.

By shifting to modern digital technology, we can increase battlespace awareness to yield increased combat power, with more targets destroyed. But if, through co-evolution of systems, organization, and doctrine, we introduce other shooters that are capable of attacking SAM sites, such as ATACMS, and employ them as part of an engagement grid, virtually all of the sites can be destroyed in the same amount of time. It is easy to focus on the number of sites destroyed, but the payoff is in the initial very high rate of change. When 50% of something important to the enemy is destroyed at the outset, so is his strategy. That stops wars—which is what network-centric warfare is all about.

Military operations are enormously complex, and complexity theory tells us that such enterprises organize best from the bottom-up. Traditionally, however, military commanders work to obtain top-down command-directed synchronization to achieve the required level of mass and fires at the point of contact with the enemy. Because each element of the force has a unique operating rhythm, and because errors in force movement needlessly consume combat power, combat at the operational level is reduced to a step function, which takes time and provides opportunity to the enemy. After the initial engagement, there is an operational pause, and the cycle repeats.

In contrast, bottom-up organization yields self-synchronization, where the step function becomes a smooth curve, and combat moves to a high-speed continuum. The "Observe-Orient-Decide-Act (OODA) Loop" appears to disappear, and the enemy is denied the operational pause. Regaining this time and combat power amplifies the effects of speed of command, accelerating the rate of change and leading to lock-out.

Self- synchronization was illustrated during the Taiwan Straits crisis. In 1995, when the People's Republic of China attempted to influence Taiwanese elections with some high- quality saber rattling, the United States quickly dispatched carrier battle groups, and the situation seemed to settle out. For our purposes, the most exciting part of that story was the fundamentally different way that command and control was exercised. Then-Vice Admiral Clemins, as Commander, Seventh Fleet, and his subordinates reduced their planning timelines from days to hours. This order of magnitude change suggests that something very fundamental is happening.

One reason we say that no plan survives initial contact with the enemy is because situational awareness does not. In platform-centric military operations, situational awareness steadily deteriorates. It is reestablished periodically, but it only then deteriorates again. Network-centric operations such as those used in the Taiwan Straits example create a higher awareness, and allow it to be maintained. Such awareness will improve our ability to deter conflict, or to prevail if conflict becomes unavoidable. This is not just a matter of introducing new technology; this is a matter of the co-evolution of that technology with operational concepts, doctrine, and organization. The enabler, of course, is technology. In the Taiwan case, Admiral Clemins was able to use e-mail, a very graphic-rich environment, and video teleconferencing to achieve the effect he wanted.

We are beginning to see the broad impact of network-centric warfare throughout the fleet, as key technology building blocks are deployed. In early 1997, a single aircraft carrier in the western Pacific sent 54,000 e-mails in one month—about half the amount of all of the traditional message traffic that was sent in Western Pacific during the same time. That is an example of a very complex outfit organizing itself from the bottom up. Now it is the norm. Such capabilities enable a move into the realm of speed of command. Questions decrease because ambiguity decreases, collegiality increases, and timelines shorten.

The Emerging Logical Model

The structural or logical model for network-centric warfare has emerged. The entry fee is a high-performance information grid that provides a backplane for computing and communications. The information grid enables the operational architectures of sensor grids and engagement grids. Sensor grids rapidly generate high levels of battlespace awareness and synchronize awareness with military operations. Engagement grids exploit this awareness and translate it into increased combat power. Many key elements of these grids are in place or available. For example, at the planning level, the elements of a DoD-wide intranet are emerging. To assure interoperability, all elements of the grids must be compliant with the Joint Technical Architecture and the Defence Information Infrastructure common operating environment. However, their full integration into a more powerful warfighting ecosystem is only partially complete.

This is not theory--it is happening now. For example, new classes of threats have required increased defensive combat power for joint forces. The combat power that has emerged-- the cooperative engagement capability (CEC)—was enabled by a shift to network-centric operations. CEC combines a high-performance sensor grid with a high-performance engagement grid. The sensor grid rapidly generates engagement quality awareness, and the engagement grid translates this awareness into increased combat power. This power is manifested by high probability engagements against threats capable of defeating a platform-centric defence. The CEC sensor grid fuses data from multiple sensors to develop a composite track with engagement quality, creating a level of battlespace awareness that surpasses whatever can be created with stand-alone sensors. The whole clearly is greater than the sum of the parts.

How to Get There

No one operates better than the U.S. Navy. Our forward presence force is the finest such force in the world. But operational effectiveness in the wrong competitive space may not lead to mission success. More fundamentally, has the underlying rule set changed so that we are now in a different competitive space? How will we revalue the attributes in our organization?

To choose a sporting example, although the objective of the game, the number of plays, and the operating environment are essentially the same, football is fundamentally different from soccer because its underlying rule set is different. Accordingly, the competitive attributes of mass, continuity of play, self-synchronization, sustained speed, and others are revalued. There are important differences between the ways a soccer coach and a football coach would recruit, train, and organize their teams.

Similarly, if we decide to fight on a network-centric rather than platform-centric basis, we must change how we train, how we organize, and how we allocate our resources. A good understanding of our competitive space, therefore, is vital to achieving success. The Navy, indeed all services, must make these strategic decisions to maximize future combat power and relevance. Because a network-centric force operates under a different, more modern rule set than a platform-centric force, we must make fundamental choices in at least three areas: intellectual capital, financial capital, and process.

Intellectual Capital. Information-based processes are the dominant value-adding processes in both the commercial world and the military. Yet the military fails to reward competence in these areas. "Operator" status frequently is denied to personnel with these critical talents, but the value of traditional operators with limited acumen in these processes is falling, and ultimately they will be marginalized, especially at mid-grade and senior levels. The war fighter who does not understand the true source of his combat power in such things as CEC, Global Command and

Control System, and Link-16 simply is worth less than those who do. The services must both mainstream and merge those with technical skills and those with operational experience in these areas. These are the new operators.

Every new revolution in military affairs produces a new elite. The inherent cultural changes are the most difficult and protracted. We must start now. While we delay, our people, our most vital asset, are deciding that they want to compete on a different team.

Financial Capital. Navy decision making across a broad front is aligning with the network-centric warfare strategy. We are moving forward rapidly with ship- and aircraft-launched weapons that have reach, precision, and responsiveness, and advanced C2 concepts are under development.

The Navy's umbrella strategy for enabling the IT elements of network-centric warfare is Information Technology for the 21st Century (IT-21). It provides for accelerated implemetation of customer-led command, control, communications, computers, and intelligence (C4I) innovations and existing C2 systems/capabilities (programs of record). The Navy's commitment to funding IT began in fiscal year 1997. For the fiscal year 1999 budget request and the Future Years Defence Program, Navy funding for IT-21-related programs exceeds $2.5 billion. Battle groups and amphibious ready groups are deploying with increasing network capabilities.

All elements of the network-centric warfare model must move forward if the promise of the revolution is to be realized. Delays will mean higher costs, reduced combat power, and, in the joint arena, failure to achieve the concepts of Joint Vision 2010.

Transformation Process. In spite of a ponderous acquisition process, technology insertion is ahead of and disconnected from joint and service doctrine and organizational development. The problem is cultural and systemic. A process for the co-evolution of technology, organization, and doctrine is required.

Service experimentation programs are a vital first step. While the temptation may be to take some units out of readiness reporting status for use in an experimental force, the result would be to isolate the larger force from the process. The objective is to create an ethos for experimentation, innovation, and a willingness to risk across the entire force. Specific top-down experimentation will be required because of cost and size or to establish overarching priorities, but these are expected to spawn experiments from the bottom up and facilitate cultural and organizational changes. That is the concept behind the Navy's Fleet Battle Experiment Program.

The concepts of network-centric operations, shifting competitive spaces, changing underlying rule sets, and co-evolution are not mere theory. They have been applied successfully under demanding conditions with encouraging results. Similarly, these concepts are not limited to a few optimum circumstances. The crime rate in New York City, for example, was reduced dramatically through the application of these concepts.

We may be special people in the armed forces, but we are not a special case. It would be false pride that would keep us from learning from others. The future is bright and compelling, but we must still choose the path to it. Change is inevitable. We can choose to lead it, or be victims of it. As B. H. Liddell Hart said, "The only thing harder than getting a new idea into the military mind is getting an old one out."

Note: *Network-Centric Warfare* derives its power from the strong networking of a well- informed but geographically dispersed force. The enabling elements are a high- performance information grid, access to all appropriate information sources, weapons reach and maneuver with precision and speed of response, value-adding command-and- control (C2) processes—to include high-speed automated assignment of resources to need—and integrated sensor grids closely coupled in time to shooters and C2 processes. Network-centric warfare is applicable to all levels of warfare and contributes to the coalescence of strategy, operations, and tactics. It is transparent to mission, force size and composition, and geography.

Speed of Command is the process by which a superior information position is turned into a competitive advantage. It is characterized by the decisive altering of initial conditions, the development of high rates of change, and locking in success while locking out alternative enemy strategies. It recognizes all elements of the operating situation as parts of a complex adaptive ecosystem and achieves profound effect through the impact of closely coupled events.

Self-Synchronization is the ability of a well-informed force to organize and synchronize complex warfare activities from the bottom up. The organizing principles are unity of effort, clearly articulated commander's intent, and carefully crafted rules of engagement. Self-synchronization is enabled by a high level of knowledge of one's own forces, enemy forces, and all appropriate elements of the operating environment. It overcomes the loss of combat power inherent in top-down command directed synchronization characteristic of more conventional doctrine and converts combat from a step function to a high-speed continuum.

THE STRATEGIC FABRIC IN THE NETWORK

An intelligent network allows an organization to more closely align its network with its processes, making the network more responsive, more flexible, and more effective at addressing everyday operations, as well as high-tempo operations experienced during contingencies and emergency responses. And it enables an organization to embed security deep within its infrastructure, to protect military assets and respond quickly to threats. Since the network can be a hacker's target, it must include appropriate security mechanisms that will allow the military to use the efficiencies and effectiveness gained by moving to a networked environment, without placing their operations at risk.

An intelligent network is the strategic fabric that streamlines and synthesizes the flow of information, integrating the complex array of proprietary networks, systems, and applications that provide support for military operations. Under an NCO model, military resources can be simply considered nodes on the network. Each of these resources or "networked vehicles" in the field of operation can enjoy complete access to voice, data, video, and command and control—to and from headquarters.

Leading military organizations are moving away from traditional centralized thinking and planning, and toward an edge-centered approach to information sharing and availability. An intelligent network provides the foundational elements, such as collaborative tools, storage, security, messaging, and mediation, creating a common platform that supports the full array of services and applications used by military forces. These services can be used across service or agency boundaries—transparently to the user. An intelligent network is also central to an environment where users can pull the information they require, without relying on a top-down, "push" approach to intelligence and decision making. This ability to "reach back" also reduces the forward footprint necessary for military operations, dramatically reducing costs and risks to personnel.

To deliver mission-critical information, the network must meet stringent requirements. It must be resilient enough to ensure that information is always available, protected from network outages, service spikes, and security breaches. And it must be responsive enough to serve up multiple types of information—including voice, video, and data—from multiple sources, to provide the highest degree of shared situational awareness.

In a defence environment, mission critical information is essential to command and control and other logistics, and can come in the form of intelligence, surveillance, or reconnaissance. Consider the advantages this information could provide if it were simultaneously broadcast from a single network across the chain of command down to battlefield operating systems.

Overcoming Challenges

Today's defence agencies must contend with a disparate communications environment. Their communications infrastructures likely include legacy equipment and systems that have accumulated over several years. Some of this equipment may be proprietary, making connectivity with other systems difficult. Or the communications infrastructure may be a collection of different systems that have been pieced together. In demanding situations, the disparity in capabilities of the networked elements can dramatically reduce the effectiveness of operations. All too often, current infrastructures are:

- Inaccessible—Legacy systems and networks offer limited capability, information accessibility, and scalability. They do not provide the necessary network intelligence to support advanced communications, security, and wireless capabilities.

- Incomplete—Because the military information domain is scattered between disparate systems, it is difficult for decision makers to obtain a complete picture. Insight and planning are hampered by proprietary enterprise systems; Command, Control, Communications, Computers, Intelligence, Surveillance, Target Acquisition, and Reconnaissance (C4ISTAR) Systems; weapons and sensor systems; and service provisioning or logistics systems—each focusing on only limited areas.
- Irrelevant—Different lines of service and coalitions use systems that are deliberately segmented, due to security constraints. Sharing relevant information between these systems in a timely manner is difficult or impossible.

Inability to provide shared situational awareness can have catastrophic results. Defence establishments need to achieve the highest degree of situational awareness to facilitate fast, accurate decisions, and promote self-synchronized action across the entire chain of command.

Seizing The Information Domain

Defence agencies recognize that immediate information is vital to mission effectiveness in military operations, and are looking to networking technology to increase the real-time availability of information. An intelligent network provides the foundation to integrate surveillance, reconnaissance, military intelligence, weapon and IT systems, and applications required to run successful command and control operations.

For example, the Royal Netherlands Army faced the challenge of replacing its European Command (EUROCOM)1-based mobile communications network with a solution that allows fully integrated services. This new solution, the Theatre-Independent Tactical Army and Air Force Network (TITAAN), uses a Cisco IP infrastructure as support for integrated voice, data, and video services. A revolutionary network solution, TITAAN is one of the first tactical military networks almost completely based on commercial off-the-shelf software and hardware components.

The U.S. Department of Defence is also actively transforming itself to take advantage of the benefits of NCO. Its "Network-Centric Warfare" report cites four main tenets:

- A robustly networked force improves information sharing
- Information sharing enhances the quality of information and shared situational awareness
- Shared situational awareness facilitates collaboration and self-synchronization, and enhances sustainability and speed of command
- These, in turn, dramatically increase mission effectiveness

NCO is changing the institutional culture of the military by enabling defence establishments to respond quickly to the changing landscape. The following benefits facilitate these changes.

Shared Situational Awareness

An intelligent network enables defence forces to deliver mission-critical information throughout the chain of command. Organizations can share situational awareness, regardless of the location or time of day.

An intelligent network enables the protection of sensitive information, helping to ensure that sensitive communications and data are available only to authorized personnel. And it streamlines the delivery of information, even from multiple sources and locations. By offering support for data, voice, and video transmissions, an intelligent network gives forces a complete picture of a combat situation.

Because it is based on standards-compliant components and technologies, an intelligent network can interoperate smoothly with existing systems. And it can scale to support thousands of users on the network at the same time.

In its report to Congress, the U.S. Department of Defence underscored the ability of NCO to provide unique advantages to armed forces:

"Network-centric operations provide a force with access to a new, previously unreachable region of the information domain.

The ability to operate in this region provides warfighters with a new type of information advantage. This advantage is enabled by the dramatic improvements in information sharing made possible by networking. With this information advantage, a warfighting force can achieve dramatically improved shared situational awareness and knowledge."

Whether at peace, at war, or engaged in a humanitarian effort, forces need information in a timely and secure fashion to make proactive decisions and successfully achieve their missions.

Greater Mission Effectiveness

An intelligent network boosts mission effectiveness. It gives defence forces the ability to understand a situation more fully, and allows dispersed personnel to simultaneously and accurately evaluate and respond to each situation. The network improves communications, coordination, and collaboration, to create greater operational efficiencies. And it boosts the effectiveness of military personnel in achieving goals or targets, enabling them to do things they couldn't do before in the field.

For example, the Royal Netherlands Army's new TITAAN system enables the organization to carry its phone traffic and several information systems over a single IP network infrastructure. According to Lieutenant Colonel Bertil Sundquest, Chief Current Ops, "With TITAAN, we can run, on any workstation, command-and-control information, planning, and support systems such as ADAMS, BICES, JOIIS, or LOCE. We can also display digital maps and aerial photos, if required, overlaid on each other, using the 3M projector systems mounted overhead in our headquarters."

Support for Ad-Hoc Operations

A network-centric strategy gives military agencies an unprecedented capability to address high-risk situations, wherever they occur. For example, a secure, ubiquitous network infrastructure can support instantaneous collaboration between military branches of service and coalition partners. Standards-based networking also allows that network to extend out to forces that are on the move, freeing them from dependence on a static location. The network's support for mobile operations can provide a tactical commander with new levels of field visibility. Because an intelligent network integrates a broad range of networks, advanced systems, and applications, defence forces can collaborate more effectively and share information as an operation unfolds.

Continuity of Operations

Continuity of operations (COOP) is a critical requirement for any defence agency. The interruption of communication, at any level, can jeopardize a mission. An NCO strategy provides the advanced technologies and best practices necessary to protect the network and information assets from unplanned outages and security threats. It also provides the critical emergency response systems to handle new threats and unforeseen situations.

Reduced Operational and Capital Costs

NCO lowers operational and capital costs by converging multiple networks together on a single intelligent network. And, because it consolidates multiple communications systems onto a common infrastructure, it enables military organizations to reduce the costs of provisioning, installing, integrating, and managing the network. An NCO strategy also allows military organizations to more easily upgrade and support intelligent network services such as converged voice and data applications—which can dramatically improve operational efficiency. With careful planning, the strategy can also reduce the costs of performing incremental upgrades, with network downtime and consumption of IT resources. One example of standards-based networks helping to reduce costs is in applying wireless in the field environment. By connecting field operations through wireless networking, field operations can save significant time and money in airlift, sealift, and excavation costs, compared to laying cable.

NCO enhances reliability and reduces troubleshooting costs, using embedded technologies and services such as integrated security, telephony, management, caching, and content management. These technologies, found on Cisco integrated services routers, protect the network from unplanned network outages, slow service, and security breaches. Training and administrative costs—a significant portion of network cost of ownership—are reduced, because network administrative staff can use a common interface to manage and administer the network. By employing open standards-based technologies, organizations can also avoid the costly pitfalls and limited interoperability associated with proprietary systems.

For example, Cisco and Scientific Research Corporation (SRC) collaborated to deliver a "push to talk" system to soldiers. The system requires minimal configuration, is self-healing, and provides ample bandwidth for military applications. By using standards-based, off-the-shelf components in the design, partners were able to create a valuable, innovative solution that cost significantly less than proprietary systems. It also improves interoperability across different vendor systems, and enables faster rollout of new capabilities. Using an open standards-based architecture gives military organizations unprecedented flexibility, enabling them to more closely attune their infrastructures to highly specific needs—and quickly adjust when those needs change.

NETWORK CENTRIC WARFARE DEFINED

NCW is the embodiment of an "Information Age" transformation of the United States Department of Defence and all the elements that support it. NCW represents a set of war fighting concepts and associated military capabilities that allow warfighters to take full advantage of all available information and bring all available assets to bear in a rapid and flexible manner. NCW is based on the following tenets:

- A robustly networked force improves information sharing,
- Information sharing enhances the quality of information and shared situational awareness,
- Shared situational awareness enables collaboration and self-synchronization, and enhances sustainability and speed of command,

Interoperability Frameworks

NCOIC streamlines systems for the elimination of interoperability issues to reduce operating costs for more effective direction of organizational resources.

Key deliverables

Systems, Capabilities, Operations, Programs, & Enterprises (SCOPE) Model

- The SCOPE interoperability assessment model is designed to characterize interoperability-relevant aspects or capabilities of a system or set of systems over a network in terms of a set of dimensions and values along those dimensions.

NCOIC Interoperability Framework (NIF)

- The NIF is a development framework that helps system architects and system engineers to embed interoperability elements throughout the life cycle of programs, beginning with requirements. Whenever possible, those resources are based upon standards.

Net Centric Patterns

- NCOIC Net Centric Patterns contain prescriptive recommendations on approaches and standards in specific interoperability domains.

Network Centric Analysis Tool (NCAT)

- NCAT is a collaborative, web-enabled questionnaire-based tool developed to assist NCOIC teams and member companies to enhance the likelihood and reduce the time and effort of member companies developing interoperable systems consistent with customers' policies and guidelines, reference models and architectures. It is also available in an excel format.

NCOIC Lexicon

- The Lexicon defines terms and expressions that are relevant to texts published by the NCOIC. This material is offered for dynamic debate, discussion and additional submissions in this online wiki. NCOIC Lexicon Custodian Working Group periodically reviews the wiki, and publishes updates of the consensed catalogue, including comments for entries that have been deleted.

NCOIC internal structure

Functional teams

Functional Teams (FTs) implement the technical roadmap of the Consortium by focusing on specific technical elements that lead to netcentricity.

The teams and their associated working groups are coordinated through a Technical Council, composed of the leaders of each Functional Team.

NIF Architecture Concepts FT

- Manages the development of the NCOIC's Interoperability Framework (NIF) and champions its use within the consortium. The NIF provides the framework through which the NCOIC will publish its prescribed use of standards and patterns in specific domains and describes the relationships between the individual Specialized Frameworks.

Specialized Frameworks FT

- Hosts and encourages the development, approval, and publication of specialized Frameworks and Patterns that contain guidelines and standards recommendations for the broad range of domains that are of interest to NCOIC members and their customers.

Building Blocks FT

- Provides a catalog of products for use by government and commercial systems engineers, which meet NCOIC criteria for the support of network centric operations requirements, network centric environments and industry standards.

Netcentric Assessment FT

- Defines, identifies, establishes and assembles the necessary criteria for measuring and assessing network centricity and network enablement in all the relevant forms.

System Engineering & Integration FT

- Helps to integrate the efforts and promote the deliverables of NCOIC Functional Teams for the accomplishment of NCOIC goals.

Integrated Project Teams

Integrated Project Teams (IPTs) serve as domain specific customer teams, who work with global NCO stakeholders in solving their interoperability problems.

The IPTs harness the expertise of the Technical Functional Teams in utilizing NCOIC tools and best practices to provide customers with the appropriate guidance to achieve their netcentric missions.

The IPTs thereby validate and refine NCOIC approaches in collaboration with customers.

Net Enabled Emergency Response IPT (NEER)

- The NEER IPT will recommend net-enabled solutions needed to bridge the gaps among the diverse organizations that need to come together to provide emergency response for day-to-day emergencies as well as for complex humanitarian disasters (CHD).

C3 Interoperability IPT

- Facilitates inter-operation and overarching coordination of the military, civil-military and civil C2-environment", promoting interoperability to achieve Situational Awareness and effective decision-making based on standards and best practices.

Sense & Respond Logistics IPT

- Provides a forum for defence and commercial stakeholders of Logistics Communities of Interest (COIs) to identify and coordinate solutions to obstacles to achieving net-centric interoperability by leveraging NCOIC solutions.

Aviation IPT

- Advocates global aviation transformation through net-centric solutions. The IPT supports this mission through industry best practices and tools to advise the use of existing and emerging standards and their patterns in support of global aviation needs.

Maritime Awareness IPT

- Establishes shared understanding of the net-centric aspects of Maritime Awareness. Advocates the enhancement of

Maritime Awareness through application of net-centric concepts and technologies.

NAPOLEON AND THE CONDUCT OF WAR

A new army emerged from the French Revolution. It had a new organisation and a new purpose, and provided Napoleon a superior instrument to wield against his enemies in Europe. This new army was capable of achieving rapid, decisive victories in battles of annihilation, which allowed Napoleon to make and enforce far-reaching demands on other states. No longer was Napoleon constrained to limited objectives as were the statesmen of the *ancien regime*. Whereas armies of the *ancien regime* tended to avoid battle, Napoleon could force battle by moving at speed on a broad front along multiple roads. Others at the end of the previous regime introduced most of the reforms that Napoleon used to such great effect. The Republican armies under Generals Francois Kellerman, Jean-Baptiste Jourdan, Jean Moreau and others refined the tactics put forward by theorists such as the Comte de Guibert, Jean-Baptiste de Gribeauval and Jean du Teil. These reforms dominated the Revolutionary and Napoleonic periods. Napoleon also inherited an officer corps that was both militarily professional and no longer restricted to the old nobility. It had become a Revolutionary officer corps, established on the principles of merit and talent for promotion. Thus, Napoleon started from a highly advantageous position with a large and experienced army and a loyal officer corps, whose fortunes and advancement were tied closely to Napoleon's own fortunes. Like Frederick, Napoleon's genius did not lie in any special or unique understanding of warfare. Instead, it lay in his ability to do what the conventional wisdom recognised should be done. Napoleon's talent lay in his expertise and the use he made of his fantastic new military instrument.

The Revolution created many enemies for France. Given the enormity of the threat, France took advantage of the new national spirit and introduced a *levee en masse* in order to raise an army of sufficient size to deal with it. The scale of the increase in size of the French army, and the speed with which the French raised it, meant that there was insufficient time and resources to devote to the degree of training given to soldiers and units of the *ancien regime*. To mitigate the lack of skill, Napoleon's armies excelled in the employment of the tactic of the assault column. Employment of the column required relatively little skill, and its flexibility and rapid employment provided a major advantage over the traditional line.

Napoleon also grasped the importance of mass in modern warfare. He used this principle, along with the greater speed and flexibility of his army, to overwhelm his enemies by using the bulk of his forces to gain local superiority and then destroy them piecemeal before they could unite. The superior mobility and agility of Napoleon's armies allowed him to position them on an enemy's rear without too much concern about them threatening his. The relative speed and mass advantage of Napoleon's armies was facilitated in part by his introduction of the *corps d'avant-garde* or *corps d'armée*. These replaced the division as the main tactical organisation of the *Grande Armée*. The corps was a self-contained army comprised of infantry, artillery and cavalry numbering anywhere from 10,000 to 30,000 men. Although not an original concept, Napoleon took full advantage of it. Each *corps d'armée* was capable of holding off greatly superior forces for several hours until support arrived. Therefore, an army made up of various corps was able to move in widely separated units. The distributed advance of multiple corps was deceptive to the enemy, easier on logistics, and is what gave Napoleon's forces a decisive mobility advantage.

The division of the *Grande Armée* into sub-elements also helped to mitigate friction. Generally, Napoleon dispersed his corps on the march so that they were in mutually supporting positions and able to come to the aid of each other in a timely manner. It also allowed Napoleon to concentrate force at the decisive point of battle without direct orders or immediate control. He issued broad but clear guidance and expected his subordinates to use their initiative. Napoleon's command system was vastly different to the direct control exercised by Frederick, and provided a degree of coherence that was previously only possible through the immediate presence of the commander. Therefore, coherence of the force was as important to Napoleon as it was to Frederick, although he achieved it in a very different manner.

All of the measures above allowed Napoleon to pursue a coherent approach to warfare that aimed at the destruction of the main body of the enemy's army in a single decisive battle. By destroying his enemy's field army, Napoleon hoped to break the national will to resist, thereby allowing him to dictate the terms of peace.

This approach, coupled with specific campaign designs derived from Napoleon's comprehensive analysis of each of his opponents, were decisive given the nature of his opponents prior to 1809. However, by the Franco–Austrian War of 1809 Napoleon's opponents had modernised, changing warfare in ways that would undermine his approach. According to historian Robert Epstein, firepower became an increasingly greater factor in battle as armies grew larger and employed greater quantities of cannon. Napoleon did not keep pace with this change in the scale of battle. Consequently, the 'god of battles, was overthrown by the dynamics of warfare that he had created but did not understand'. While he was still pursuing battles of annihilation, campaigns of attrition were becoming the norm. Therefore, Napoleon seems to amplify the imperatives of context and design raised during the analysis of Frederick.

Napoleon's genius related closely to his personality. Napoleon was an egotist. He was supremely confident and optimistic. He possessed great energy, ambition, and willpower. He was unperturbed under stress. He possessed a vivid imagination, which allowed him to envisage how things might be after a series of possible actions and events, similar to the skill of a master chess player. Napoleon had an amazing capacity for work. He could apply his mind for extraordinarily long hours, often going with little to no sleep for extended periods. According to Martin Van Creveld, daylight hours saw ceaseless and prodigious activity: travelling, inspecting, reviewing, meeting with subordinates and with other dignitaries, reconnoitering, gathering intelligence, questioning prisoners and local inhabitants, all of which enabled him to see and hear for himself and prevented him from becoming the prisoner of his staff.

The nature of Napoleon's qualities (and those of Frederick) seems to suggest that personal qualities are an important factor in the nature of command. In fact, Napoleon's character was such that his whole command system was tailored to it to an extent like no other. Therefore, a superior intellect was a critical aspect of Napoleon's command.

Van Creveld contends that it was the 'emperor's brain that served as the *Grande Armée*'s central information-processing machine', which explains why speed and decisiveness were so characteristic of Napoleon's way of warfare. Napoleon eliminated intermediate tiers, conjecture and discussion from the decision-making process and command function. An insight into Napoleon's style of command and way of warfare are to be gleaned from his words, 'One jumps into the fray, then figures out what to do next.' Napoleon would concede to risk and limited understanding, and use action to compensate. In a way, it was a tendency to experiment and accept the unexpected, including negative consequences. Napoleon's method was to avoid planning operations through to a logical conclusion, seeking to create opportunity through action. His emphasis on action to create the opportunities that he could not foresee must have depended largely on a robust character that could accept the risks inherent in such an approach.

Nevertheless, the weakness of the command system built around Napoleon was its dependence on a single man. Napoleon's health, wellbeing, state of mind or death could clearly affect the command system in catastrophic ways, which suggests that some redundancy in the command system is important, or even necessary. Yet this deduction would miss the point presented by Napoleon's case. Napoleon and the command system built around him were effective. Taken as a whole, the command system, coupled with Napoleon's character, and given the political and social conditions of the time, was coherent, relevant and very effective. Napoleon's effectiveness as a commander relates to his particular context.

One of the most important factors of Napoleon's personality and its effect on his abilities as a commander was his capacity to inspire others. Napoleon was a charismatic leader. He was adept at motivating individuals. He believed in the maxim that 'moral force rather than numbers, decides victory'. Napoleon instituted a system of awards, which encouraged greater effort and greater loyalty. He promoted those who performed well regardless of their social background, thereby linking the fortunes of his officers to his own continued success and maintenance of power. Napoleon was sceptical of the value of rhetorical speeches at the moment of battle.

It is not set speeches at the moment of battle that render soldiers brave. The veteran scarcely listens to them, and the recruit forgets them at the first discharge. If discourses and harangues are useful, it is during the campaign; to do away with unfavorable impressions, to correct false reports, to keep alive a proper spirit in the camp, and to furnish material and amusement for the bivouac. Napoleon's inspiration was as important to the *Grande Armée* as it was to Frederick's army, although the manner with which they provided the inspiration and maintained their informal authority over their respective armies was very different. Both inspired largely because of the manner with which they presented themselves.

NEW WEAPON OF THE INFORMATION AGE

The term network-centric warfare broadly describes the combination of emerging tactics, techniques and procedures that a networked force can employ to create a decisive warfighting advantage. According to John Keegan, author of *A History of Warfare,* it is similar to the significant warfighting developments of the industrial age and agrarian age in that network-centric warfare seeks to exploit an order of magnitude change in an underlying source of power to increase warfighting advantage dramatically.

Paula Kaufman, in an article she wrote for *IEEE Spectrum,* agrees with this opinion. In the industrial age, power was primarily derived from mass and the sources of power for moving mass. In the information age, power is increasingly derived from information sharing, information access and speed, she says. The advantages network-centric warfare brings to the battlespace are particularly relevant to the tactical and operational levels of war, but they impact all levels of military activity from the tactical to the strategic. Although the construct of an information advantage may seem somewhat intangible, it can be measured, and its impact on military operations can be evaluated in terms of mission effectiveness, survivability and lethality—coins of the realm used by warfighters across the ages.

Evidence of the power of network-centric warfare accumulated from a wide range of activities, including combat operations, training events, exercises and demonstrations, continues to strengthen and reinforce its existing tenets. A U.S. Defence Department 2001 report to Congress about network-centric warfare enumerates several specific points: A robustly networked force improves information sharing; information sharing and collaboration enhances the quality of information and shared situational awareness; shared situational awareness enables collaboration and self-synchronization and enhances sustainability and speed of command; and these in turn dramatically increase mission effectiveness.

Although the margin of victory has varied across mission areas, the outcome has consistently been decisive in favor of forces that are robustly networked. In some tactical engagements, superior platforms were decisively defeated by less capable platforms that leveraged the order of magnitude improvement in information sharing that networking enables. In other engagements, digitized and networked ground forces with a reduced number of platforms were able to substitute information for mass and outperform units that had fought with a larger number of platforms not similarly digitized and networked. Even more impressive, the combination of networked and digitized ground and air forces was able to defeat an opposition force decisively with unprecedented lethality by creating and leveraging an information advantage.

Most recently, military operations in support of operation Enduring Freedom highlighted the emergence of near-real-time information sharing as a source of warfighting advantage. The source of power was not new platforms, but rather the networking of the legacy platforms with special operations forces (SOF). The extent to which ground-based SOF were able to share precision information with command and control aircraft and fighter, bomber and attack aircraft was unprecedented in military operations. It represented an order of magnitude increase in information sharing over what had been previously demonstrated anywhere in the world in combat operations.

Two of the more noteworthy and documented examples of the power of network-centric warfare are drawn from the air-to-air mission. In this mission area, a major contributor to enhanced survivability and lethality is an increase in shared situational awareness and enhanced situational understanding. With audio-only communications, pilots and controllers must share information generated by onboard sensors about opposing forces as well as their own position and status via voice. Communicating the minimum essential information required to take offensive or defensive actions takes time, and the resulting situational awareness can often differ significantly from reality.

In contrast, when datalinks are employed on fighter aircraft, digital information on blue and red forces is shared instantaneously, enabling all participants to share a common tactical picture. This improved information position constitutes a significant information advantage vis-à-vis an adversary fighting with voice-only communications. This information advantage in turn enables a cognitive advantage in the form of dramatically increased shared situational awareness and enhanced situational understanding. The result is that pilots flying datalink-equipped aircraft can achieve much higher levels of shared situational awareness and understanding on a timeline previously unachievable with voice-only communications. They can translate these advantages into increased survivability and lethality.

One of the best examples of how networking and digitization can be leveraged to create an information advantage took place in a training exercise in the mid-1990s when Royal Air Force (RAF) Tornado aircraft from U.K. 29 Squadron with tactical datalinks defeated U.S. Air Force F-15Cs with voice-only communications in a series of air-to-air engagements that took place during a red flag exercise in the airspace over the Nellis Air Force Base range.

Historically, the most favorable outcome that the absolute best RAF pilots could manage when flying against F-15Cs was a draw. However, when the RAF introduced a datalink in the form of Link-16, U.K. 29 Squadron pilots, flying with new innovative tactics, were able to increase their kill ratio over the F-15C equipped with voice-only communications to approximately 4-to-1.

The power of information sharing to increase survivability and lethality in the air-to-air mission was substantiated by the Air Force again in the mid-1990s during a joint tactical information distribution system (JTIDS) operational special project. Air Force pilots flying F-15Cs with and without datalinks clearly demonstrated an order of magnitude increase in information sharing enabled by the datalinks. This operational special project consisted of hundreds of tactical engagements, ranging in size from two-versus-two to eight-versus-16 aircraft, which were conducted during day and night conditions. During the more than 12,000 sorties and more than 19,000 flying hours, the average kill ratio for F-15Cs equipped with datalinks increased by more than 150 percent over F-15Cs fighting with voice-only communications, according to a JTIDS operational special project report to Congress.

An analysis of the growing body of evidence highlights a very strong relationship between information advantage, cognitive advantage and increased lethality and survivability at the tactical level. It shows that these relationships are not unique to the air-to-air mission but rather that they were demonstrated first in this mission area as a result of the relative maturity of the application of networking technology in this arena.

This same story line of increased warfighting effectiveness enabled by networking has been played out in counter special operations forces mission Fleet Battle Experiment Delta; counter anti-access, Fleet Battle Experiment Foxtrot; multinational rapid reaction forces, Allied Command Europe Mobile Force–Land; and combined arms maneuver warfare, Division Capstone Exercise–Phase I (DCX-I).

During DCX-I, the blue force was digitized and networked to an unprecedented degree. Equally important, these forces were highly trained on this digital equipment and in many cases had developed new tactics, techniques and procedures to leverage their improved capability to operate in the information domain. The digitized and networked ground forces demonstrated significantly improved warfighting capabilities and were able to prevail over the opposing forces in a number of engagements.

For example, during one phase of the exercise, the blue force was in a defensive posture with the opposing force moving to contact under the cover of darkness.

A significant column of armor was detected by the joint surveillance target attack radar system and positively identified as hostile by a Hunter unmanned aerial vehicle, Col. Fred Stein, USA (Ret.), explains. An analysis of the real-time blue ground picture indicated that the attacking opposing force column was located approximately 10 miles from the brigade combat team's defensive positions. The brigade commander, in consultation with the division commander, decided to engage the hostile force, and the fire mission was assigned to close air support. At this point, the engagement departed from the usual script, which had been characterized in the past by some as an exercise in futility, according to an internal correspondence from the Air National Guard Air Force Reserve Test Center.

F-16s and A/OA-10s of the Arizona Air National Guard equipped with the situational awareness data link (SADL) performed a close-air-support mission. The networking of these aircraft enabled them to exchange real-time targeting information as well as to receive and display a forward trace of the blue ground picture. The result of this networking was more than an order of magnitude improvement in the ability of ground and air forces to share information.

In addition to being equipped with SADL, the F-16s were equipped with Lightening II targeting pods and a mixed weapons load of GBU-12s and AGM-65D Mavericks. The Forward Air Controller–Airborne (FAC-A) determined that employing the F-16s as a coordinated pair would maximize combat power. In engaging the ground targets, the A/OA-10 FAC-A identified targets of interest and distributed sensor points of interest over SADL to facilitate sensor cueing by the F-16's Lightening II targeting pod. Employing these tactics enabled each wave of two-ship pairs to engage tanks selectively and avoid dropping ordnance on less significant targets.

The battle damage assessment of the first wave of F-16s was "two battalions rendered combat ineffective." Follow-on flights of F-16s were equally lethal, according to the Air National Guard correspondence. The net result of this engagement was that this phase of the training exercise had to be recocked to enable ground forces to accomplish their training objectives for hasty defence and counterattack successfully, Col. Stein says. This transformation of close air support at night from an exercise in futility to devastatingly effective combat highlights the efficacy of network-centric warfare.

The impact of digitization and networking on the combined arms fight, specifically the impact of digital close air support, is described in an Army evaluation of DCX-I. "The National Training Center is a playing field that often humbles the visiting team," it reports. "However, during the U.S. Army's Division Capstone Exercise–Phase I, the visiting team, in the form of the U.S. Army's 4th Infantry Division, supported by elements of the U.S. Air Force, including elements of the Arizona Air National Guard, were able to leverage the power of an order of magnitude increase in information sharing to turn the tables on the opposing forces on at least two occasions. Of particular significance was a devastating defeat of opposing forces at night by F-16 and A/OA-10 aircraft performing the close-air-support mission."

Worldwide, militaries are crafting their individual responses to the challenges and opportunities of the information age. They are taking actions that demonstrate an increased understanding of the sources of information age warfighting advantage. A new vocabulary has developed that reflects the subtle variations in underlying strategies and core missions of militaries worldwide. To varying degrees, these actions also are reflected in emerging concepts and doctrine, focused investments in key enablers and well-crafted programs of experimentation.

CYBERNETIC WARFARE AND THE COMPUTER

As the intensity and breadth of the battlefield grew along with its logistical requirements, new communication technologies became necessary to achieve the required integration and coordination of increasingly large and intricate military systems.

The harnessing of electromagnetic forces for telecommunication purposes proceeded with telegraphy and telephony, simultaneously stimulating growing scientific interest in the concept of information. Cybernetics emerged from the unprecedented technological and industrial effort of the Second World War, in particular the work on the automation of anti-aircraft defences. The selfproclaimed 'science of communications and control' promised to manage chaos and disruption through self-regulating mechanisms of negative information feedback. By being defined in terms of negative entropy (negentropy), information became conceptualized as the source of all order. The computer, also developed during the war for the purposes of code-breaking and the computation of nuclear physics, emerged as the new dominant technology and abstract model through which the world came to be understood chiefly in terms of information processing.

The drive for complete predictability and centralized control over armed conflict was renewed under cybernetic warfare with the deployment of computers and automated control technologies, and the widespread application of the analytical tools of operations research and systems analysis.

The Cold War and the constant threat of nuclear annihilation required ever greater levels of automation and centralization of the war machine; and cybernetics, with its promise of stability in the face of perturbation, appeared best suited to the containment and management of a conflict of potentially apocalyptic proportions.

Vast command and control architectures were established to organize the global projection of armed force and the rapid mobilization of military systems within the shrinking windows of opportunity afforded by nuclear weaponry. Scientific methodology was applied to warfare more systematically than ever, with operations research and systems analysis applied comprehensively to both tactical and strategic questions. The first two decades of the postwar era saw the rise of the defence intellectuals and their analytical tools in the United States, culminating in the nomination of Robert McNamara as Secretary of Defence.

In its most pristine form, cybernetic warfare fuelled wild yet enduring fantasies of omniscience and omnipotence on the battlefield. In 1969 General William Westmoreland, commander-in-chief of US forces in Vietnam, formulated his vision of the military's future, encapsulating this cybernetic ideal:

On the battlefield of the future, enemy forces will be located, tracked, and targeted almost instantaneously through the use of data links, computer assisted intelligence evaluation, and automated fire control. With first round kill probabilities approaching certainty, and with surveillance devices that can continually track the enemy, the need for large forces to fix the opponent becomes less important.

Towards Chaoplexic Warfare

Since the mid-1970s, the cybernetic mode of warfare has come under increasing challenge from the military reversal for US forces in Vietnam, geopolitical transformation following the end of the Cold War, and novel scientific developments growing out of the original corpus of cybernetics.

The increasing application of computers to the study of scientific problems, the exploration of non-linear mathematics, and an extension of the cybernetic analysis of systems to questions of self-organization opened the way for novel scientific approaches which eventually crystallized into the theories of chaos and complexity (here referred to together as *chaoplexity*). Information remains the central concept, and in this sense chaoplexity is an outgrowth of cybernetics; but the focus on change, evolution and positive feedback breaks with the cybernetic pioneers' concern for stability.

Chaos is seen no longer as simply a threat to order which must be averted at all costs, but as the very condition of possibility of order. The key notions here are those of non-linearity, self-organization and emergence, and the pivotal technological figure is that of the network, the distributed model of information exchange perhaps best embodied by the internet.

The Science of Chaoplexity

Although still firmly set in the informational paradigm, chaos theory and complexity science departed from cybernetics in shifting the focus away from the stabilizing self-regulation (or homeostasis) underlying the persistence of existing systems towards runaway processes of change leading to the emergence of new systems or patterns of behaviour.

Non-linear dynamics and positive feedback processes, whereby small causes can amplify into large effects, are crucial here. Chaos theorists have used computer simulations of non-linear systems to reveal how initially minute variations can ramp up into dramatic changes in the long-term behaviour of the system. The popular image invoked to illustrate this phenomenon is the 'butterfly effect': the notion that a butterfly flapping its wings in (say) Tokyo can cause a tornado in (say) California. While chaos theory has imposed serious limits on the ability to predict the long-term behaviour of systems, it has also provided new insights, uncovering a subtle order and structure to phenomena previously believed to be completely devoid of recognizable patterns, such as the turbulence of fluids or plate tectonics.

Building on the original insights of chaos theory, complexity scientists turned to the interactions of the different component parts of living systems, and particularly to the new properties and behaviours constituted through the networked selforganization of autonomous agents.

Self-organization is the process by which the autonomous interaction of individual entities results in the bottom-up emergence of complex systems, systems composed of many parts which are connected in a non-linear fashion.

The notion of the network is central to describing the patterns of interaction which are constituted by the interplay of entities in a complex system: 'The first and most obvious property of any network is its non-linearity— it goes in all directions. Thus the relationships in a network pattern are non-linear relationships. In particular, an influence, or message, may travel along a cyclical path, which may become a feedback loop. The concept of feedback is intimately connected with the network pattern.'

Of special interest are the 'complex adaptive systems' which display the ability to change and learn from experience. Complexity theorist John Holland defines a complex adaptive system as a dynamic network of many agents acting simultaneously, constantly both acting and reacting to what the other agents are doing.

Since the control of a complex adaptive system tends to be highly dispersed and decentralized, any coherent behaviour in the system arises from competition and cooperation among the agents themselves. It is the accumulation of all the individual decisions taken by the multitude of agents which produces the overall behaviour of the system, which can thus be said to be emergent. Complex adaptive systems include living organisms, insect colonies, bird flocks, ecosystems, businesses, stock markets and other forms of social organization; the constituent agents may be cells, species, individuals, firms or nations. From the perspective of chaoplexity, the most successful systems are those that retain flexibility and openness in the interaction and organization of their parts within environments which elude complete predictability.

No longer is order to be sought in a natural tendency towards equilibrium. On the contrary, it is with non-equilibrium that order emerges from chaos, at the point where instability and creative mutation allow for the genesis of new forms and actions. As Ian King puts it, 'networking [is] a way of maintaining a low-level chaotic substrate so that—as in the brain—the chaos will from time to time give birth to an intellectual self-organizing structure'.

Decentralized self-organizing systems are inherently better equipped than centralized systems to deal with limited predictability and contingency. According to the biologist Christopher Langton, 'since it's effectively impossible to cover every conceivable situation, top-down systems are forever running into combinations of events they don't know how to handle. They tend to be touchy and fragile, and they all too often grind to a halt in a dither of indecision.' In contrast, decentralized systems of quasi-autonomous units can operate more effectively and with a greater degree of adaptability on the basis of the local calculations of the networked agents constituting them. For Stuart Kauffman, 'networks in the regime near the edge of chaos—this compromise between order and surprise—appear best able to coordinate complex activities and best able to evolve as well'.

Chaoplexity has challenged some of the most deeply held scientific convictions about the natural world and opened up whole new areas of research. It is now also increasingly weighing on the debates about military organization, heralding a new era in the scientific way of warfare.

The Dawn of Chaoplexic Warfare

Cybernetic warfare experienced its first serious reversal with the Vietnam War, where its analytical techniques and military systems foundered in the conditions of a low-intensity conflict. James Gibson has written persuasively about the failure in the jungles of South-East Asia of 'technowar', an approach to military conflict in which war was viewed as 'a production system that can be rationally managed and warfare as a kind of activity that can be scientifically determined by constructing computer models'.

The conduct of the war was blighted by the attempts of the military and political hierarchy to micro-manage the conflict and by an obsession with statistical evaluation and information-gathering which frequently created assessments of the war that were completely at variance with the reality on the ground.

Despite the deployment of an unprecedented telecommunications network in the field of operations, command and control technologies failed to perform as expected, with saturation and bottlenecks preventing information on Vietcong positions and movements from arriving in time to be actionable.

Perhaps most seriously, a misguided faith in the powers of technoscience to grant military omnipotence led policy-makers to embrace armed force more willingly as the means to solve complex strategic problems. Such hubris was perfectly encapsulated by Henry Kissinger's claim in 1968 that 'a scientific revolution has, for all practical purposes, removed technical limits from the exercise of power in foreign policy'.

The debacle in Vietnam provoked some soul-searching among strategists and military men but did not result in an immediate abandonment of the central principles of cybernetic warfare, which continued to dominate military thinking through the 1980s. All the early contributions to the debate on the revolution in military affairs were premised on the idea that computers, telecommunication links and precision-guided munitions would finally deliver the frictionless, automated battlefield promised by Westmoreland. However, new thinking drawing on the emerging non-linear sciences did begin to penetrate military theory, at first espoused only by isolated individuals but entering the mainstream at the turn of the century.

The late US air force colonel John Boyd is perhaps the most prominent pioneer of chaoplexic warfare, and increasingly is considered to be one of the most important military thinkers of recent times. Boyd is best known for his formulation of the OODA loop (observe–orient–decide–act), describing the decision-making process of the warfighter engaged in combat. Although this is at first sight reminiscent of a typical cybernetic feedback loop, whereby a system adjusts its behaviour to incoming information from its environment in order to meet a desired objective, Boyd was insistent on the need for the analytical frameworks used during the orientation phase to be continually challenged and reinvented through a perpetual process of 'destruction and creation'.

No predetermined automated response can prevail for long in a world that is 'uncertain, everchanging, unpredictable'. Boyd went on to contribute to US Marine Corps doctrine, which displays clear signs of the influence of chaoplexity in asserting that 'the best we can hope for is to impose a general framework of order on the disorder, to prescribe the general flow of action rather than to try to control each event', and that 'like a living organism, a military organization is never in a state of stable equilibrium but is instead in a continuous state of flux—continuously adjusting to its surroundings'.

If the earlier proclamations of an imminent revolution in military affairs remained firmly tributary to cybernetic conceptions, the ascent of network-centric warfare (NCW) marked the onset of a shift towards chaoplexic notions on the centre ground of debates over military doctrine. With its ideas couched in the language and concepts of the non-linear sciences, NCW first appeared on the scene within the US navy in the late 1990s before rapidly rising to become the new official Pentagon gospel under the agenda of 'Transformation' with the founding of the Office of Force Transformation in 2001 under the stewardship of its original formulator Vice Admiral Arthur Cebrowski.

According to Cebrowski, networkcentric warfare views war as a 'complex, adaptive system where non-linear variables continuously interact'. Since 'coordination from the top down inevitably results in delays and errors in force dispositions', the military should seek to acquire 'the ability of a well-informed force to organize and coordinate complex warfare activities from the bottom up'. For Cebrowski, what is being proposed is nothing less than a 'new theory of war'.

Such a new theory can emerge only by breaking with the command and control principles that governed cybernetic warfare during the Cold War, as suggested by Alberts and Hayes:

Control Theory requires both prediction and the existence of an adequate set of levers of control ... [But] having effective, centrally managed levers that can control or even predictably influence a complex, adaptive system is far from guaranteed ... In the Information Age, control needs to be thought about and approached differently.

Control is not something that can be imposed on a complex adaptive system, particularly when there are many independent actors. Control, that is, ensuring that behavior stays within or moving to within acceptable bounds, can only be achieved indirectly.

The most promising approach involves establishing, to the extent possible, a set of initial conditions that will *result* in the desired behavior. In other words, control is not achieved by imposing a parallel process, but rather emerges from influencing the behaviors of independent agents. NCW theorists claim that through the distribution of information across the battlefield and the constitution of a common operational picture via an overarching 'Global Information Grid', command and control will be decentralized and individual troops will be freed to act on their own initiative, leading to self-synchronization, a clear nod to the chaoplexic notion of self-organization.

New tactical schemes denied to their hierarchical counterparts are seen as the emergent properties that will be unlocked by fully networked self-synchronizing forces. Drawing further from the writings of complexity theorists and deploying biological metaphors, military theorists appeal to the 'swarm', the networks of distributed intelligence that enable bees, ants and termites to evolve complex forms of collective behaviour on the basis of the simple rules of interaction of their individual members.

Of particular interest are the resilience and flexibility of these swarms as amorphous ensembles whose continued existence and successful operation is not critically dependent on any single individual. Military swarms promise not only more adaptable and survivable forces but also new offensive and defensive tactics better suited to the contemporary battlespace.

According to Alberts and Hayes, decentralization and information-sharing will permit military platforms to 'evolve from being networked entities to being nodes in the network, to organizing efforts resembling "packs" and "swarms"'. The ensembles of different entities making up fighting forces, whether human or robotic, will 'ultimately become dynamically reconfigurable packs, swarms, or other organizations of highly specialized components that work together like the cells of our bodies' and will be 'less mechanical and more organic, less engineered and more "grown"'.

Beyond the flexibility and evolutionary capability that are attributed to military swarms, it is also claimed that they will be able to bring force to bear in a new manner.

Rather than throwing themselves onto the enemy in 'waves', forces will be able to converge on their target from all directions in offensive bursts, thereby maximizing the shock effect.

For Arquilla and Ronfeldt, the full effects of swarming are achieved when the dispersed nodes of a network of small (and also perhaps some large) forces can converge on an enemy from multiple directions, through either fire or maneuver. The overall aim should be *sustainable pulsing*—swarm networks must be able to coalesce rapidly and stealthily on a target, then dissever and redisperse, immediately ready to recombine for a new pulse. A swarm network should have little to no mass as a rule (except perhaps during a pulse), but it should have a high energy potential—like a swarm of bees that can fell a mighty beast, or a network of antibodies that can attack a spreading virus.

Troops that can disperse swiftly after an attack or 'pulse' also have the advantage of being less vulnerable to enemy attacks, particularly in the context of the high lethality and precision characteristic of contemporary and future battlefields. The promises of network-centric warfare are bold and, for all its deployment of chaoplexic language, the doctrine suffers from a number of potentially critical weaknesses. In several respects it has not significantly broken with cybernetic warfare and therefore may not in fact implement all the features of a truly chaoplexic way of warfare.

While 'decentralization' is the order-word of the day, the networking of troops may in fact provide the technological infrastructure for greater micro-management than ever by a military brass which will have access to data feeds from anywhere in the battlespace.

Second, dependence on a unified 'Global Information Grid' could both create a critical vulnerability likely to be targeted by competent adversaries and deprive troops of the skills required to respond creatively to situations in which only limited local information is available (as most of the complex adaptive systems studied are found to do).

Furthermore, NCW advocates fall back all too often on impoverished conceptions of Boyd's OODA loop which substitute speed of execution of predetermined responses for creative thinking and adaptability to the unforeseen. Finally, there persists a tendency to see information technology as the panacea which will permanently lift the friction and fog of war which has plagued all past militaries, when in fact chaoplexity points to the irreducible contingency and unpredictability of war and the need to organize so as to tolerate and even take advantage of this uncertainty.

Ultimately chaoplexic warfare will depend more on doctrinal and organizational commitments than on any particular information technologies, which are liable to be employed to quite contrary purposes. The full arrival of chaoplexic warfare may therefore still lie ahead; but the debates around network-centric warfare clearly show an impetus towards greater decentralization and the use of the network form of organization within armed forces. NCW now has its counterparts in most major western militaries, including Network Enabled Capabilities (NEC) in the United Kingdom, NATO Network Enabled Capabilities (NNEC), and Network Enabled Operations (NEOps) in Canada. Where such militaries have encountered recent setbacks, for example in Iraq, Afghanistan or Lebanon, it has been against opponents that have employed decentralized networks to good effect against better-equipped forces, thereby further stimulating discussion about their merits and underlining the limitations of established modes of operation. Just as the ideas of mechanism, thermodynamics and cybernetics inspired past military thought and practice in association with their respective paradigmatic technologies, a new set of scientific theories are now occupying a central role within the doctrinal and organizational changes of the armies of the early twenty-first century. Our network age is therefore also that of chaoplexity.

9

Space Warfare and Weapon Technology

There are good lexicographic reasons not to use terms like "the military geography of space" or "the terrain of space warfare". In both case the words "geography" and "terrain" have their origins in the Greek and Latin terms for Earth. If space can be described as anything, it is definitely "not of the Earth." The term "space as a theater of war" is still not completely satisfactory, but for the moment it will have to do. Cislunar space, give or take a few million kilometers, is for the next few decades the only place where space warfare is going happen. The most important fact about this area is that Earth has a deep gravity well and the Moon has one six times smaller. John Collins' 1989 study "Military Space Forces: The Next Fifty Years" divides it into four military regions: Earth and its atmosphere, circumterrestrial space, the Moon and its environs, and the outer envelope.

The vulnerabilities of Earth-based space installations are evident and need little emphasis here. Questions are still being raised, particularly on Capitol Hill, about the Air Force's efforts to exploit the upper atmosphere or what is called "near space". Circumterrestrial space, basically low Earth orbit (LEO) and geosynchronous orbit (GEO), is where almost all of today's military space activity takes place.

It is the last two regions, the Moon and beyond, as defined by Collins, that deserve a new look. The Outer Space Treaty may prohibit certain types of military activity of the Moon, but that is not to going to stop the place from being used for all sorts of quasi-military roles. For example, what happens when lunar-produced hydrogen is used to fuel military spacecraft in LEO? Is the fuel manufacturing facility of the Moon a legitimate target? The treaty itself may not survive past the time when two or more nations have bases on or below its surface.

Proposals to use the surface of the Moon for a set of observatories that will both look outwards towards the rest of the solar system and inwards towards the Earth have a definite paramilitary aspect. The size of the apertures that can be created on the Moon are huge and they could produce sets of detailed environmental data that would be extremely valuable for military purposes. Such observatories would be under civilian control, but the products of their observations would be controlled by the nation or nations that built them and thus available for military purposes, just like data from environmental satellites in LEO.

In the area Collins calls "the Moon and its environs", also sometimes referred to as "cislunar space", there are the Lagrange points. So far there has not been any serious known plan to use these for military purposes, but there has been speculation over the years that these could become bases for space surveillance systems or even for space control weapons. The stable L-4 and L-5 points might be especially useful for these roles, but, on the other hand, these locations are so well known that any military spacecraft or facility placed there would lack any camouflage whatsoever.

The nature of the new generation of US and foreign "non-kinetic" space weapons is already changing the nature of space warfare. There are basically three types of these weapons: jammers, such at the counter-communications device that the US currently has; disablers, such as medium- or high-powered lasers or high-powered microwaves (HPM) that can disable a target spacecraft; and electromagnetic pulse (EMP) weapons.

These last types of weapons are not strictly space weapons since they could also disable electronic systems over large swaths of the Earth as well as knocking out any satellites within range. Since EMP weapons are powered by nuclear explosions they can be classified as weapons of last resort. Any state that used them would have to expect a nuclear response.

It is the question of range that determines the new shape of the theater of space operations. Expensive and delicate surveillance satellites in LEO, such at the US KH-12 series, are vulnerable to laser or HPM attack, yet they need to fly relative low in order to get the best resolution for their optical systems. The same holds true for radar imaging satellites. Protecting these satellites from kinetic and non-kinetic attack is a difficult problem: it requires them to have plenty of propellant to maneuver out of the way of "normal" ASATs and to carry shielding of various kinds that will be effective against lasers and HPMs. Such defenses will inevitably degrade the performance of these spacecraft or, if ignored, will make them into strictly peacetime assets.

Navigation and communications satellites in higher orbits, including GEO, may be vulnerable to the same laser and HPM weapons, but obviously it will be more difficult for Earth-based beams to maintain their coherence at such ranges. If the beams were to come from laser- or HPM-equipped satellites then it will be more difficult to defend these craft, but the platforms for such weapons would themselves be targets. In the future it may be that the US and other space powers will try to hide both operational and reserve satellites in cislunar space or beyond. Using complex orbits that depend on minute changes in the gravitational environment, such steathly satellites could remain undetected for many years. They would have to use nuclear power since solar arrays have an easily identified signature. They would also have to use "extremely low probability of intercept" communications. Another requirement is that they have a powerful "dash" capability to be able to change orbits quickly in response to a crisis. Another new factor is the need for a new kind of space navigation system. GPS, and later Galileo, will not be all that useful in GEO orbit or beyond, and the current generation of star trackers, though obviously pretty good, represent what engineers call a "single point failure". One alternative is to find a way to use the sixteen or so powerful pulsars that are easily detectable from our solar system as a sort of natural space GPS.

In space warfare, it must be assumed that some satellites and spacecraft are going to be destroyed by the enemy. Therefore, it is simply prudent to have reserves in place. So far the GPS system is the only military asset with any significant on-orbit reserves. In the near future the US is going to have to start planning to hide some reserve satellites in cislunar space or even in the "outer envelope" of the Earth-Moon system. Reconstituting a satellite network after an attack will be a lot faster if there are spares already in orbit that can be moved into an operationally suitable position when needed. This may be one answer, among others, to the question of what are "Operationally Responsive" space activities.

SPACE WARFARE

Space warfare is combat that takes place in outer space, i.e. outside the atmosphere. Space warfare therefore includes *ground-to-space warfare,* such as attacking satellites from the Earth, as well as *space-to-space warfare,* such as satellites attacking satellites. It does not include the use of satellites for espionage, surveillance, or military communications, however useful those activities might be. It does not technically include *space-to-ground warfare,* where orbital objects attack ground, sea or air targets directly, but the public and media frequently use the term to include any conflict which includes space as a theatre of operations, regardless of the intended target. For example, a rapid delivery system in which troops are deployed from orbit might be described as "space warfare," even though the military uses the term as described above.

A film was produced by the U.S. Military in the early 1960s called *Space and National Security* which depicted space warfare. From 1985 to 2002 there was a United States Space Command, which in 2002 merged with the United States Strategic Command.

There is a Russian Space Force, which was established on August 10, 1992, and which became an independent section of the Russian military on June 1, 2001. Only a few incidents of space warfare have occurred in world history, and all were training missions, as opposed to actions against real opposing forces. In the mid-1980s a USAF pilot in an F-15 successfully shot down the P78-1, a communications satellite in a 345 mile (555 km) orbit. In 2007 the People's Republic of China used a missile system to destroy one of its obsolete satellites, and in 2008 the United States similarly destroyed its malfunctioning satellite USA 193. To date, there have been no human casualties resulting from conflict in space, nor has any ground target been successfully neutralized from orbit. International treaties governing space limit or regulate conflicts in space and limit the installation of weapon systems, especially nuclear weapons.

History

Early efforts to conduct space warfare were directed at space-to-space warfare, as ground-to-space systems were considered to be too slow and too isolated by Earth's atmosphere and gravity to be effective. The history of active space warfare development goes back to the 1960s when the Soviet Union began the Almaz project, a project designed to give them the ability to do on-orbit inspections of satellites and destroy them if needed.

Similar planning in the United States took the form of the Blue Gemini project, which consisted of modified Gemini capsules that would be able to deploy weapons and perform surveillance.

One early test of electronic space warfare took place in 1963 when the United States exploded a ground-launched nuclear weapon in space to test the effects of an electromagnetic pulse. The result was a deactivation of many then-orbiting satellites, both American and Soviet. The deleterious and unfocused effects of the EMP test led to the banning of nuclear weapons in space in the Outer Space Treaty of 1968.

1970s–1980s

Through the 1970s, the Soviet Union continued their project and test-fired a cannon to test space station defence. This was considered too dangerous to do with a crew on board, however, so the test was conducted after the crew had returned to Earth.

Space warfare strongly influenced the final design of the United States Space Shuttle. The distinctive delta wing shape was needed if the shuttle were to launch a military payload towards the Soviet Union and perform an immediate de-orbit after one rotation to avoid being shot down.

Both the Soviets and the United States developed anti-satellite weaponry designed to shoot down satellites. While early efforts paralleled other space-to-space warfare concepts, the United States was able in the 1980s to develop ground-to-space laser anti-satellite weapons. None of these systems are known to be active today; however, a less powerful civilian version of the ground-to-space laser system is commonly used in the astronomical technique of adaptive optics.

2000s

China successfully tested a ballistic missile-launched anti-satellite weapon on January 11, 2007. This resulted in harsh criticism from the United States of America, Britain, and Japan.

Space warfare system

A space system has three segments, each of which, in principle, offers opportunities for attack to an enemy. The system comprises: (i) the satellite, perhaps the constellation of satellites in orbit; (ii) the up and down links to and from the orbiting vehicle, commands from the ground stations and information flow from the satellite; (iii) and the ground station that controls the behaviour of the satellite and distributes its information to the users."

MILITARY TECHNOLOGY IN SPACE WEAPONS

On Tuesday April 24 at 7pm Global Network (GN, Global Network against Weapons and Nuclear Power in Space) members and supporters gathered at the Continuing Education Building of the University of New Mexico to protest. Just a few days previously the campus paper had announced the award of a 'defence' grant to its Electrical and Computer Engineering department for work on a super laser weapon project.

Also, just a few blocks away at UNM's Institute for Space and Nuclear Studies, work is being carried out on nuclear power supplies for space vehicles and platforms. What have these two projects in common? The answer lies in the Space-Based Laser Integrated Flight Experiment, which forms what George Bush calls the "next generation weaponry" and is at the heart of our campaign against "weapons and nuclear power in space". Part of the 'experiment' is to build a Space-Based Laser Readiness Demonstrator - this is a scaled down version (at an estimated cost of $1. billion) of the proposed weapon system which would eventually be deployed for theater ballistic missile defense and as an anti-satellite weapon.

If the SBL IFX is successful, the US Department of Defense will decide whether to deploy a fully operational network of 20-30 laser battle stations giving global coverage. The first launch of an operational system could occur in 2020 and it could take several years to launch the full constellation of spacecraft around Earth. The Pentagon estimates that the total SBL program will cost $30 billion.

Why the nuclear connection? Any pace-based laser will require tremendous amounts of power and, as a study commissioned by the US Congress notes "nuclear reactors thus remain the only known long-lived, compact source able to supply military space forces with electric power"... nuclear reactors "could meet multimegawatt needs of space-based lasers, neutral particle beams, mass drivers, and railguns."

Also - New World Vistas: Air And Space Power For The 21st Century, states: "In the next two decades, new technologies will allow the fielding of space-based weapons of devastating effectiveness... These advances will enable lasers with reasonable mass and cost to effect very many kills." But "power limitations... currently make large space-based radars and space-based weapons relatively unfeasible... A natural technology to enable high power is nuclear power in space." This is the reason why nuclear power is being developed for use in outer space. So - the development of a SBL is already well underway - and forms a major part of the US Space Command plans to "dominate" and "master" space. As international weapons expert John Pike has said:

> *"Whoever controls space has control of Earth... the United States is unable to resist it. If the U.S. is in a position to control Earth from outer space, there's nothing to stop us. Of course we're going to do it."*

In January this year US Defense Secretary Donald Rumsfeld spoke of a "space Pearl Harbor" and a commission he formerly headed unveiled a report calling for tighter security for American space systems. "The US... needs to take seriously the possibility of an attack on US space systems," said the report "... The US is more dependent on space than any other nation" and the report called for a 'technological push' to foil threats from foreign nations or terrorists.

However, as reported in the Spring 2001 GN Newsletter, the environmental assessment for the SBL refers to the possibility of a catastrophic explosion that could result in a sudden release of a large quantity of toxic materials and/or destruction of surrounding structures with additional environmental consequences - although no reason for such an assessment of risk is given. Just another reason why the SBL is nicknamed "Death Star". It is a frighteningly ambitious component of Star Wars to be used as a boost-phase missile interceptor and satellite destroyer

Boost-Phase Missile Interception

Lasers are very attractive to the military because they travel so fast - at the speed of light. Therefore they are being seriously considered for intercepting missiles during their boost-phase. Apart from the SBL, two other methods of achieving this with lasers are currently being funded - airborne and ground based High Energy Laser systems. Of course, one major difficulty with this approach (apart from the fact that it might be technically difficult - if not impossible - and extremely expensive) is that boost-phase defences would break the ABM Treaty (if it still exists at the time of this presentation!). However - as we know - a number of influential US generals and politicians believe that the laser weapon provides such a valuable defense that it is worth abrogating the treaty.

The stated advantages of a boost-phase system for Ballistic Missile Defence Systems are that it would:

- provide another tier of missile defence;
- remove the problem of debris falling over the target area (as occurs with "terminal intercept");
- prevent the deployment of multiple warheads;
- does not require the ability to differentiate between warheads and decoys;

- would deter the use of payloads through threat of "country of origin impact of debris".

It also, of course, enhances the US first strike capability and its ability to knock out other nation's space hardware. The SBL can also be used for NMD as well as TMD - in fact strategic missiles would be more vulnerable to laser attack in boost phase than theatre missiles because of their longer boost times. They also have higher burn-out altitudes which reduces the atmospheric effects that would interfere with laser beam propagation from space.

An alternative space based system would incorporate fewer SBL platforms (perhaps 3) with a number of orbiting relay mirrors (perhaps 24) to direct the beams. A number of configurations are possible and this type of configuration is favoured by many military.

Military Lasers

The Air Force, Army and Navy all started working on lasers in the mid-1960s, and the idea of a SBL has been around since 1977. Initial tests involve a megawatt-class chemical laser with a large, multi-segmented mirror that unfurls and locks into place to create a 13-foot (4-meter) diameter reflecting surface. The entire spacecraft would weigh between 45,000 and 50,000 pounds (20,455 and 22,700 kilograms). The competing lasers are hydrogen fluoride (HF), deuterium fluoride (DF), and chemical oxygen iodine (COIL).

The HF laser uses atomic fluorine and molecular hydrogen to produce excited hydrogen fluorine molecules producing several simultaneous wavelengths in the range of 2. - 2. microns. At these wavelengths the beam is mostly absorbed by the earth's atmosphere and can only be used above the earth's atmosphere e.g. for the SBL. A HF laser has been test fired at the TRW San Juan Capistrano test facility in California.

The DF laser uses deuterium (an isotope of hydrogen) and atomic fluorine. Longer wavelength laser light than for HF lasers is produced (3. - 4 microns), giving better transmission through the atmosphere but requiring larger optical surfaces to shape and focus the beam. The Chemical Oxygen Iodine Laser (COIL) was developed at the Air Force Research Laboratory in Albuquerque in 1977. It is the basis of the $1. billion Air Force Airborne Laser Attack Aircraft - scheduled for anti-missile tests in 2003.

On October 1997 the Pentagon conducted a "laser dazzler" test against one of its satellites using the Army's MIRACL DF laser (Mid-Infrared Advanced Chemical Laser) based at White Sands Missile Range, N.M. In 1996 a MIRACL laser shot down a rocket at the same site.

A new, lightweight, "all gas" Iodine Laser, or AGIL has also been developed by the Air Force Research Lab. This laser uses nitrogen chloride and iodine which are mixed in a vacuum chamber. AGIL has a better atmospheric transmission, which is important for a laser weapon required to reach targets in the atmosphere or even near the surface of the Earth. A basic weapon-size AGIL laser will take at least until 2003 to develop, demonstrate and test.

The Army's Tactical High Energy Laser (THEL) system is designed by a team led by TRW Corp. After the war in Lebanon in April 1996, Israel was promised by the Clinton administration that the U.S. would help develop a laser-based anti-missile system capable of destroying incoming Katyusha rockets. The US Army and the Israeli Ministry of Defense paid weapons contractor TRW $200 million to build a HF laser to generate a powerful infrared beam that can pass through the atmosphere.

On 6 June 2000 the THEL intercepted and destroyed an armed Russian made Katyusha rocket at White Sands Missile Range, N.M. and on Aug. 28 and Sept 14 the demonstrator shot down two rockets launched in succession. The system detected the 10 foot long, 5 inch diameter rocket with its radar before shooting it down. THEL has a range of about 12 miles and costs about $3,000 per destroyed rocket to use.

The U.S. military's first high energy weapon is likely to be the Airborne Laser mounted on a Boeing 747, it is being designed to acquire, track, and destroy theatre ballistic missiles. The system is expected to be deployed in 10 years. The Air Force has proposed spending $11 billion to develop a fleet of seven airborne lasers that could be used for battlefield anti-missile defense at a cost of about $10,000 per shot, based on the price of the laser fuel.

Last month Raytheon Electronic Systems, a subcontractor to Lockheed Martin Space Systems, carried out a 'first light' test of the Track Illuminator Laser (TILL) at the High Energy Laser Centre in El Segundo in California. The TILL is part of the Beam Control/ Fire Control system for the US Air Force's Airborne Laser (ABL) programme, which will aim and fire a high-energy laser at a target missile in its boost phase.

However, also last month Nathan Kopeika of Ben-Gurion University told a conference in Florida that he believes engineers working on the Airborne Laser (ABL) project have overlooked the effect of tiny dust particles in the atmosphere, called aerosols. These could scatter and weaken the laser beam, making it incapable of destroying incoming missiles. "We found that, after a propagation of 100 kilometres, aerosols can widen a laser beam up to a cross section one kilometre wide—several orders of magnitude worse than optical turbulence," he said.

The Space Based Laser represents the ultimate in current military thinking about space weaponry and demonstrates the extent to which the US Space Command is prepared to go to realize their vision of domination. We must continue to bring these issues to the attention of the citizens of the world - this is no way to spend our limited resources, no way to increase global security, no way to take our first steps outside our own planet. We must strive to keep space for peace.

On 21 December, 2000, the Stennis Space Center, Mississippi, was selected as the site of the SBL performance test facility. Local people will be holding a vigil at the site on 12 May and on 13 October there will be an action at Stennis as part of the GN International Day of Action.

THEORETICAL SPACE WEAPONRY

Ballistic warfare

In the late 1970s and through the 1980s the Soviet Union and the United States theorized, designed and in some cases even tested an astonishing variety of bizarre and exotic weaponry designed for warfare in outer space. Space warfare was seen primarily as an extension of nuclear warfare, and so many theoretical systems were based around the destruction or defence of ground and sea-based missiles. Space-based missiles were not a target due to the Outer Space Treaty, which banned the use, testing or storage of nuclear weapons outside the Earth's atmosphere.

Systems proposed ranged from measures as simple as ground and space-based anti-missiles to railguns, space based lasers, orbital mines and other such futuristic weaponry. Deployment of these systems was seriously considered in the mid-1980s under the banner of the Strategic Defence Initiative (popularly known as Star Wars). If the Cold War had continued, then many of these systems could have seen deployment: the United States got as far as developing working railguns, and a laser that could destroy missiles at range, though the power requirements of both were phenomenal, and the ranges and firing cycles utterly impractical.

Electronic warfare

With the end of the Cold War and continued development of satellite and electronics technology, attention was focused on space as a supporting theatre for conventional warfare. Currently, military operations in space primarily concern either the vast tactical advantages of satellite-based surveillance, communications, and positioning systems or mechanisms used to deprive an opponent of said tactical advantages.

Accordingly, most space-borne proposals which would traditionally be considered "weapons" (a communications or reconnaissance satellite may be useful in warfare but isn't generally classified as a weapon) are designed to jam, sabotage, and outright destroy enemy satellites, and conversely to protect friendly satellites against such attacks. To this end, the US (and presumably other countries) is researching groups of small, highly mobile satellites called "microsats" (about the size of a refrigerator) and "picosats" (approximately 1 cubic foot (H"27 litres) in volume) nimble enough to manoeuvre around and interact with other orbiting objects to repair, sabotage, hijack, or simply collide with them.

Kinetic bombardment

Another theorized use involves the extension of conventional weaponry into orbit for deployment against ground targets. Though international treaties bar the deployment of nuclear missiles outside the atmosphere, other categories of weapons are largely unregulated. Traditional ground-based weapons are generally not useful in orbital environments, and few if any would survive re-entry even if they were, but as early as the 1950s, the United States has toyed with kinetic bombardment, i.e. orbiting magazines of non-explosive projectiles to be dropped onto hardened targets from low-earth orbit. Kinetic weapons have always been widespread in conventional warfare—bullets, arrows, swords, clubs, etc.—but the energy a projectile would gain while falling from orbit would make such a weapon rival all but the most powerful explosives. A direct hit would presumably destroy all but the most hardened targets without the need for nuclear weapons.

Such a system would involve a 'spotter' satellite, which would identify targets from orbit with high-power sensors, and a nearby 'magazine' satellite to de-orbit a long, needle-like tungsten dart onto it with a small rocket motor or just dropping a very big rock from orbit (such as an asteroid). This would be more useful against a larger but less hardened target (such as a city). Though a common device in science fiction, there is no publicly-available evidence that any such systems have actually been deployed by any nation.

Directed-Energy Weapons

Weapon systems that fall under this category include lasers, linear particle accelerators or particle-beam based weaponry, microwaves and plasma-based weaponry. Particle beams involve the acceleration of charged or neutral particles in a stream towards a target at extremely high velocities, the impact of which creates a reaction causing immense damage. Most of these weapons are theoretical or impractical to implement currently, aside from lasers which are starting to be used in terrestrial warfare. That said, directed-energy weapons are more practical and more effective in a vacuum (i.e. space) than in the Earth's atmosphere, as in the atmosphere the particles of air interfere with and disperse the directed energy. Obviously, that problem would not occur in space.

Practical considerations

Space warfare is likely to be conducted at far greater distances and speeds than terrestrial combat. The vast distances involved pose difficult challenges for targeting and tracking, as even light requires a few seconds to traverse ranges measured in hundreds of thousands of kilometres. For example, if attempting to fire upon a target at the distance of the Moon from the Earth, the image one sees reflects the position of the target slightly more than a second earlier.

A projectile from a railgun recently tested by the US Navy would take over eighteen hours to cross that distance (making the simplifying and optimistic assumption that it will travel in a straight line at a constant velocity of 5.8 km/s along its entire trajectory). Even a laser will need approximately 1.28 seconds, meaning a laser-based weapon system would need to lead a target's apparent position by 1.28×2 = 2.56 seconds.

Three factors conspire to make engaging targets in space very difficult. First, the vast distances involved mean that an error of even a fraction of a degree in the firing solution could result in a miss by thousands of kilometres. Second, space travel involves tremendous speeds by terrestrial standards—a geostationary satellite moves at a speed of 3.07 km/s whereas objects in low earth orbit can move at up to 8 km/s.

Third, though distances are large, targets remain relatively small. The International Space Station, currently the largest artificial object in Earth orbit, measures slightly over 100m at its largest span. Other satellites can be orders of magnitude smaller, e.g. Quickbird measures a mere 3.04m. External ballistics for stationary terrestrial targets is enormously complicated—some of the earliest analog computers were used to calculate firing solutions for naval artillery, as the problems were already beyond manual solutions in any reasonable time—and the issues in targeting objects in space make a difficult problem even harder. Additionally, though not a problem for orbital kinetic weapons, any directed energy weapon would require large amounts of electricity. So far the most practical batteries are lithium batteries, and the most practical method of generating electricity in space is through photovoltaic modules, which are currently only 5-18% efficient, and fuel cells, which have limited fuel. Current technology might not be practical for powering effective lasers, particle beams, and railguns in space.

Regardless of one's reasons for going to war, at present those reasons are not likely to suggest major targets located in space. Most of the main theories which attempt to explain human proclivity for warfare—psychological, sociological, demographic, economic, political, or otherwise—would not indicate space as a likely location of conflict until a significant population is engaged in large-scale activity there. Until then, space warfare is likely to take a supporting role to conventional, terrestrial warfare. Aside from applications such as communications, reconnaissance, GPS, and the like, which would be difficult or impossible without satellites, there do not appear to be any major advantages to basing weapons systems in space. The main reason is simply cost. Space warfare that involves humans being deployed in space to fight each other is not currently practical because of the difficulty and cost of sustaining human life in space, especially over long periods of time.

Additionally, there are few things that could be accomplished by space warfare that any nation wealthy enough to finance them cannot accomplish far more cheaply through conventional means. Raising any significant mass beyond Earth's gravity will always require a large amount of energy, and the cost increases with mass. For example, though kinetic bombardment potentially offers the ability to strike any target anywhere in the world within minutes, both the United States and Russia, possibly the only nations with the resources and facilities necessary to implement such a system, have sufficiently long-range supersonic bombers that the same target could already be deployed in a matter of hours at a mere fraction of the cost.

SPACE TECHNOLOGY

It is becoming more difficult to guard against casualties in outer space. All space technology is dual-use; however, the capabilities of dual-use space125 based technologies are increasing and can be used directly for a range of space system protection and negation purposes. On the one hand, newer, more adaptable technologies such as small satellites are facilitating more active space system defences. Small satellites can provide key protection capabilities such as on-orbit servicing, greater manoeuvrability in space, inorbit space surveillance, faster hardware replacement in the event of satellite failure, and clusters of defensive satellite configurations. On the other hand, the same benefits of size and manoeuvrability can also support more active negation activities. Small satellites are easy to hide and difficult to detect. They can be discreetly released into orbit, approach other satellites and cause physical harm.

Projects that are developing close-proximity, rendezvous, and spacebased surveillance capabilities for protection purposes include the joint German–Russian–Canadian on orbit servicing programme Technology Satellite for Demonstration and Verification of Space Systems (TECSAS), the ConeXpress Orbital Life Extension Vehicle (CS-OLEV) being developed by Orbital Recovery and the European Space Agency (ESA), the Orbital Express mission jointly managed by the US Defense Advanced Research Projects Agency (DARPA) and NASA, and the US Air Force's Autonomous Nanosatellite Guardian for Evaluating Local Space (ANGELS). There is no evidence to suggest that these programmes are being developed for space systems negation purposes. Nonetheless, the destructive potential of manoeuvrable small satellite technology were demonstrated when NASA's Demonstration of Autonomous Rendezvous Technologies (DART) spacecraft unexpectedly collided with the target satellite during its 15 April 2005 mission. Dedicated military programmes that are developing similar advanced dual-use technologies include the US Air Force's Experimental Satellite System 11 (XSS-11) and the Microsatellite Demonstration Science and Technology Experiment Program (MiDSTEP) sponsored by DARPA, the US Air Force and the US Navy.

These programmes are developing spacebased technologies that could support a variety of protection and negation activities. Like the technology behind them, the line between protection and negation activities in outer space is ambiguous; the difference between protection and negation is increasingly not clear, and not shared. The ambiguity of more active space-based protection and negation technology and activities is a challenge for space security. The difficulty in distinguishing between protection and negation capabilities and intent reduces transparency, can fuel negation/

protection spirals and cause fear and mistrust that can trigger confrontation in outer space or pre-emptive responses. However, regulation of new technologies is both impractical and undesirable because such advancements cut across all space applications. This is an area where technology has outpaced diplomacy.

MILITARY SPACE TECHNOLOGY

One has to look to beyond forefront military space technologies in order to begin to map the future of space warfare. This is partly due to the fact that in recent years, research and development partnerships related to sensitive military space systems and dual-use commercial systems have grown broader and more inclusive. This trend has resulted in greater access for the United States to talented minds from all over the world and low-cost scientific contributions from university-based researchers and small commercial operations. It has also resulted in a greater probability for technologies developed in the U.S. to leak outside its borders. The realignment of the global economy stands to further shift the international balance of space power in the years to come. For nations that possess the relative wealth, infrastructure, and knowledge to develop space warfare technologies, their ability to become a leading military space power requires only the will to do so. The "brain drain" that hampered the space programs of many nations in decades past is weighing less on them today. The stagnancy of foreign economies that resulted in a flood of scientific minds to the U.S. is slowly ebbing, as many are now returning home to profitable jobs in booming defence and space industries.

This situation is compounded by increased competition in the launch services industry, which has resulted in reduced costs to place assets into orbit, as well as a decrease in the size and weight of satellites and space systems—developments that are conducive to space warfare. Consequently, access to space is no longer limited to nations with massive military budgets. In this rapidly changing environment, the greatest influence on the development of space warfare may rest on our ever-growing dependency upon satellites—for both military and commercial purposes—and their inherent vulnerabilities.

Furthermore, as we venture forward into a globalized security environment fueled by advances in technologies such as directed energy (DE) systems, artificial intelligence (AI), and nanomanufacturing, both the warfighter and the diplomat will be presented with new tools to respond to security crises.

Military space technologies currently in development are the precursor to a world where threats can be neutralized at the speed of light and conflicts may escalate at a rate too fast to curtail.

Accordingly, adjustments will soon have to be made across the entire spectrum of diplomatic and military affairs. If we fail to draft international treaties now that are in line with the pace of advancements in military space technology, a global technology free-for-all could result. This could contribute to a climate in which a spacefaring nation such as the U.S. would be bound to engage in a constant race against itself in order to maintain an effective defensive capability. The purpose of the following military space technology forecast and analysis is to provide new insights and specific recommendations that might protect peaceful cooperation in outer space. This forecast assumes that there are no binding constraints from international treaties. It depicts the current and future state of science related to military space systems, specifically systems that could lead to scenarios that could be precursors to or causes of warfare in space.

In the years leading up to 2020, tensions among military space powers have been mounting. This has been due, in part, to broad-spectrum advances that have materialized internationally in the "Five Ds" of counter-space operations: Deception, Disruption, Denial, Degradation, and Destruction. Even as nations flaunt their military space abilities as a means of intimidating and deterring space rivals, instances of space systems failures, though still uncommon, are slowly rising due to space-warfare systems testing and the increasing amount of space debris. Space systems failures in this new era are triggering accusations of systems disruption and sabotage between nations. The means to achieve an offensive and defensive military space capability in this heady space environment can be found in various force-multiplying arenas of technology.

2020

We enter 2020 to find that the disparities that existed in decades past regarding global space warfare capabilities have been fundamentally and irreversibly altered. Many leading nations are now operating on a near-level playing field. Complementary technologies are driving one another's progress; for example, as robotics concepts top out and undergo a momentary pause, they are soon catapulted ahead by explosive growth in the field of supercomputing.

The arrival and subsequent establishment of strong artificial intelligence is approaching. Key strategists of military space warfare systems are chasing full-spectrum, real-time, and seamless situational awareness of sea, ground, air, and space. The world's brightest minds are reaching new heights as human intelligence is fused with intelligent agents and neural networks. These are the systems that will deliver humanity to the next echelon as nations become increasingly reliant on AI systems and their ability to process a now humanly unmanageable stream of information–a torrent to which our military is now inextricably connected.

The five theaters of combat: Cyber, Space, Air, Land, and Sea, now resemble a unified battlesphere. The international space community is being led by drivers such as the still plummeting cost of computational power, the continued free exchange of knowledge, and the refinement of nanomaterials applications, which are resulting in stronger, lighter, faster and more responsive space systems. Featured most prominently in this transition process is the influence of the smaller commercial space systems companies and non-military R&D providers, such as universities.

The roles of large military and governmental-based, space-systems providers have been challenged effectively by the private space industry. This challenge was inspired in part by successes in the fields of launch services, satellite development, and niche emerging systems. During this era, the commercial launch industry in the United States is now spending as much as four times the total annual budget of NASA, with wide spread commercial space travel seeming more plausible than ever.

The threat spectrum for potential space-attack scenarios is no longer a distant hypothesis, nor does it seem an abstract possibility because the technology is unknown–in 2020 various advanced space-warfare technologies are openly displayed and touted as offensive attack systems. For many nations there is an ominous and increased probability of sustaining a space asset attack; running in parallel with such concerns are increasing fears of worst-case scenarios related to the accidental launch of nuclear forces. This is also due to measurable increases in space debris and the confusion that could arise should space systems be attacked or time-out for extended periods without explanation. As more countries than ever are now realizing their mounting reliance on space, and as tensions run higher, the range of possible deterrents and responses to a space systems attack are increasingly severe and include the possible use of nuclear weapons. Full-scale attacks on space systems can now deliver catastrophic effects upon economies, societal functions, and military operations that would take decades to recover from–even limited acts of space warfare could result in rapid conflict breakout and light-speed escalation scenarios. Intolerable demands have now been placed upon the government and military officials of the leading space powers, as the remaining human factors across the entire spectrum of military space operations must come to terms with the prospect that their continued presence might only serve as an impediment to the realized potential of computational efficiency.

Artificial Intelligence & Cyber Warfare

In light of the convergence process that is now taking place between AI and cyber warfare systems and their corresponding areas of responsibility relating to military space systems and space warfare technologies internationally, their sections have been merged to reflect this evolution.

Human-machine interactions and interfaces are radically changing many aspects of the military space command and control structure. In many cases, specific combat operations are now being conducted by human and artificial operators working together in a virtual environment, which delivers a real-time view of the target area with semi-autonomous and autonomous attack options just a blink or a voice-command away. In 2020, AI-driven systems are now supplying consolidated information and refined military options to high-level decision makers, who are now unable to decipher and analyse vast data flows alone. The role of the war planner is now found to be most critical during the process of selecting war fighting strategies generated and provided by AI systems.

The entire sphere of global military operations in 2020 has the potential to be fully interconnected for those with the means and the desire to do so, as successful military operations are decided by this complex network of systems.

Vast protection measures have been taken to guard these systems, including actions to greatly reduce the number of network access points into military and national security systems and to centralize individual architectures in an attempt to prevent unauthorized access and lessen the probability of cyber attacks. This will prove to be a critical decision for many advanced military powers.

As governmental network access points are reduced and their decentralized layout is eventually integrated, the potential for security breaches is greatly decreased.

However, should a cyber denial of service or brute force attack prove successful, a full or near-full spectrum catastrophic failure could result. Scenarios such as these must be considered before the complete consolidation of information architectures is achieved. Decentralized systems lead to an increased potential for vulnerabilities; however they defuse the effects of successful attacks, thus minimizing the potential for significantly debilitating operational effects. Threats posed to computer networks that support critical military satellite systems are in 2020 becoming increasingly complex and are occurring more frequently. Specifically, attacks targeting ground stations and command centres threaten military connectivity and the seamlessness of the Command, Control, Communications, Computer, Intelligence, Surveillance, and Reconnaissance systems (C4ISR).

Such attacks have the potential to effectively induce a systems blackout. A military's ability to adequately secure C4ISR systems and protect ground segments ensures success not only in space, but in all dimensions of warfare. Advances in cryptology, quantum cryptology, and related technologies such as ciphers and crypto-keys for performing encryption and decryption of these data streams are vital to space-systems security. Specifically, the preservation of secure crosslink/uplink/downlink data transmissions will require constant enhancement efforts due to the availability of advanced computer processing capabilities and the adaptive nature of highly skilled adversaries.

As with all military space-supporting computer systems, threat sources are not limited to code breakers and hackers trying to exploit weaknesses from outside government facilities in faraway lands, but from within the host government as well. In an environment where trust is everything, a weakness in the human element of security could jump all other protection measures.

Additionally, if an attack were to succeed against the C4ISR supporting space systems, a self-healing capability or Self-Regenerative Systems (SRS) solution must be executed immediately in order to repair and secure the effected network. Such abilities to survive a debilitating space systems attack will be made possible by advances in AI.

Nanotechnology

In 2020 it is nearly impossible to find nanotechnology detractors as universal applications are benefiting countless industries in this multidisciplinary field.

Up to this point, nanotechnology discoveries that improved space warfare capabilities had appeared mostly in the form of materials improvements, which enhanced solar power generation, survivability, and structural integrity. Now, micro-electro-mechanical systems (MEMS) and micro-opto-electro-mechanical systems (MOEMS) are beginning to lead to further improvements in sensors, such as Attitude Determination and Control (ADCS) and other components, such as actuators.

Meaningful research into the materials sciences has now been underway for nearly twenty-five years and novel applications are currently appearing and addressing key challenges. Specifically, developments made in the areas of carbon nanotubes (CNT) are resulting in materials capable of thermal and electrical conduction. Additionally, CNT in the proper configurations have led to the creation of materials with unprecedented ballistic protection and heat-shielding and load-bearing strength, including the ability to defuse and insulate against the effects of high-energy lasers. For example, 3D aerogels and xerogels are in 2020 capable of withstanding load-bearing pressures as extreme as 75,000psi. One can imagine numerous applications for such materials, especially when we factor in advances in oxide options. Nanocomposite materials such as those utilizing silica or polystyrene even demonstrate an ability to shield against the effects of high-power microwaves (HPM) and radio frequency (RF). This field of science is also delivering applications that provide the ability to blend an asset's thermal, visual, and radar appearance into its background. Through this research, advanced photovoltaics and power generation methods are evolving as well.

More elaborate, yet feasible, concepts are being pursued such as a Faraday Cage built on a nanoscale level, which would require doped and multi-walled carbon nanotubes (MWCNT). This concept uses carbon nanotubes to develop an enclosure for satellite subsystems and smaller satellite classes such as picosats and nanosats and would provide insulation against various DE threats. Such an enclosure could deter the effects of an electromagnetic pulse (EMP), electrostatic discharges and various other directed energy threats.

Also, self-healing materials are being researched by universities, industry, and militaries to develop self-repairing technologies to address damages such as those that could be sustained in space as a result of space debris or destructive space-asset attacks. Such impacts could lead to a satellite failure, and so a technology like this reaching the development stage would prove invaluable. These materials would use composite structures that contain nanoscale spheres, which encapsulate an unhardened polymer resin. When a satellite is hit, the resin would spread and then fill the cracks to prevent further damage. Such systems could also provide shielding.

Flexible nanoelectronic devices that are as thin as paper and mounted to a thin flexible substrate such a as a plastic would provide a flexible, conductive, and multiuse material, which could then be integrated into countless space systems. A very attractive manifestation of this application would be in the form of a substrate on which electronic circuits could be printed on demand. Such a nanomaterial would also be durable and could be rolled up and stored.

Flexible substrates and the use of various conductors could lead to thin-film solar cells for space applications or thin-film semiconductors. The next level: Molecular nanotechnology (MNT) promises to revolutionize countless products by engineering mechanical and electronic systems, including advanced materials, at the molecular scale. Such a capacity for discovery will touch upon every aspect of military technology in the realm of space warfare.

POSSIBLE WARFARE OVER SPACE

Most of the world's communications systems rely heavily on the presence of satellites in orbit around Earth. Protecting these assets might seriously motivate nations dependent upon them to consider deploying more space-based weaponry, especially in conflicts involving advanced countries with access to space. Even without the further militarization of space, a future conflict conducted largely on the ground through conventional means might well be sparked by actions conducted entirely in space. Alternatively, the very threat of space warfare may be enough to put considerable pressure on the political system of a nation, such as the pressure which caused the formation of the Outer Space Treaty.

Relatedly, though no infrastructure or economic interests exist at the moment to warrant the occupation of terrain on other terrestrial bodies within the Solar system, or to occupy orbital trajectories in outer space, some futurists have predicted that should such infrastructure be deployed, space-faring nations may go to war for control of extra-planetary resources. Such a conflict could easily involve warfare both within and outside the Earth's atmosphere. One suggested point of conflict is the helium-3 resources in the south polar region of the Moon. Russia has already stated its intention of developing this resource, and the Chinese lunar mission is scheduled to land in that area in 2024. However, the high abundance of this isotope would make war quite unlikely.

Space warfare in fiction

Space warfare is a topic often touched upon in science fiction, with a wide range of realism and plausibility, from stories based on anticipated future technology and tactics, to fantasy or historically based scenarios that happen to take place in a science-fiction background. Some portray a space-borne military will be similar to an Air Force, whereas others depict a more naval analog. Still others suggest forces more like marines: highly mobile forces engaged in interplanetary and interstellar warfare but with most of the actual conflict occurring in terrestrial environments.

Both kinetic energy and directed energy weapons are often portrayed, along with various military space vessels. The Lensman series by E. E. Smith is an early example, which also inspired the term Space Opera due to the grandiose scales of the stories. The Ender's Game series by Orson Scott Card is a notable example in that it makes conjecture as to what sort of tactics and training would be required for war in outer space. Other science fiction authors have also delved into the tactics of space combat, such as David Weber in his Honorverse series as well as Larry Niven and Jerry Pournelle in their Mote in God's Eye series. A more recent example would be Alastair Reynolds' Revelation Space universe, which explores combat at relativistic speeds. Robert A. Heinlein's Starship Troopers is perhaps one of the best-known and earliest explorations of the "space marine" idea. Space-based vehicular combat is portrayed in many movies and video games, most notably Star Wars, the Halo Series, Descent, Macross and Star Trek. Games such as the Homeworld series provide interesting concepts for space warfare, such as the use of plasma-based projectors that receive their energy from a ships propulsion system, and automated unmanned space combat vehicles. Other series, such as Gundam, prominently feature vehicular combat in and among many near future concepts, such as O'Neill cylinders.

The distinct fictional settings in which space warfare occurs are far too numerous to list, but popular examples include Star Trek (in all of its various incarnations), Warhammer 40,000, Star Wars, Babylon 5, Buck Rogers, Flash Gordon, Battlestar Galactica, Mass Effect, Stargate, the Halo Series and many comic book franchises. Video games have frequently touched the subject, with the Wing Commander franchise serving as a prototypical example. Note that very few games attempt to simulate an environment with realistic distances and speeds, though Independence War and Frontier: Elite II both do, as does the board game Attack Vector: Tactical.

THE SPACE TECHNOLOGY PARADOX IN THIRD BATTLE

During the past decade, technology has grown exponentially in key areas that would seem custom suited to the design of more capable space systems. One example is computing power, commonly measured by "Moore's Law", which has seen the number of transistors on an integrated circuit rise from 2,250 in 1971 to 410,000,000 in 2004 while processor performance has improved by six orders of magnitude in the same period. Another example is miniaturization. In building space systems, the limiting factor is almost always weight due to the excessive costs of lifting a spacecraft to orbit. Technologies such as micro electro mechanical systems (MEMS) and nanotechnology offer great promise for reducing weight on spacecraft.

Launch costs continue to be the largest drag on space systems. The U.S. launch business has seen not only a reduced launch demand, but the drive toward economic launch costs has been largely unproductive. According to Benjamin Lambeth in his article *Footing the Bill for Military Space,* the constant-dollar price of getting a satellite to orbit has not changed much over the past two decades. Putting a satellite in low earth orbit continues to cost between $3,600 and $4,900 per pound, while getting to geostationary Earth orbit runs $9,200 to $11,200 per pound. Through micro-technology advances in industry, materials have become lighter. Power, a definite limiting factor in space, has become more efficient with smaller more capable devices requiring less electrical power. However, trends in military satellite development have not kept up with those in industry. Mass and power on defense spacecraft have leveled out. The average weight of a commercial geostationary communications satellite over the past 10 years has slowly come down, stabilizing at about 3750 pounds. Military communication satellites on the other hand have tended to be heavier with Milstar weighing in at 10,000 pounds and the new Wideband Gapfiller Satellite at 6,615 pounds. This weight differential is partly due to military unique components required to assure survivability or add jam resistance. Despite significant breakthroughs in electronics and miniaturization, we have yet to see corresponding improvements in our national security space systems. Like the advent of stealth technology and precision weapons transformed airpower, the U.S. must seize on the chance to develop leap-ahead technologies in space.

A large reason behind the lag in DoD space technology is driven by the way it does space acquisition. Because space systems are typically complex in nature, acquisition leaders commit to technology decisions early in a program in order to stabilize the future production cost and schedule. This creates what Douglas Lee calls a "technology paradox" in that any technical advantage a program gains is lost before launch of the first satellite. In the end, long development cycles and risk averse practices couple to make technology obsolescent before it reaches orbit.

Combined with typically long satellite development and production schedules (often 10 years from start to first launch), this paradox makes it especially difficult to respond with agility to a changing threat. Art Cebrowski, Director of the Office of Force Transformation pushes for tactically responsive space systems, claiming "What we want...are space capabilities in weeks and months and not decades." To date, the space acquisition system has not adjusted to this new timeline. Revolutionary transformation will require revolutionary new acquisition processes—and a solution to the technology paradox. Based on recent space system acquisition results, the U.S. space acquisition system is not moving in that direction. Failures in developing replacements for legacy systems raise serious questions about whether the U.S. national security space system can support more complex acquisition programs such as space tracking and targeting systems and space weapons.

WEAPONS AND NEXT GENERATION LAUNCH SYSTEMS

Ground-based (GB) DEWs are in 2025 abundant and can be found in the arsenals of many nations, as they have by now achieved adequate power levels and have clearly demonstrated an ability to strike space assets. For the few nations that have the ability and choose to deploy in space (covertly or overtly), ground targets can be reached from the heavens as well. DEW has redefined warfare, with speed-of-light attack capabilities and a psychological factor second only to nuclear, biological, and chemical (NBC) weapons.

It can be expected that the number of nations with deployed DEW weapons will continue to grow exponentially, as the methods to develop such tools of war and the means to reduce the challenges that hamper development-ready systems will find their way to virtually any nation that seeks to acquire their awesome power.

A thought-provoking combat scenario surrounding GB-DEWs in 2025 begins with the fact that many GB-DEW installations are fixed stationary systems with a large foot print. These fixed systems will likely require massive amounts of energy to provide an effective beam strength that can be capable of sustained offensive and defensive effects.

Because of such constraints, many GB-DEWs are directly wired into nuclear plants and municipal power stations. Accordingly, it should be noted that in 2025, should a nation be faced with a threat to their military forces or space systems by GB-DEWs, there will be few options but to attack these power sources. Clearly then, it is difficult to deny that DEWs powered by fusion sources place a very unique set of challenges upon the war planner.

By 2025 military DE efforts are not only limited to directly improving weapons effects, but rather innovations in the field of DE are also advancing areas such as propulsion. Examples of promising systems in this field include, solar thermal propulsion (STP), which could provide a highly efficient alternative to hydrazine for micro-scale (and larger) space systems that require high Delta-V maneuvers. Another method is based on the concept of using energy generated by a laser to heat a gas, such as hydrogen for example, to a very high temperature.

As a result of this interaction, the gas then rapidly expands and delivers thrust. At this time, lasers have a demonstrated ability to reach the power levels required to deliver this concept to the military in a truly beneficial sense. Just as affordability, reductions in weight, and sheer innovation drove the satellite industry forward in prior decades, those same satellites and their dramatically reduced size and cost has, in turn, provided new opportunities for discovery in the field of space exploration.

In keeping with this spirit of innovation, other methods of propulsion that have been in the R&D stream for many years, such as the Lorentz force ion thruster, are now coming into full fruition. This method delivers a lift capability via the energy created when an electric current is combined with magnetic energy to generate thrust. In 2025, this concept may be already integrated into various space crafts. Other DE propulsion methods such as plasma-based, pulse-detonation engines (PDE), which received much attention in the past, may now be seen regularly preparing for take off.

The rapidly growing threat spectrum against space systems is further expanded by the increasing number of nations and non-state actors with access to ballistic missile technology. At the same time, the ballistic missile defence (BMD) methods deployed in decades past are in some cases now seen as unable to fully respond to the challenges presented in 2025 and beyond. In particular, BMD systems such as the kinetic energy interceptor (KEI) and the miniature kill vehicle (MKV) require elaborate sensor suites, such as infrared, radar, and optics to ensure an accurate trip to the threat. Additionally, components that add weight and systems complexity such as thrusters and guidance systems can now be avoided with the aid of DE missile defence solutions.

Other methods for ballistic missile intercepts such as ground-based lasers (GBL) and space-based laser (SBL) programs have now existed for many years and have proven to be successful for the few nations that possess the resources to employ DE as a BMD system. Though also welcomed are complementary alternatives that help meet the increasing challenges while at the same time preventing threat leakage caused by advanced countermeasures, maneuverable in-flight warheads, and hypersonic global-strike platforms.

One such DE system that may emerge as a complementary BMD application involves a laser-propulsion system named Lightcraft, which could by 2025 deliver a Kinetic Kill Vehicle (KKV) to a target at hypersonic speeds. Such a KKV could be ground, air, or space launched, though its effectiveness is reliant on the overall quality of the DE source that propels it. The structure of the KKV resembles a parabolic-like shape, with an interior consisting of highly reflective mirrors that channel heat away from the laser, resulting in explosive energy that ultimately generates thrust. Such a technology could theoretically be used to deliver lightweight space systems into LEO, without a launch vehicle, resulting in immeasurable cost reductions.

THEORETICAL SPACE WEAPONRY

Ballistic Warfare

In the late 1970s and through the 1980s the Soviet Union and the United States theorized, designed and in some cases even tested an astonishing variety of bizarre and exotic weaponry designed for warfare in outer space. Space warfare was seen primarily as an extension of nuclear warfare, and so many theoretical systems were based around the destruction or defence of ground and sea-based missiles. Space-based missiles were not a target due to the Outer Space Treaty, which banned the use, testing or storage of nuclear weapons outside the Earth's atmosphere. Systems proposed ranged from measures as simple as ground and space-based anti-missiles to railguns, space based lasers, orbital mines and other such futuristic weaponry. Deployment of these systems was seriously considered in the mid-1980s under the banner of the Strategic Defence Initiative (popularly known as Star Wars). If the Cold War had continued, then many of these systems could have seen deployment: the United States got as far as developing working railguns, and a laser that could destroy missiles at range, though the power requirements of both were phenomenal, and the ranges and firing cycles utterly impractical.

Electronic warfare

With the end of the Cold War and continued development of satellite and electronics technology, attention was focused on space as a supporting theatre for conventional warfare. Currently, military operations in space primarily concern either the vast tactical advantages of satellite-based surveillance, communications, and positioning systems or mechanisms used to deprive an opponent of said tactical advantages.

Accordingly, most space-borne proposals which would traditionally be considered "weapons" (a communications or reconnaissance satellite may be useful in warfare but isn't generally classified as a weapon) are designed to jam, sabotage, and outright destroy enemy satellites, and conversely to protect friendly satellites against such attacks. To this end, the US (and presumably other countries) is researching groups of small, highly mobile satellites called "microsats" (about the size of a refrigerator) and "picosats" (approximately 1 cubic foot (H"27 litres) in volume) nimble enough to manoeuvre around and interact with other orbiting objects to repair, sabotage, hijack, or simply collide with them.

Kinetic bombardment

Another theorized use involves the extension of conventional weaponry into orbit for deployment against ground targets. Though international treaties bar the deployment of nuclear missiles outside the atmosphere, other categories of weapons are largely unregulated. Traditional ground-based weapons are generally not useful in orbital environments, and few if any would survive re-entry even if they were, but as early as the 1950s, the United States has toyed with kinetic bombardment, i.e. orbiting magazines of non-explosive projectiles to be dropped onto hardened targets from low-earth orbit. Kinetic weapons have always been widespread in conventional warfare—bullets, arrows, swords, clubs, etc.—but the energy a projectile would gain while falling from orbit would make such a weapon rival all but the most powerful explosives. A direct hit would presumably destroy all but the most hardened targets without the need for nuclear weapons.

Such a system would involve a 'spotter' satellite, which would identify targets from orbit with high-power sensors, and a nearby 'magazine' satellite to de-orbit a long, needle-like tungsten dart onto it with a small rocket motor or just dropping a very big rock from orbit (such as an asteroid). This would be more useful against a larger but less hardened target (such as a city). Though a common device in science fiction, there is no publicly-available evidence that any such systems have actually been deployed by any nation.

Directed-Energy Weapons

Weapon systems that fall under this category include lasers, linear particle accelerators or particle-beam based weaponry, microwaves and plasma-based weaponry. Particle beams involve the acceleration of charged or neutral particles in a stream towards a target at extremely high velocities, the impact of which creates a reaction causing immense damage. Most of these weapons are theoretical or impractical to implement currently, aside from lasers which are starting to be used in terrestrial warfare. That said, directed-energy weapons are more practical and more effective in a vacuum (i.e. space) than in the Earth's atmosphere, as in the atmosphere the particles of air interfere with and disperse the directed energy. Obviously, that problem would not occur in space.

Practical considerations

Space warfare is likely to be conducted at far greater distances and speeds than terrestrial combat. The vast distances involved pose difficult challenges for targeting and tracking, as even light requires a few seconds to traverse ranges measured in hundreds of thousands of kilometres. For example, if attempting to fire upon a target at the distance of the Moon from the Earth, the image one sees reflects the position of the target slightly more than a second earlier.

A projectile from a railgun recently tested by the US Navy would take over eighteen hours to cross that distance (making the simplifying and optimistic assumption that it will travel in a straight line at a constant velocity of 5.8 km/s along its entire trajectory). Even a laser will need approximately 1.28 seconds, meaning a laser-based weapon system would need to lead a target's apparent position by 1.28×2 = 2.56 seconds.

Three factors conspire to make engaging targets in space very difficult. First, the vast distances involved mean that an error of even a fraction of a degree in the firing solution could result in a miss by thousands of kilometres. Second, space travel involves tremendous speeds by terrestrial standards—a geostationary satellite moves at a speed of 3.07 km/s whereas objects in low earth orbit can move at up to 8 km/s.

Third, though distances are large, targets remain relatively small. The International Space Station, currently the largest artificial object in Earth orbit, measures slightly over 100m at its largest span. Other satellites can be orders of magnitude smaller, e.g. Quickbird measures a mere 3.04m. External ballistics for stationary terrestrial targets is enormously complicated—some of the earliest analog computers were used to calculate firing solutions for naval artillery, as the problems were already beyond manual solutions in any reasonable time—and the issues in targeting objects in space make a difficult problem even harder. Additionally, though not a problem for orbital kinetic weapons, any directed energy weapon would require large amounts of electricity. So far the most practical batteries are lithium batteries, and the most practical method of generating electricity in space is through photovoltaic modules, which are currently only 5-18% efficient, and fuel cells, which have limited fuel. Current technology might not be practical for powering effective lasers, particle beams, and railguns in space.

Regardless of one's reasons for going to war, at present those reasons are not likely to suggest major targets located in space. Most of the main theories which attempt to explain human proclivity for warfare—psychological, sociological, demographic, economic, political, or otherwise—would not indicate space as a likely location of conflict until a significant population is engaged in large-scale activity there. Until then, space warfare is likely to take a supporting role to conventional, terrestrial warfare. Aside from applications such as communications, reconnaissance, GPS, and the like, which would be difficult or impossible without satellites, there do not appear to be any major advantages to basing weapons systems in space. The main reason is simply cost. Space warfare that involves humans being deployed in space to fight each other is not currently practical because of the difficulty and cost of sustaining human life in space, especially over long periods of time.

Additionally, there are few things that could be accomplished by space warfare that any nation wealthy enough to finance them cannot accomplish far more cheaply through conventional means. Raising any significant mass beyond Earth's gravity will always require a large amount of energy, and the cost increases with mass. For example, though kinetic bombardment potentially offers the ability to strike any target anywhere in the world within minutes, both the United States and Russia, possibly the only nations with the resources and facilities necessary to implement such a system, have sufficiently long-range supersonic bombers that the same target could already be deployed in a matter of hours at a mere fraction of the cost.

Bibliography

Ahuja, Vijay: *Network and Internet Security*. Academic Press, Inc.: Boston, 1996.

Ajey Lele: *Strategic Technologies for the Military : Breaking New Frontiers*, Sage, Delhi, 2009.

Alexander, J : *Military Technology and Equipment Technology*, Omega Pub, Delhi, 2008.

Amoroso, E. : *Fundamentals of Computer Security Technology*, Prentice Hall, Englewood Cliffs, 1994.

Bajpai, G.S. : *On Cyber Crime and Cyber Law*, Serials Publications, Delhi, 2011.

BloomBecker, Buck: *Spectacular Computer Crimes*. Dow Jones-Irwin: Homewood, IL, 1990.

Brenner, Susan W. : *Cybercrime : Criminal Threats from Cyberspace*, Pentagon Press, Delhi, 2012.

Chandra, R.: *Judicial System in Mechanical Warfare*, Lucknow, Print House (India), 1992.

Crichton, Michael: *Electronic Life, How to Think About Computers*, New York, Alfred A. Knopf, 1983.

David Post : *The Rise of Law in Cyberspace*, 48 Stan, L. Rev. 1367, 1996.

Dery, Mark. *Escape Velocity: Cyberculture at the End of the Century* . Grove Press, 1997.

Digumarti Bhaskara Rao: *Military Conversion : Impact on Science and Technology*, Discovery, Delhi, 2003.

Dudeja, V. D. : *Crimes in Cyber Space-Scams and Frauds: Issues and Remedies*, Commonwealth, Delhi, 2003.

Erbschloe, Michael: *Information Warfare : How to Survive Cyber Attack*. New York: Osborne/ McGraw-Hill, 2001.

Frederick B.: *Protection and Security on the Information Superhighway*. John Wiley & Sons, Inc.: New York, 1995.

Friedman, G.: *The Future of War: Power, Technology and American World Dominance in the 21st Century*, N.Y., Random House, 1996.

Godwin, Mike: *Cyber Rights: Defending Free Speech in the Digital Age*. Times Books, 1998

Harish, Chander : *Cyber Laws and It Protection*, PHI Learning, Delhi, 2012.

Hoffman, Bruce: *Inside Terrorism and Internet Crime*, New York: Columbia University Press, 1998.

Jones, W.H.: *Government and Politics of India Military*, London, Hutchinson, 1971.

Karanjit Siyan: *Internet Firewalls and Network Security*. New Riders Publishing: Indianapolis, 1996.

Keane J.: *Democracy and Cyber Crimes*, London, Verso, 1988.

Kumar, Raj : *Weapons and Military Technology*, Sumit Enterprises, Delhi, 2009.

Laquer, Walter: *Terrorism Attack from Computer Hacking*, Oxford: Oxford University Press, 1999.

Mary, W.: *Military Space Force: the Cultural Dimensions of Authority*, Cambridge, Belknap Press, 1985.

McMahon, David: *Cyber Threat: Internet Security for Home and Business*. Warwick Publishing Inc.: Toronto, 2000.

Mehra, Raman : *Information Technology and Cyber Laws*, Global India Publications, Delhi, 2010.

Nagia, Rajan : *The Transnational Dimension of Cyber Crime and Terrorism*, Cyber Tech, Delhi, 2010.

Paul T Augastine: *Combating Cyber Crime*, Crescent Pub, Delhi, 2007.

Radhakrishna: *Military Ethics: Guidelines for Peace and War*, Sumit Enterprises, Delhi, 2009.

Raj Kumar: *Weapons and Military Technology*, Sumit Enterprises, Delhi, 2009.

Rajan Nagia: *Cyber Laws and Computer Crimes*, Cyber Tech Pub, Delhi, 2009.

Rizvi, Askari : *Nuclear Terrorism and South Asia*, Albuquerque, NM: Sandia National Laboratories, February 2003.

Rosen, P.: *Societies and Military Power: India and its Armies*, Ithaca, Cornell University Press, 1996.

Schroeer, Dietrich: *Science, Technology, and the Cyber Crimes*, Ontario: John Wiley & Sons, 1984.

Singh, Y.K. : *Cyber Crime and Law*, Shree, Delhi, 2005.

Taylor, Paul: *Hackers: Crime in the Digital Sublime* . Routledge, 1999

Verton, D. : *Black Ice: The invisible Threat of Cyber-terrorism*, New York: McGraw-Hill/Osborne, 2003.

Zanini, M.: *Countering the New Terrorism*, Santa Monica, CA: RAND, 1999.

Index

R

S

T

W

❑❑❑